AF764189

"This monograph is certainly a timely and enlightening response to the post-pandemic economic order, constituted both by fast growing AI technology, which poses a challenge to the anthropocentric worldview, and the era of Trump 2.0, that is undermining longstanding international alliances and diplomatic protocol. The author, by referring to 'China Shock' and 'China Factor', effectively exposes the fragility of the current US-centric political-technological-economic hegemony. She then, relying on the 'Two-Level Game Theory', critically investigates how China's domestic and international political perspective on equality and independence crystallises into its constructive subversion of existing worldwide trade practices. The book, in short, is trying to deterritorialize the rigid and essential rhizomatous connection between the current US-centric political-technological-economic hegemony and changing international trade discourse."

—Chiu Man-Chung, *Chair Professor at the Law School, Beijing Normal University*

The Two-level Games in China's Foreign Trade Policies

Applying two-level game theory and rational decision-making analysis, this book explores how China navigates domestic constraints and international pressures to achieve optimal outcomes in its foreign trade policy.

The author examines China's accession to the WTO and the evolving trade tensions between China and the US. She analyzes some of the most contentious trade issues in the contemporary landscape, such as China's economic model, technology restrictions, and non-tariff barriers. Through a case study on China's solar photovoltaic (PV) manufacturing sector, she illustrates how these trade issues influence policy-making within a specific industry. In conclusion, the book evaluates China's strategies for navigating its foreign trade within the broader global trading system – it considers the prospects for a potential "win-set" in future trade negotiations, offering insights into how China might navigate these complexities moving forward.

The book will appeal to academics specializing in international trade law, international relations, and China studies.

Zuozhen Liu is Associate Professor of Law whose research focuses on cultural heritage law, international trade law, and Chinese constitutional law. She holds a PhD in Art and Law from the University of Amsterdam and also practices law part-time. Dr Liu serves as a legal consultation expert for local governments' rule-of-law initiatives, with her policy reports earning repeated commendations from various departments. Her work bridges academic inquiry and legal practice, with a focus on the intersection of culture, law, and development.

The Two-level Games in China's Foreign Trade Policies

Zuozhen Liu

Routledge
Taylor & Francis Group
LONDON AND NEW YORK

First published 2025
by Routledge
4 Park Square, Milton Park, Abingdon, Oxon OX14 4RN

and by Routledge
605 Third Avenue, New York, NY 10158

Routledge is an imprint of the Taylor & Francis Group, an informa business

© 2025 Zuozhen Liu

The right of Zuozhen Liu to be identified as author of this work has been asserted in accordance with sections 77 and 78 of the Copyright, Designs and Patents Act 1988.

All rights reserved. No part of this book may be reprinted or reproduced or utilised in any form or by any electronic, mechanical, or other means, now known or hereafter invented, including photocopying and recording, or in any information storage or retrieval system, without permission in writing from the publishers.

Trademark notice: Product or corporate names may be trademarks or registered trademarks, and are used only for identification and explanation without intent to infringe.

British Library Cataloguing in Publication Data
A catalogue record for this book is available from the British Library

Library of Congress Cataloging in Publication Data
Names: Liu, Zuozhen, author.
Title: The two-level games in China's foreign trade policies / Zuozhen Liu.
Description: Abingdon, Oxon [UK] ; New York, NY : Routledge, 2025. |
Includes bibliographical references and index.
Identifiers: LCCN 2025003129 (print) | LCCN 2025003130 (ebook) | ISBN 9781041063803 (hardback) | ISBN 9781041067931 (paperback) | ISBN 9781003637110 (ebook)
Subjects: LCSH: Foreign trade regulation--China. | Investments, Foreign--Law and legislation--China.. | China--Commercial policy.
Classification: LCC KNQ3405 .L58 2025 (print) | LCC KNQ3405 (ebook) | DDC 382/.30951--dc23/eng/20250128
LC record available at https://lccn.loc.gov/2025003129
LC ebook record available at https://lccn.loc.gov/2025003130

ISBN: 978-1-041-06380-3 (hbk)
ISBN: 978-1-041-06793-1 (pbk)
ISBN: 978-1-003-63711-0 (ebk)

DOI: 10.4324/ 9781003637110

Typeset in Times New Roman
by Deanta Global Publishing Services, Chennai, India

Contents

List of Figures

List of Tables

Introduction

For mercantilists, wealth and power are the ultimate objectives of nations, with each reinforcing the other (Viner, 1948). Since the 16th century, trade and war have been the two primary forces shaping both domestic politics and the international system. War redistributes power among states, while trade redistributes economic activity and wealth (Wallerstein, 2011). Today, trade remains a cornerstone of the global economic agenda. A central issue in current debates is the so-called "China shock," which has become a key factor fueling tensions and disputes in international trade (Autor et al., 2016). These escalating conflicts over trade policies and governance are emblematic of the broader struggles over the shifting balance of power in the global system.

China's Rise in Global Trade

Foreign trade has transformed China from a virtually closed economy into a leading global trading power, particularly following its accession to the WTO in 2001. In 2001, China's exports of goods amounted to $266.16 billion, representing approximately 4.3% of the global market share. Since 2009, China has been the world's largest exporter of goods. By 2020, its exports surged to $2.6 trillion, growing at an average annual rate of 12.7%, and accounting for 15.2% of global exports. Alongside this export growth, China's import capacity has expanded significantly. The value of its imports grew from $243.61 billion in 2001 to $2.1 trillion in 2020, with its share of global imports increasing from 3.8% to 11.8%. These figures underscore China's growing influence in international trade and its emergence as a key player in the global economy.[1]

Oswaldo de Rivero describes the free trade model as a form of "international Darwinism," in which globalization transforms the global economy into a "global jungle." In this environment, international free trade promotes the growth of supranational authorities while pushing "Third World" countries to the margins. Technological advancements are also diminishing the traditional advantages of

1 Data quoted from: Zhou Mi, "Over the 20 years since joining the WTO, China has become a critical hub of global connectivity." [入世"20年，中国成为全球互联的重要路口]. *China.com.cn* (December 11, 2021)

DOI: 10.4324/9781003637110-1

developing nations – such as abundant unskilled labor and natural resources – making many of these countries economically unstable and pushing them toward the status of "quasi-nation-states" with unrealized national goals (De Rivero, 2001). When China entered this "global jungle," it was a developing country, yet it has achieved remarkable economic growth over the two decades. How has China not only survived but thrived in the highly competitive global market in such a short period?

From the perspective of economies of scale, China's vast market size enables its companies to produce at significantly lower costs, providing a substantial competitive edge. Historically, China has undergone a remarkable transformation from an ancient agricultural civilization to a global manufacturing powerhouse. Its success within the global free trade system is largely attributed to its ability to harness scalability and production efficiency. Historian Shi Zhan, in his widely acclaimed book *The Hub: Three Thousand Years of China*, argues that this vast scalability is key to understanding China's rise. In ancient times, China's large scale allowed emperors to accumulate substantial administrative resources at relatively low costs, which helped suppress local resistance and establish a unified state. This historical foundation continues to support China's growth and international competitiveness. Since the Song Dynasty, China has largely avoided prolonged political fragmentation, unlike Europe and the Middle East. This unity is deeply rooted in traditional Chinese culture, where politics and culture reinforce one another. As a result, China is the only ancient civilization that has continuously developed into the modern era (Shi, 2018). When China entered the global economy in the late 20th century, its immense scale was fully realized, cementing its status as the hub of manufacturing (Shi, 2018).

Beyond scalability, targeted industrial policies and government support have been crucial to China's trade expansion. China is often cited as a prime example of leveraging export-driven strategies to accelerate industrialization and economic growth, drawing inspiration from the East Asian development models of Japan, South Korea, and Singapore. A key feature of these East Asian economies is the proactive role of government. Recognizing the limitations of market mechanisms in allocating resources, these governments have strategically intervened to promote economic development (Aoki et al., 1997; Wei 2020). Data from the Global Trade Alert indicate that, between 2009 and 2022, China implemented approximately 5,400 subsidy policies – nearly two-thirds of the measures introduced by G20 advanced economies combined. These subsidies have proven effective in boosting exports, with subsidized products experiencing a 1% increase in export levels compared to non-subsidized products. Simultaneously, imports of subsidized products have declined, suggesting some degree of domestic substitution.[2]

Lastly, Chinese enterprises excel in iterative innovation, a strategy that contrasts with the disruptive, groundbreaking technologies emphasized by Silicon Valley

2 Data quoted from: Gourinchas, P. et al. "Trade Balances in China and the US Are Largely Driven by Domestic Macro Forces," *IMF Blog*. (September 12, 2024).

ventures. Rather than focusing solely on visionary breakthroughs, Chinese enterprises prioritize adaptation and optimization, refining existing models to meet specific demands. This "learning by doing" approach enables continuous, incremental improvements, eventually leading to larger, more impactful innovations (Zhang & Liu, 2008). The success of this model is evident in sectors such as e-commerce, information technology, and manufacturing, including solar photovoltaics, electric vehicles, and wind power. Chinese enterprises consistently deliver high-quality products at lower costs while driving advancements within their industries. By emphasizing practical, incremental innovation, Chinese enterprises effectively balance technological progress with market relevance, securing a competitive edge both domestically and globally.[3] Additionally, intense domestic competition forces companies to prioritize cost management, flawless execution, and strategic business planning. This challenging environment has cultivated a generation of resilient entrepreneurs, equipped to compete on the global stage.

In summary, a combination of macro factors –such as China's enormous market size and supportive industrial policies – and micro factors like the resilience and competitive edge of Chinese enterprises has contributed to the success of Chinese manufacturing.

Foreign Responses and Pressures

The mass production of Chinese enterprises has raised concerns about overcapacity in advanced economies. US and EU officials have repeatedly criticized China's overcapacity, particularly in green technology sectors such as photovoltaic manufacturing. For example, during her 2024 visit to China, US Treasury Secretary Janet Yellen expressed concern about excessive investments in these sectors, warning that production was exceeding domestic demand. She emphasized the need for a coordinated US-EU approach to address China's industrial overcapacity.[4] These criticisms often targeted alleged market-distorting practices and China's unique economic model, referred to as "China, Inc." or "state capitalism." Economist Justin Yifu Lin explains that such "overcapacity" is part of a "wave phenomenon." According to Lin (2007), firms in developing countries often converge on industries they see as promising, leading to a surge in capital inflows. While this behavior initially drives growth, it can eventually result in overcapacity and a range of economic challenges. This has prompted varied responses from other nations, including traditional trade remedy measures, strategic partnerships, heightened scrutiny, and trade sanctions.

3 See "Lee Kaifu: Chinese Entrepreneurs Excel at 'Iterative Innovation' [李开复：中国企业家擅长的是'迭代式创新']. *The Time Weekly*. (August 30, 2013); "Qian Yingyi: Innovation is not just about going from 0 to 1; it is also about expanding from 1 to N [钱颖一：从0到1是创新，从1到N也是创新]." Available at: <http://finance.people.com.cn/GB/n1/2016/0121/c1004-28073565.html>

4 Rich McKay and David Lawder, "Yellen to Warn China on Excess Production Capacity, Wants Constructive Talks." *Reuters*. (March 28, 2021)

Since becoming the world's second-largest economy in 2010, China's economic rise has reshaped the global balance of power, increasingly seen as a challenge to US global leadership. In its 2022 National Security Strategy, the US identified China as the only competitor with both the intent to reshape the international order and the economic, diplomatic, military, and technological power to do so. Managing or curbing China's expanding influence has become a bipartisan priority in the US Economic and trade interactions, once considered a stabilizing force in US-China relations, have now become one of the most contentious issues between the two nations.

On the international stage, the US has taken actions to weaken the WTO's rule-based system, notably by blocking consensus and obstructing appointments to the Appellate Body, the core mechanism for resolving trade disputes within the organization. By April 2024, this blockage had occurred 75 times, effectively paralyzing the WTO's dispute settlement system and undermining multilateral trade governance.[5] Simultaneously, the US has pushed for reforms in the WTO that align with its strategic interests, such as the US-EU-Japan trilateral cooperation, aimed at establishing new rules on industrial policies. These efforts reflect broader US attempts to reshape global trade governance in response to emerging economic challenges. Additionally, the US and its allies have sought to restructure global supply chains through initiatives like the Indo-Pacific Economic Framework for Prosperity and reshoring strategies. These measures aim to reduce dependence on specific countries, particularly China, and foster economic resilience among allied nations.

The US has also frequently resorted to unilateral measures, including additional tariffs, trade sanctions, and technology bans. During his first term, President Trump initiated a "tariff war" against China (2018–2019) by imposing substantial tariffs on Chinese goods. The move aimed to address longstanding trade imbalances, reduce the US trade deficit, and tackle concerns over intellectual property theft. Prior to this, the average US tariff rate on Chinese imports was approximately 2.68%.[6] As of December 2024, the US continues to impose elevated tariffs on Chinese imports, including 100% on electric vehicles, 50% on solar cells and semiconductors, 25% on steel and aluminum products, and 50% to 100% on various medical products.[7] In response, China has maintained an average tariff rate of approximately 20% on US goods.[8] By comparison, the average US tariff rate on imports from all countries was around 1.5% in 2022, while China's corresponding figure stood at 3.1%.[9]

5 "WTO: US Blocks Appellate Body Vacancies for 75th Time, DSS Reform in Crisis." *TWN Information on WTO and Trade Issues*. (May 4, 2024)

6 Data quoted from: Torfi Smith, Tom Lee, "Section 301 (China) Tariffs Causing a Fourfold Increase in Tariff Rates." *American Action Forum*. (July 18, 2018).

7 The White House, "Fact Sheet: President Biden Takes Action to Protect American Workers and Businesses from China's Unfair Trade Practices." (May 14, 2024).

8 Data quoted from: Chen Xing, "How flexible is the adjustment of tariffs on exports to the United States?" [对美出口关税，调整的弹性有多大？]. *Yicai*. (November 15, 2023).

9 Data quoted from: World Bank Group.

These figures highlight the significantly higher tariffs imposed by both nations on each other's goods compared to imports from other trading partners. This trend is expected to intensify with Trump's return to the presidency.[10]

Trump's victory in the 2024 presidential election has raised concerns about the potential introduction of new tariffs, as he has made trade a top priority. During his campaign, he proposed imposing hefty tariffs on foreign goods entering the US, calling himself "Tariff Man" and declaring that "tariffs are the greatest thing ever invented." Trump has threatened to unilaterally impose a 60% tariff on Chinese goods, raising anxiety among Chinese exporters.[11] In November 2024, prominent members of Congress introduced the Restoring Trade Fairness Act, a bill aimed at revoking China's Permanent Normal Trade Relations (PNTR) status, a key component of the China-US economic relationship. Trump also threatened to revoke China's Most Favored Nation status.[12]

In response to these threats, China's Vice Commerce Minister, Wang Shouwen, addressed the issue at a press conference on November 22, 2024. He reiterated China's willingness to engage in constructive dialogue with the United States, emphasizing that mutual respect forms the foundation for advancing bilateral economic and trade relations. Wang also highlighted the resilience of China's economy and its ability to withstand external shocks, presenting a strategy aimed at mitigating and withstanding such impacts. This strategy is anchored in a new development paradigm that prioritizes domestic circulation while promoting a mutually reinforcing relationship between domestic and international circulations.[13]

Since President Donald Trump resumed office in January 2025, trade tensions between the US and China have escalated significantly. In February, the US imposed an additional 10% tariff on Chinese imports, initiating a broader trade conflict. On April 2, the US announced "reciprocal tariffs" ranging from 10% to 49% on all its trading partners, which took effect on April 9.[14] Although the US government granted a 90-day implementation pause for over 75 countries, it imposed a new 125% tariff on Chinese goods following China's retaliation. On April 11, China announced that it would raise tariffs on US imports from 84% to 125%, effective April 12. It also stated that, at these tariff levels, US exports to China are effectively unmarketable, rendering any further US tariff increases economically

10 Trump's trade policy emphasized boosting exports over imports as a means to increase national wealth. He regarded exports as inherently beneficial and imports as potentially harmful, advocating for "strict reciprocity" in trade relations.

11 Paul Wiseman, "Trump Favors Huge New Tariffs. What are They, and How Do They Work?" *AP News*, (September 27, 2024).

12 Currently, four countries – Russia, Belarus, North Korea, and Cuba – do not have PNTR status with the US See Lili Pike, "Trump's Threat to Revoke China's Trade Status, Explained." *Foreign Policy*. (December 4, 2024)

13 Xinhua, "China Open to Dialogue, Cooperation with US to Promote Steady Economic Relations: official." *ENGLISH.GOV.CN*. (November 22, 2024).

14 The White House, "Regulating Imports with a Reciprocal Tarriff to Rectify Trade Practices that Contribute to Large and Persistent Annual United States Goods Trade Deficits". (April 2, 2025).

meaningless.[15] As a result, China declared that it would not respond to future tariff hikes. Nevertheless, it emphasized its readiness to "fight to the end" if tensions continue to escalate, while still advocating for dialogue based on mutual respect.[16] Trump's "reciprocal tariffs" strategy has drawn in nearly all major global economic players. How will US–China trade relations evolve? How might these developments reshape the international trade system and global economic order? These concerns now extend far beyond China and the US – they are matters of global significance, with far-reaching implications for the international community.

In Chinese political discourse, the sweeping geopolitical changes of the present era are often referred to as the "great changes unseen in a century."[17] This phrase aptly captures the profound transformations reshaping the global landscape – an era characterized by intensified rivalry, shifting power dynamics, and a reordering of the international trade system. In light of these complex challenges and growing external pressures, a critical question arises: How will China navigate these turbulent waters? Specifically, how will foreign pressures shape China's foreign trade policies? These questions lie at the heart of this book, which seeks to analyze China's strategies for managing foreign trade in the face of such pressures.

Theoretical Framework: Two-level Game Theory

At times, external pressures lead to visible shifts in a nation's foreign policy. For example, Japan has often been characterized as a "reactive state" in relation to US interests, with its foreign policy frequently responding to international stimuli rather than to domestic needs (Vidal, 2022). Caught between the US and China, Japan faces complex strategic, economic, and political pressures from both major powers. A recent example of this was China's ban on Japanese seafood imports following the discharge of treated water from the Fukushima nuclear power plant into the Pacific Ocean. China justified this ban on the grounds of "radioactive contamination" and the need to "ensure food safety and protect public health." However, after several rounds of talks, China agreed on September 20, 2024, to "gradually resume" Japanese seafood imports.[18] Many in Japan perceive such Chinese trade

15 The White House, "Modifying Reciprocal Tariff Rates to Reflect Trading Partner Retaliation and Alignment". (April 9. 2025).

16 Ministry of Finance of the People's Republic of China, "Announcement of the Customs Tariff Commission of the State Council on Adjusting Tariff Measures on Imports Originating from the United States[国务院关税税则委员会关于调整对原产于美国的进口商品加征关税措施的公告]". (April 11, 2025); Xinhua, "Ministry of Commerce: We are open to negotiations, but if it comes to a trade war, we are prepared to fight to the end. [商务部：谈，大门敞开；打，奉陪到底]". (April 10, 2025).

17 Quoted from Xi Jinping's speech at the opening ceremony of a training program for younger officials at the Central Party School (National Academy of Governance) during its 2019 fall semester (September 3, 2019).

18 Ministry of Foreign Affairs of the PRC, "China and Japan Reach Agreement on Ocean Discharge of Fukushima Nuclear-Contaminated Water" (September 20, 2024). Available at: <https://www.mfa.gov.cn/mfa_eng/xw/wjbxw/202409/t20240920_11493511.html>

measures as a form of "economic coercion," arguing that China's actions are less about consumer safety and more about pressuring Japan to alter its policies or make strategic concessions (Ferguson & Igata, 2024).[19]

In contrast, foreign pressures can also prompt significant opposition, leading to the formation of national alliances aimed at resisting or accommodating external demands. Historically, China struggled to reconcile its identity as a central, universal civilization with the reality of existing within a world of nation-states. Since the late 19th century, China has oscillated between integrating into the international community and pursuing self-reliance. Following the reform and opening-up policy, China's approach has shifted from isolation to active participation. However, the historical experience of humiliation has deeply influenced Chinese intellectuals and political leaders, prompting them to reconsider their approach to international relations. Two key propositions have emerged from this reflection: first, that the course of human history is driven by competition among nation-states, and second, that a nation's well-being is closely tied to its ability to compete effectively on the global stage (Kaufman, 2011).

This sense of humiliation has shaped China's political mindset and its responses to foreign pressures. Confronted with external challenges, the Chinese Communist Party (CPC) has often adopted a "resistance" approach, positioning itself as the defender of national interests and striving to assert China's identity on the world stage. At the same time, China has increasingly integrated into the global economy, with more than 600,000 enterprises engaging in foreign trade, providing millions of jobs.[20]The question then arises: to what extent do foreign pressures influence China's foreign trade policies? Will China continue to take a hardline, resistance-based approach, or is there room for compromise through diplomatic bargaining? In recent years, China has pursued strategies such as institutional opening-up and dual circulation, as well as testing new high-standard trade rules. Are these policies a response to external pressures, or do they reflect a broader, more strategic vision?

Theoretical frameworks help shed light on these dynamics. In his influential article, Gourevitch introduced the concept of "the second image reversed," which suggests that the international system influences domestic politics as much as, if not more than, domestic politics shapes international relations. Gourevitch argues that the international system is not merely a consequence of domestic structures, but also a driving force behind them. This raises the important question: to what extent does the international system shape a nation's foreign policy? In theory,

19 See "China might be expressing domestic frustration through the treated water issue, suggests Professor Ichiro Korogi of Kanda University of International Studies." [in Japanese]. (28 August 2023). Available at <https://www.iza.ne.jp/article/20230828-HNYOX7CIGVLO5M3ASWWCYMMZXI/>

20 According to data, in 2023, China had 645,000 foreign trade entities engaged in import and export activities. Among these, private enterprises have maintained their position as the largest foreign trade operators for five consecutive years. The share of private enterprises reached 86.2%, setting a new record. Data quoted from: "Foreign Trade Showcases New Highlights in China's Economic Performance." [从外贸"成绩单"看中国经济新亮色]. *People.cn.* (January 16, 2024).

there is always flexibility in how a nation responds to external pressures, making it essential to understand the rationale behind these responses. This examination inevitably involves analyzing domestic politics, particularly the competition among different actors advocating for different responses to international pressures (Gourevitch, 1978).

Further enriching this analysis is Robert D. Putnam's two-level game theory, introduced in 1988. This framework offers a way to understand the interaction between domestic and international politics. According to this model, international negotiations involve simultaneous negotiations at both the international and domestic levels. On the international level, national governments seek agreements with other countries on matters of mutual concern. On the domestic level, societal actors apply pressure on their governments to secure favorable policies. The central concept of this model, the "win-set," refers to the set of international agreements that are acceptable at the domestic level (Putnam, 1988). Although much of the literature on two-level games focuses on established trade and military powers, there is a notable gap in research regarding rising powers. Given the shifting balance of power in global trade, applying two-level game theory to rising powers such as China is a crucial area for future research. [21]

In two-level game theory, the chief negotiator – typically the head of state or government – is modeled as a rational actor who evaluates constraints and opportunities at both the domestic and international levels to achieve a favorable outcome. This framework highlights that the rational decision-making process at the international level (e.g., securing a deal) is heavily influenced by domestic politics. To reach a deal that satisfies both international partners and gains domestic political acceptance (the "win-set"), the chief negotiator must rationally evaluate the trade-offs between international concessions and domestic approval, ultimately aiming to maximize the national interest.

The rational actor model, as outlined by Allison (1991), provides a systematic approach to this decision-making process. A central premise of this model is that all actors behave rationally, aiming to maximize their payoffs. The model involves four key steps:

(1) Identifying the problem: Clearly defining the issue that requires resolution.
(2) Defining the desired outcomes: Establishing specific objectives to guide decision-making.
(3) Evaluating the potential consequences of various policy options: Analyzing the costs, benefits, and implications of alternative strategies.
(4) Choosing the option that maximizes utility or benefits: Selecting the most advantageous course of action to achieve the desired outcomes.

21 Eugénia da Conceição-Heldt, Patrick A. Mello, "Two-Level Games in Foreign Policy," *Oxford Encyclopedia of Politics*, 2017.

By following these steps, the chief negotiator can systematically navigate the dual pressures of domestic and international demands. Within this theoretical framework and decision-making model, this book assumes that the chief negotiator – represented by the Chinese government – is a rational, informed actor who strategically evaluates options to optimize the state's interests and perceived benefits. The analysis focuses on the negotiator's decision-making process within the broader interplay of domestic and international politics, providing insights into how these dynamics shape policy choices.

Additionally, as a non-native speaker, the author acknowledges the use of ChatGPT-4.0 to assist with language enhancement and refinement in the preparation of the book.

Structure of the book

This book examines how China navigates domestic constraints and international pressures to achieve optimal outcomes in its foreign trade policy. The analysis is organized into six chapters, structured around the logical steps of decision-making. Chapter 1 identifies the key problems and defines the desired outcomes of China's foreign trade policy, tracing its evolution from early struggles with foreign powers to its eventual integration into the global trading system, particularly following its accession to the WTO. To provide a deeper understanding of these problems and objectives, Chapter 2 explores trade tensions between China and the US, comparing China's responses to similar challenges faced by Japan. Chapters 3 and 4 assess the potential consequences of various policy options by analyzing some of the most contentious trade issues in the contemporary landscape, such as China's economic model, technology restrictions, and non-tariff barriers. Chapter 5 provides a focused case study on China's solar photovoltaic (PV) manufacturing sector, illustrating how these trade issues influence policy-making within a specific industry. Finally, Chapter 6 evaluates China's strategies for selecting the most rational course of action to achieve beneficial outcomes, addressing the challenges posed by shifting international trade dynamics and domestic pressures. This chapter also considers the prospects for a potential "win-set" in future trade negotiations, offering insights into how China might navigate these complexities moving forward.

Chapter 1 examines China's accession to the WTO and its far-reaching impacts over the past two decades. The chapter begins with a historical overview of China's trade policies, tracing its journey from the Haijin (sea ban) policy to its gradual integration into the global trade system. It highlights the ideological and systemic challenges China faced in joining the WTO, particularly the persistent issue of market economy status, which remained a barrier to its full acceptance by Western economies. The chapter also explores the economic, social, and political implications of China's WTO membership, emphasizing its transformation into a global manufacturing superpower. This growth has led to security concerns and populist backlash in the West, fueled by negative impacts on labor markets and rising income inequality. These tensions have contributed to the marginalization of the WTO and the rise of protectionist sentiments.

Chapter 2 discusses the evolving trade tensions between China and the United States, drawing comparisons to the US-Japan trade frictions in the second half of the 20th century. It provides a historical overview of US-China trade relations, noting the rapid growth of bilateral trade since the normalization of diplomatic ties in 1979. This chapter identifies key sources of trade tensions, including the widening trade deficit and national security concerns. A critical comparison is made with Japan's conciliatory Gaiatsu model of the 1980s, contrasting it with China's more assertive stance, which resists US unilateralism and "trade hegemonism." The chapter explores the cultural and political factors behind these differing strategies, emphasizing China's focus on equality, independence, and national pride. The chapter concludes that US-China trade tensions transcend economic issues, reflecting deeper clashes of nationalism and power dynamics. It highlights the challenges of achieving meaningful trade cooperation and reform amid ongoing geopolitical rivalry and ideological differences.

Chapter 3 examines the intersection of trade policy and competition policy, with a focus on China's state-owned enterprises (SOEs) and industrial policies. This chapter looks into China's state-driven economic model, often referred to as "China Inc.," and its frequent clashes with global trade norms. It explores the role of SOEs in strategic sectors and the rapid growth of China's private enterprises since its WTO accession. The chapter also discusses the concept of competitive neutrality policies as a potential solution to address distortions caused by SOEs, drawing examples from Australia's framework and the CPTPP's SOE chapter. While China has undertaken reforms, including mixed ownership models, it is unlikely to relinquish control over its SOEs. This chapter underscores the broader challenge of reconciling market liberalization with state-led economic policies in the evolving global trade environment.

Chapter 4 explores the impact of technology export controls and the growing integration of non-trade values in trade policies. The chapter traces China's shift from a strategy of exchanging market access for foreign technology to an emphasis on self-reliance in technology as a key component of its development strategy. It also addresses the increasing use of trade sanctions tied to human rights concerns and the EU's carbon border tax. The chapter argues that while blending trade with non-trade values carries significant normative weight, it poses challenges for developing economies and risks becoming a tool for trade protectionism. It highlights the need for a balanced approach to trade and non-trade values, with implications for international trade law.

Chapter 5 presents a case study of China's PV industry, illustrating how targeted industrial policies and technological advancements have propelled China to the forefront of global PV manufacturing. The chapter examines how subsidies and strategic policies initially fueled the industry's growth, and how China's move towards a more sustainable development model has led to a reduction in subsidies. It also examines the challenges posed by trade restrictions from other economies, which have spurred both consolidation and expansion in the domestic market. The case study offers insights into how Chinese enterprises have driven technological innovations and utilized industrial policies to emerge as global leaders in renewable energy.

In **Chapter 6**, the author examines China's strategies for navigating its foreign trade within the broader global trading system. The chapter emphasizes the principle of sovereign equality of states, which remains central to the consensus-based decision-making process within the WTO, despite its inherent inefficiencies. While it argues that the consensus mechanism is unlikely to undergo significant transformation, China has increasingly turned to alternative approaches, such as the Multi-Party Interim Appeal Arbitration Arrangement (MPIA). Additionally, the chapter explores China's engagement with other trade mechanisms, including regional and bilateral agreements like the Regional Comprehensive Economic Partnership (RCEP) and its pursuit of high-standard agreements, such as the Comprehensive and Progressive Agreement for Trans-Pacific Partnership (CPTPP). Despite these efforts, the chapter highlights the ongoing challenge of reforming China's economic model, particularly in terms of reducing state intervention in the market. The chapter concludes by forecasting that competition in advanced industries will intensify, especially in light of global shifts and the lack of political will among major powers to pursue meaningful reforms within the WTO.

This comprehensive analysis is expected to provide a nuanced understanding of China's foreign trade policies, highlighting the complexities and challenges the country faces as it navigates an ever-changing global landscape.

References

Allison, G. (1991). *The Essence of Decision: Explaining the Cuban Missile Crisis*. Pearson.

Aoki, M., Kim, H., & Okuno-Fujiwara, M. (Eds.). (1997). *The Role of Government in East Asian Economic Development: Comparative Institutional Analysis*. Oxford University Press.

Autor, D. H., Dorn, D., & Gordon, H. H. (2016). The China shock: Learning from labor-market adjustment to large changes in trade. *Annual Review of Economics*, 8, 205–240.

De Rivero, O. (2001). *The Myth of Development: The Non-Viable Economies of the 21st Century*. Zed Books.

Ferguson, V., & Igata, A. (2024). Consumer buycotts and supply chain diplomacy: Japan's responses to China's seafood ban. *The Asan Forum*, September 12, 2024.

Gourevitch, P. (1978). The second image reversed: The international sources of domestic politics. *International Organization*, 32(4), 881–912.

Kaufman, A. A. (2011). The 'century of humiliation' and China's national narratives. Testimony before the US-China Economic and Security Review Commission Hearing on "China's Narratives Regarding National Security Policy," March 10. https://www.uscc.gov/sites/default/files/3.10.11Kaufman.pdf.

Lin, J. Y. (2007). Wave phenomenon and the reconstruction of macroeconomic theories for developing countries. *Economic Research*, 1, 126–131 (in Chinese).

Putnam, R. D. (1988). Diplomacy and domestic politics: The logic of two-level games. *International Organization*, 42(3), 427–460.

Shi, Z. (2018). *Shu Niu: 3000 Nian de Zhongguo* [The Hub: 3000 Years of China]. Guanxi Normal University Press.

Vidal, L. L. i. (2022). Beyond the Gaiatsu model: Japan's Asia-Pacific policy and neoclassical realism. *Journal of Asian Security and International Affairs*, 9(1), 26–49.

Viner, J. (1948). Power versus plenty as objectives of foreign policy in the seventeenth and eighteenth centuries. *World Politics*, 1(1), 1–29.

Wallerstein, I. (2011). *The Modern World-System*. University of California Press.

Wei, J. (2020). China's industrial policy: Evolution and experience (UNCTAD/BRI PROJECT/RP11). https://unctad.org/system/files/official-document/BRI-Project_RP11_en.pdf.

Zhang, P., & Liu, X. (2008). . *The Chinese Economy*, 41(4), 54–76.

1 Two Decades after China's Accession to WTO

China's Path to WTO Membership

After 15 years of negotiations, China officially became the 143rd member of the WTO on December 11, 2001. Its entry into the global economy was celebrated as a triumph for free trade and economic liberalization. However, two decades later, the sentiment in the Western world has shifted, with some now describing the relationship as a seemingly happy marriage gone sour (Mavroidis & Sapir, 2021).

The Legacy of the Century of Humiliation and Its Influence

Traditional China prioritized agriculture but restricted commerce, resulting in rare discussions of foreign trade prior to the 19th century.[1] From a political and economic standpoint, private commerce and industry consistently threatened the stability of the feudal social structure, which was rooted in a small-scale peasant economy, often contributing to its breakdown. Ethically, private commerce was viewed as a disruptive force that undermined the feudal hierarchy, the "equitable" social order, and the values of frugality, leading to potential confusion in social status and ranks (Fan et al., 1996).

However, since the second half of the 19th century, foreign trade began to take a central role in Chinese economic thought, marking a significant shift from earlier periods. China was compelled to integrate into the global trade system, prompting Chinese elites to reconsider their stance on free trade. The desire to catch up with Europe and America, along with the pressing need to ensure national survival, became key factors shaping modern Chinese intellectual perspectives. They gradually abandoned traditional ideas based on the closed, self-sufficient peasant

1 During the Song Dynasty (960–1279), foreign trade reached its peak, with Song China emerging as the wealthiest nation in the Far East and one of the richest in the world. Despite this, the impact of foreign trade on China – both in terms of goods and ideas – remained relatively limited. Robert Hartwell estimates that around 1100, foreign trade accounted for only about 1.7% of China's total GNP. The primary imports were spices and herbs, while exports included silks, tea, salt, and various manufactured goods. See Robert M. Hartwell (1988). "The Imperial Treasuries: Finance and Power in Sung China." *Bulletin of Sung-Yüan Studies*. Vol.20: 18–89.

DOI: 10.4324/9781003637110-2

economy, instead recognizing Western advancements and seeking to learn from their successes (Yuan & Guo, 2001).

The Impact of the Haijin Policy on China's Trade History

The decline of the Qing court is often attributed, in mainstream Chinese historical narratives, to the series of isolationist policies known as *haijin* (海禁), or the sea ban. This policy can be traced back to the Yuan dynasty and was formally instituted by the Hongwu Emperor (1368–1398), the founder of the Ming dynasty. Hongwu aimed to make *haijin* a lasting cornerstone of Ming policy, serving two key purposes: securing the coast by restricting private Sino-foreign interactions and establishing a state monopoly over foreign imports such as spices, aromatics, silver, and other exotic goods through the tribute trade system. The strict enforcement of *haijin* allowed the Ming court to control all foreign trade, effectively creating a vacuum in the regional trade network that had flourished since the Tang dynasty (Lim, 2013). The policy began to relax in the early 1550s, when informal trade liberalization was permitted in Guangdong, which supported the argument that opening access to trade would decrease the frequency of pirate attacks (Lim, 2013).

The Qing court inherited the *haijin* policy from its predecessors. During much of the Qing dynasty, particularly from 1757 until the First Opium War (1839–1842), the Qing court implemented a policy known as the Canton System, under which Guangzhou (Canton) was the only port designated for legal foreign trade, and all foreign merchants were required to conduct their business exclusively through a government-licensed group of merchants known as the Thirteen Factories. This policy aimed to control foreign trade and limit foreign influence by centralizing and restricting interactions with foreign merchants. In an effort to access China's lucrative markets, Western traders resorted to military force. This culminated in the First Opium War, which ended with the signing of the Treaty of Nanjing in 1842, widely regarded as the first of the "unequal treaties" imposed on China. Key provisions of the treaty included the cession of Hong Kong to Britain and the opening of five major Chinese port cities to foreign trade. The Second Opium War (1856–1860) similarly concluded with a series of unequal treaties that further weakened the Qing court, forcing the opening of an additional 11 treaty ports to international commerce.[2]

Development of Foreign Trade Thoughts in China

China's market was opened to Western trade as a direct result of the Qing dynasty's military defeats and foreign coercion in the late 19th century. During this period, China's national capitalists were just beginning to emerge. The Qing court's

2 Office of the Historian, "The Opening to China Part I: the First Opium War, the United States, and the Treaty of Wangxia, 1839–1844"; "The Opening to China II: the Second Opium War, the United States, and the Treaty of Tianjin, 1857–1859." *Milestones: 1830–1860.*

failures, compounded by the signing of unequal treaties, gave rise to new ideas and perspectives on foreign trade.

Initially, foreign trade thinking was shaped by mechanistic views, encapsulated by the slogan "saving the nation through commerce." The question of how to address China's trade deficit was central to Chinese intellectuals, who argued that achieving a trade surplus required a strong domestic production base, reflecting an awareness of an import substitution strategy. Following the Qing navy's defeat in the Sino-Japanese War of 1894–1895, Chinese intellectuals realized that without social and political reform, pursuing commerce or development alone was insufficient. They resolutely called for the restoration of tariff sovereignty and the abolition of unequal treaties. Sun Yat-sen, one of the most prominent advocates for reclaiming customs sovereignty, believed that imperialist control over China's customs was the root cause of the country's silver outflow, trade deficit, and industrial failures. China gradually regained customs sovereignty and abolished unequal treaties in the 1930s and 1940s. During this period, foreign trade thinkers were keenly aware of the need for economic development and linked their foreign trade ideas to China's industrialization efforts.

Earlier Chinese intellectuals also opposed government control over commerce, advocating for greater commercial autonomy. The debate over the role of government intervention versus private enterprise significantly influenced their discourse, a topic that continues to shape Chinese economic thought today. For instance, Yan Fu (1854–1921), a staunch proponent of laissez-faire principles and minimal government intervention in the market, translated Adam Smith's *Wealth of Nations* into Chinese in 1902. Yan criticized the Qing court's state-controlled approach to commerce, advocating instead for granting more freedom to the people. His translation had a profound impact on the development of Chinese thought at the turn of the century (Yuan & Guo, 2001; Li, 1979).

China's Quest for GATT/WTO Membership

Between 1946 and 1948, the government of the Republic of China (ROC) took part in negotiations that led to the creation of the International Trade Organization (ITO) and the General Agreement on Tariffs and Trade (GATT). In 1947, the ROC signed the Final Act of GATT. However, since the US Congress did not ratify the ITO Charter, the GATT provisions were implemented through the Protocol of Provisional Application. The ROC, along with other contracting parties (except Chile), signed the Protocol and became one of the 23 original Contracting Parties. However, following the Communist Party of China's (CPC) victory in the civil war and the establishment of the People's Republic of China (PRC) in 1949, the ROC government withdrew from GATT in 1950 under Article 5 (Chan, 1994; Qin, 1993).[3]

3 GATT/CP/54. According to Chinese sources, the ROC government's withdrawal from the GATT was primarily driven by US pressure. The US feared that China, under the leadership of the CPC, might

After the ROC's withdrawal, China suspended its relations with the GATT for over three decades. This break was due to both ideological opposition during the Cold War – rooted in China's socialist economic policies – and the PRC's misunderstandings of GATT's role and functions (Yang & Cheng, 2001). When the PRC regained its seat at the United Nations in 1971, the PRC government opted not to join the GATT for two main reasons, according to Shi Guangsheng, former Minister of Foreign Trade. First, Chinese policymakers viewed GATT as an exclusive club for wealthy Western nations, making it unnecessary for China to join. Second, GATT required its members to operate under a market economy system, a concept seen as equivalent to capitalism, which was incompatible with China's socialist system at the time (Shi, 2011).

In line with its "leaning to one side" (一边倒政策) foreign policy, the PRC concentrated its foreign trade efforts on the socialist bloc, primarily with the Soviet Union and Eastern European socialist countries. Between the 1950s and 1970s, China's foreign trade volume remained relatively modest. In 1950, the total import and export value was only USD 1.135 billion, representing 0.9% of the world's total trade volume. By 1960, this figure had risen to USD 3.809 billion, reaching USD 4.586 billion by 1970, and further increasing to USD 14.804 billion by 1977. In the early years of the PRC, over 80% of the country's exports consisted of primary products, while imports were mainly machinery and other production materials.[4]

In 1982, China began internal preparations to enter GATT. By 1984, it obtained observer status, emphasizing that this interim status would not undermine its future legal standing within the organization. Notably, Hong Kong's accession to GATT influenced the PRC's decision to seek membership (Shi, 2011).[5] In 1986, China formally applied to resume its membership in GATT. On January 1, 1995, with the official establishment of the WTO, China's efforts shifted from seeking the "resumption of GATT membership" to negotiating "WTO accession." However, unlike the relatively smooth and positive experiences China encountered when joining most international and multilateral organizations (Feinerman, 1996), the process of resuming GATT membership and subsequently gaining WTO accession turned into a 15-year marathon. One major hurdle contributing to the prolonged negotiations was the conflict over China's economic system.

---

exploit the tariff reductions and trade benefits offered by the GATT. The ROC had gained observer status in GATT in 1965 but lost this status following the passage of UN General Assembly Resolution No. 2758. (Shi, 2011).

4 Data quoted from the National Bureau of Statistics of the PRC. Available at: <https://www.stats.gov.cn/zt_18555/ztfx/qzxzgcl60zn/>

5 The Sino-British Joint Declaration on Hong Kong, signed in 1984, stated that Hong Kong "will retain the status of a free port and a separate customs territory." To enable Hong Kong to continue benefiting from GATT membership, which it had enjoyed under British colonial rule, the PRC expressed its willingness to allow Hong Kong to join GATT independently. As a result, Hong Kong became a separate GATT member in 1986.

Blending Market Economy with Planned Economy: A Unique Approach

The CPC adopted the Stalinist model of a centrally planned economy when the PRC was founded, characterized by central authority controlling all economic activities. In this system, the central government maintained a state monopoly on foreign trade to prevent capitalist influences from undermining the planned economy. In 1950, the Ministry of Foreign Trade issued the *Implementation Rules for the Provisional Regulations on the Administration of Foreign Trade*, mandating that all foreign trade activities be placed under unified state management, with the Ministry of Foreign Trade overseeing these activities nationwide.

With the launch of the reform and opening-up policy, Deng Xiaoping emphasized the importance of decentralizing economic management authority to stimulate growth and efficiency. As a result, 19 departments under the State Council and various local governments established foreign trade companies involved in both trade and industrial production activities. Between 1979 and 1987, the number of foreign trade companies grew rapidly, reaching 2,200 – 11 times the total in 1979 (Huang et al., 2019). Deng also dismantled the long-standing prohibition against China's participation in the international division of labor, underscoring that engaging in global trade and competition was vital for driving economic development (Ma, 2003). Despite the reform, the negotiations on China's resumption of GATT membership stalled due to the conflict between the market economy and the planned economy, a point of contention that continues to this day.

According to UNCTAD, a market economy refers to "a national economy of a country that relies heavily upon market forces to determine levels of production, consumption, investment, and saving without government intervention." In contrast, planned economies, also known as command economies, are systems in which a central authority, typically the government, controls production, consumption, investment, and saving, instead of allowing these decisions to be governed by market forces. It was widely perceived that the GATT system, along with the OECD, functioned as a "club" of market economies, in contrast to the Council for Mutual Economic Assistance (Comecon), which represented centrally planned economies (Thorstensen & Ramos, 2013).

To gain acceptance within GATT, China initially described its economic system as a "commodity economy system that combines a planned economy with market forces" during the negotiations. However, this concept was not accepted. Deng's Southern Tour at the beginning of 1992 dismantled the belief that a planned economy is the defining feature of socialism and that a market economy is exclusive to capitalism. His emphasis on the idea that a market economy could function within a socialist framework was pivotal for China's negotiations. Deng's assertion that a market economy could function within a socialist framework is widely regarded as a theoretical breakthrough in China and had a profound impact on China's economic reforms (Long, 1998). In October 1992, the 14th CPC National Congress declared that the goal of China's economic restructuring was to establish a socialist market economic system.[6] This strategic decision paved the way for the GATT Working Party to officially conclude its review of China's foreign trade system, moving the negotiations into the critical phase of market access discussions. This transition was a key step toward China's eventual accession to the WTO.

Adapting to WTO Rules: Challenges and Progress

It has been widely reported that China made significant compromises during the negotiations. As the Chinese reformer and Minister of Foreign Trade, Chen Deming, remarked, "We paid a high price for the membership."[7] This "high price" refers to the substantial reforms China had to undertake to adjust to a new economic order, as there was a gap between its commitments and its actual trade practices (Kong, 2000; Shi, 2011).

China's membership in the WTO has been described as "unfavorable, non-reciprocal, and asymmetric," as outlined in its Protocol of Accession (Wu, 2011). This characterization highlights the stringent and unequal conditions China faced during its accession, requiring significant concessions and reforms that were not equally imposed on other members.[8] China undertook "WTO-plus" commitments, requiring it to implement obligations beyond standard WTO rules, such as heightened transparency and stricter reforms of state-owned enterprises (SOEs). At the same time, China accepted "WTO-minus" rights, meaning it was denied some flexibilities typically granted to other developing countries, such as certain trade remedy protections (Grieger, 2016; Kanungo, 2011).

More than two decades after its accession to the WTO, extensive debates have emerged regarding China's compliance with WTO commitments. These discussions highlight significant discrepancies between China's self-assessment and the views held by many of its Western trading partners, particularly the US and the EU.

Assessing Gaps in China's WTO Compliance

The Chinese government and officials emphasized that China has fully met its WTO accession commitments in three main areas: market access, alignment with WTO rules, and compliance with WTO rulings. First of all, China has significantly

6 In 1993, the CPC issued the "Decision on Issues Concerning the Establishment of a Socialist Market Economy." This document outlined that a socialist market economy allows the market to play a central role in resource allocation, while the state retains macroeconomic control. A key aspect of this transition was the reform of state-owned enterprises, which was considered crucial for developing a socialist market economy.

7 Zhang Danhong . "Global membership." *DW*. (12 December, 2011)

8 The Protocol distinguishes China's membership from other WTO members both in form and substance. Formally, it includes legally binding provisions from China's Working Party Report, which deviates from typical WTO practice, as such reports are usually not legally enforceable. Substantively, unlike other members that simply commit to following WTO rules, China agreed to a more rigorous framework (Grieger, 2016).

reduced its average import tariff on goods, from 15.3% in 2001 to 9.8% in 2010, and further to 7.4% by 2021, lower than the 9.8% China promised when acceding to the WTO. Additionally, it opened nearly 120 sectors in the services industry, far beyond opening 100 sectors China promised, reflecting significant progress in liberalizing its markets.[9] Secondly, China undertook comprehensive legal reforms to align its domestic laws with WTO standards. At the national level, the State Council and its departments reviewed over 2,300 laws, regulations, and departmental rules. At the local level, more than 190,000 regional laws, regulations, and policy measures were evaluated, with necessary amendments or repeals implemented to ensure compliance (Yang, 2021). China has maintained an impressive track record in complying with WTO dispute settlement rulings. As of October 1, 2021, China had participated as a complainant in 22 cases, as a respondent in 47 cases, and as a third party in 190 cases. Among the 47 disputes where China was a respondent, 34 distinct issues were addressed. Of these 34 cases, 27 have been resolved, either through mutually agreed solutions (15 cases) or by China implementing the WTO rulings (12 cases). The remaining seven cases are at different stages: six are still under litigation, and one case has lapsed (Zhou, 2023). There has not been a single instance where China refused to comply with a ruling, prompting a complainant to request retaliatory measures.

The US has sharply criticized China's compliance with WTO obligations, characterizing it as poor. In its 2023 annual report on China's WTO compliance, the US Trade Representative (USTR) argues that China has a long record of violating, disregarding, and evading existing WTO rules. It specifies that the primary harm to other WTO members stems not from China's occasional non-compliance with specific WTO rules but from the structural impact of China's state-led, non-market economic model. This model, according to the USTR, heavily relies on government and CPC interventions in the market, which have intensified in recent years.

The differing conclusions between the US and China regarding China's compliance with WTO rules highlight a key issue: the incorporation of the WTO rules and its commitments in laws and policies is the easier part for the Chinese government, but non-market factors and domestic legal constraints present significant challenges to their implementation (Kong, 2000). China maintains that it has revised its domestic laws and policies in alignment with WTO rules and reduced tariffs, whereas the US argues that China's market-oriented reforms remain incomplete, pointing to ongoing state intervention, subsidies, and the dominance of SOEs. The EU aligns with the US position, particularly regarding China's market economy status. In a 2016 resolution by the European Parliament, the EU emphasized that China had committed, through its Accession Protocol, to allowing market forces to determine all prices. However, the resolution asserts that China cannot be considered a market economy, as it has yet to meet the five criteria established by the EU

9 Data quoted from Xinhua. 2021. "China's accession to WTO Benefits World, says Chinese ambassador." *China Daily*. (December 9, 2021)

to define market economies.[10] This ongoing friction over China's socialist market economy model will likely remain a significant issue in future trade negotiations and global economic governance.

The Impacts of China's WTO Accession

Over the past two decades, China has transitioned from a developing nation to a global economic powerhouse, fundamentally reshaping the global economy. Simultaneously, Western governments have become increasingly concerned, viewing competition with China as "unfair" due to perceived advantages in its economic model and policies.

Economic Impacts: Transforming China's Global Role

China is widely regarded as one of the greatest beneficiaries of its accession to the WTO, as its economic development has often been credited to its rapid expansion in international trade (Yao, 2019). Since joining the WTO, China has experienced remarkable and sustained economic growth, alongside notable industrial advancements. In 2001, China's GDP stood at 9.59 trillion RMB, which skyrocketed to 114.9 trillion RMB by 2021, securing its position as the world's second-largest economy since 2010. This impressive economic growth has been accompanied by a significant rise in living standards, with GDP per capita increasing from $1,053 in 2001 to $20,407 in 2021 (see Table 1.1). Exports were estimated to account for 11–15 percent of China's GDP, considering both net exports and the associated forward and backward linkages (Lau et al., 2007). By comparison, the contribution of net trade to annual growth ranks significantly below that of investment and consumption (Al-Haschimi & Spital, 2024).

A recent quantitative case study by Li et al. (2023), found that WTO accession had a positive impact on China's economy, supporting the widely accepted view that trade drives growth. The study suggests that, without joining the WTO, China's growth would have been significantly slower. While China's growth trajectory was initially comparable to other economies that joined the WTO around the same time, it became notably stronger after 2008, when the Great Recession affected other economies much more severely than China. Several factors contributed to

10 See the European Parliament Resolution of 12 May 2016 on China's Market Economy Status (2016/2667(RSP)). Section 15 of China's Accession Protocol permits WTO members to treat China as a non-market economy in anti-dumping investigations and to apply alternative methods for determining the normal value of Chinese exports. A major point of contention was that paragraph 15(a)(ii) was set to expire on December 11, 2016. China has argued that, after this date, members should no longer treat it as a non-market economy. Under EU law, the five criteria required for market economy status include minimal government intervention in enterprises, fair implementation of the rule of law, the absence of state control over resource allocation and production, independent financial institutions, free access to market-determined inputs, and transparent business practices and regulations.

China's sustained growth during this period, including the rapid expansion of its expressway network, an increase in university graduates, a rise in Foreign Direct Investment (FDI), the stimulus package introduced during the global financial crisis, and the economic boost from the 2008 Beijing Summer Olympics (Li et al., 2023). China's export-to-production ratio reached its peak at 18% in 2004 but had declined to 13% by 2020, returning to levels close to the 1995 figure of 11%. This drop is mainly due to the rapid rise in domestic consumption, which has absorbed an increasing share of China's manufacturing output since 2004.

According to Yao (2019), China's remarkable economic growth has been attributed to its effective focus on the key drivers of economic development: labor, capital formation, and technological progress. Before joining the WTO, from 1979 to 2001, China experienced rapid expansion in its overall economic output, achieving an average annual GDP growth rate of 9.4%. The implementation of reform and opening-up policies allowed China to quickly integrate into global value chains, capitalizing on its low-cost labor advantage. This integration led to a substantial increase in labor-intensive manufacturing exports. Capital formation has played a central role in China's growth, following an investment-driven growth model that has been financed by high domestic savings, a result of several government policies. Over the three decades leading up to 2010, the share of investment in China's GDP steadily increased from 35% to 47% (Yao, 2019; Al-Haschimi & Spital, 2024).

In 2001, China's trade volume stood at 4.22 trillion RMB, accounting for 4.6% of global exports of goods. By 2009, China had surpassed Germany to become the world's largest exporter, and since 2013, it has overtaken the US as the largest trading nation. By 2021, China's trade volume had grown to 39.1 trillion RMB, cementing its dominant position in international trade. Accompanied by the export boom, China's foreign exchange reserves increased from $212 billion in 2001 to $3.25 trillion in 2021. The country's appeal to foreign investors grew significantly, with Inward FDI rising from $46 billion in 2001 to $173.5 billion in 2021, as global investors were drawn to China's expanding market and manufacturing capabilities. During the same period, China's outward FDI surged from a modest $2.7 billion to $178.82 billion, reflecting its emergence as a major international investor with substantial projects and investments abroad, particularly under the Belt and Road Initiative (see Table 1.1).

Table 1.1 A Comparison of China's Economic Indicators in 2001 and 2021

Year	*GDP (trillion RMB)*	*GDP per capita (USD)*	*Trade volume (trillion RMB)*	*Share of global exports of goods (%)*	*Foreign exchange reserves (trillion USD)*	*Inward FDI (billion USD)*	*Outward FDI (billion USD)*
2001	9.59	1,053	4.22	4.6	0.212	46	2.7
2021	114.9	20,407	39.1	15.7	3.25	173.5	178.82

Source: China National Bureau of Statistics, China General Administration of Customs

Becoming the World's Manufacturing Superpower

One of the most remarkable economic impacts since China's WTO accession has been the rapid development of its industries and the significant enhancement of its industrial competitiveness. China's rapid industrialization has been widely reported domestically: it is the only nation in the world to encompass all industrial categories outlined by the United Nations industrial classification. From 1978 to 2017, the manufacturing sector consistently played a key role in driving China's economic growth. During this period, industrial output contributed over 50% to GDP growth in 17 years, with contributions exceeding 60% in three of those years. Conversely, the industrial contribution fell below 30% in only nine years, while it remained between 40% and 50% in 14 years. By 2023, the total added value of China's industrial sector surpassed 48 trillion *yuan*, accounting for 38.2% of the country's GDP.[11]

The manufacturing industry has been a pillar of China's macro-economy, consistently holding the top global position since 2007. In a 2024 research report by Richard Baldwin, the author asserts that while the US remains the world's sole military superpower, China has emerged as the world's only manufacturing superpower. China's manufacturing output now surpasses that of the next nine largest producers combined (see Table 1.2). Baldwin's analysis shows that China's share of global manufacturing exports increased from just 3% to 20% by 2020 (Baldwin, 2024).

China's expansion in the manufacturing sector is largely attributed to technological development, which was greatly accelerated by its integration into global value chains. This integration allowed China to access advanced technologies, knowledge, and expertise from developed countries, facilitating rapid industrial upgrading. China maintained a high level of imports, driven in part by the need for intermediate goods used in the manufacturing of export products, as well as the import of investment goods, such as machinery, to upgrade its production capabilities (Al-Haschimi & Spital, 2024). This technological advancement was crucial for China's shift toward more sophisticated industries. The increasing sophistication of China's industries is evident in its export trends, with high-value products like machinery and electronics gradually replacing traditional exports such as clothing and footwear. By 2023, China's exports of electromechanical products had

Table 1.2 Global Trade Share of the World's Largest Manufacturing Economies (2020)

Country	*China*	*US*	*Japan*	*Germany*	*India*	*South Korea*	*Italy*	*France*
Gross Production (% of world)	35%	12%	6%	4%	3%	3%	2%	2%

Source: Baldwin (2024)

11 Data quoted from the National Bureau of Statistics of the PRC.

reached 13.92 trillion RMB, accounting for 58.6% of the country's total exports. Additionally, in 2023, exports of the "new three major items" – battery electric vehicles (BEVs), lithium batteries, and photovoltaic products – surpassed 1.06 trillion RMB for the first time, growing by 29.9%.[12]

Political and Social Impacts of China's WTO Membership

Most economists agree that trade liberalization benefits the US economy overall but imposes adjustment costs for certain sectors and regions (Akhtar et al., 2024). The term "China Shock" has been coined to encapsulate the substantial impacts of China's WTO accession faced by industries and communities in developed economies, notably the US This phenomenon has led to job losses, wage pressure, economic dislocation in manufacturing regions particularly sensitive to increased global competition, as well as security concerns.

Security Concerns and Strategic Challenges

In the United States, trade occupies a pivotal position at the intersection of two key national priorities: economic growth and foreign policy. Increasingly, foreign trade and economic policy are deeply interconnected with other pressing issues such as national security, job creation, and environmental sustainability, among others. China's accession to the WTO not only accelerated its economic rise but also had far-reaching social and political consequences.

In the same year that China joined the WTO, John J. Mearsheimer's book **The Tragedy of Great Power Politics** was published, offering a detailed account of offensive realism. In the book, Mearsheimer argues that one of the key foreign policy challenges for the US is the question of how China might act if its rapid economic growth persists, effectively transforming it into a "giant Hong Kong" (2001 & 2014). With China's rapid economic growth, the term *Thucydides' Trap* has surged in popularity in international politics, fueled by rising geopolitical tensions between China and the US Coined by Graham Allison, the term draws from the ancient historian Thucydides, who described how Athens' rise and the resulting fear in Sparta made war nearly inevitable. Allison applied this historical insight to contemporary US-China relations, suggesting that as China's economic and military power grows, a similar dynamic could challenge US dominance (2017). Mearsheimer has echoed this view, observing that the US-led order once stabilizing the Asia-Pacific region is shifting. Economic changes are redistributing strategic power, with China's ascent significantly altering the global balance and steadily closing the power gap with the US (2010 & 2019).

While expectations of imminent conflict have eased somewhat since *Thucydides' Trap* entered the public discourse, US-China relations remain challenging. The

12 Data quoted from the Chinese government, available at: <https://www.gov.cn/lianbo/fabu/202401/content_6925700.htm>

Biden administration, through statements by Jake Sullivan, the US security advisor, has stressed that the so-called "China shock" that hit pockets of our domestic manufacturing industry especially hard – with large and long-lasting impacts – wasn't adequately anticipated and wasn't adequately addressed as it unfolded. The Biden administration has advocated for alliances and partnerships that create shared advantages for US economic and security strategies. As Mark Wu explains, as China's economic success expanded, it created spillover effects in the security domain, prompting mixed reactions from the West. On one hand, Western countries have benefited from China's growth, which has contributed to addressing global public issues. On the other hand, concerns have emerged that China's advances in trade and technology may spill over into non-trade areas, such as military and national security. The US, in particular, feels the impact of these spillover effects and fears that China's growing influence could eventually shift the international power structure, weakening the Western security alliance (Wu, 2019).

Impacts on the US Labour Market

The Stolper-Samuelson theorem suggests that trade liberalization benefits the abundant factor of production in a country while harming the scarce factor (Stolper & Samuelson, 1941).[13] In general, developed countries have relatively abundant capital and knowledge, while low-skilled labor is scarcer. In contrast, developing countries typically have an abundance of labor, particularly low-skilled labor, and a scarcity of capital and advanced technology. According to the Stolper-Samuelson theorem, trade liberalization would thus harm low-skilled labor in developed countries by increasing competition from labor-abundant developing countries.

During his political campaigns and presidency, Donald Trump frequently blamed China for "stealing" American jobs, arguing that its economic policies and trade practices were central to the decline in US manufacturing employment. Similarly, the Biden administration has adopted a "worker-centered" trade policy, which seeks to ensure that the benefits of international trade are distributed more fairly among American workers, addressing some of the economic disruptions attributed to globalization and trade with China. The Biden administration also acknowledges the significant and lasting economic impact of the "China Shock," particularly on the American manufacturing sector. In public statements, the US National Security Advisor, Jake Sullivan, emphasized that the effects of China's economic rise were neither fully anticipated nor effectively addressed as they unfolded, resulting in

13 The Stolper and Samuelson theorem posits that an increase in the price of a good will lead to an increase in the price of the production factor that is intensively used in its production, and a decrease in the price of the other factor. The theorem is derived from the Heckscher-Ohlin (H-O) model, which attributes the inequality effect of trade openness to differences in productivity, the country's relative factor endowments, and individuals' reliance on either labor or capital income. Bertil Ohlin first explained the H-O model in the book *Interregional and International Trade* published in 1933. However, he credited Heckscher as a co-developer due to Heckscher's earlier work on the issue and the significant influence of Ohlin's doctoral thesis, which was supervised by Heckscher.

considerable job losses and economic displacement in specific US regions. Autor et al. find that employment has declined in US industries more exposed to import competition, as expected; however, compensating job growth in other sectors has yet to materialize. Gaining a clearer understanding of when and where trade incurs costs, as well as how and why it might offer benefits remains a central focus for trade and labor economists (2016).[14]

Widening income inequality in the US has been influenced by increased trade with lower-wage countries, especially China. For instance, Josh Bivens (2013) argues that while trade liberalization can increase overall national income, often framed as a "win-win" scenario, it also drives specialization. This leads the US economy to expand production in capital-intensive industries while scaling back output in labor-intensive sectors. As a result, in a country like the US, the majority of workers – especially those in lower-skilled, labor-intensive industries – are likely to be net losers from increased trade with poorer nations, where labor is more abundant and cheaper. Bivens attributes one-third of the increase in US income inequality from 1973 to 2011 to trade with low-wage countries, with a significant portion of this effect – about one-third – specifically linked to increased trade with China (Bivens, 2013).

By contrast, some findings reveal that the connection between free trade and income inequality should not be overstated. International knowledge flow and technology, along with financial globalization, play a more significant role in increasing inequality (e.g., Grossman & Helpman, 2018; Jaumotte & Papageorgiou, 2013). Some empirical research findings indicate that the negative distributional effects of international integration are primarily driven by knowledge flows rather than trade itself. Innovation is a key driver of growth, but within a country, income inequality is worsened by knowledge sharing, as spillovers enhance innovation productivity and incentivize the expansion of knowledge-generating sectors globally. In the presence of partial or complete international knowledge spillovers, an R&D subsidy in one country accelerates growth across all nations while also increasing income inequality within countries worldwide Grossman and Helpman (2018). Similarly, Jaumotte and Papageorgiou's research also finds that while income inequality has risen in most countries and regions over the past decades, trade liberalization and export growth are associated with lower income inequality. Increased financial openness is linked to higher inequality. However, the combined contribution of trade and financial globalization to rising inequality has been much lower than that of technological change, both globally and especially in developing countries. Although the spread of technology is related to increased globalization, technological progress is seen to have a separately identifiable effect on inequality (2013).

14 A 2015 report by the Economic Policy Institute (EPI) highlighted that the US lost 3.4 million jobs, most of them in manufacturing, between 2001 and 2015 due to the growing trade deficit with China. This report has been central to the ongoing debate over the economic impact of US-China trade relations, particularly regarding job losses and wage stagnation in the US.

Challenges Confronting the Multilateral Trading System

China's integration into the global trade system through joining the WTO was initially seen as a potential avenue for further economic liberalization and engagement. However, over time, Western countries have expressed increasing concern about China's trade practices and China's economic model, which are perceived as inconsistent with WTO rules and principles.

The Deadlock of the WTO Appellate Body

Since its establishment in 1995, the World Trade Organization's (WTO) dispute settlement mechanism has been instrumental in resolving numerous trade disputes, earning it the reputation as the "crown jewel" of the global trading system. However, beginning in 2017, the United States started blocking the appointment of new judges to the Appellate Body, leading to its inoperability in December 2019. As of May 28, 2024, the US has obstructed proposals to initiate the selection process for filling these vacancies 76 times, holding to its position that its longstanding concerns remain unaddressed.[15] This prolonged paralysis has significantly undermined the WTO's capacity to enforce trade rules effectively.

The US frustrations with WTO have accumulated over time for several reasons, including both procedural and systemic concerns (Payasova et al., 2018). While procedural issues may be more easily resolved, the main US concerns are rooted in systemic issues, which require greater political will to address. Two key systemic issues lie at the heart of the current crisis. First, the US and some other members have accused the Appellate Body of "overreaching" in its interpretations, creating what they perceive as new rules rather than simply applying existing ones. This runs counter to the Appellate Body's mandate under Articles 3.2 and 19.2 of the Dispute Settlement Understanding (DSU), which prohibits it from creating or abolishing rights and obligations for WTO members. Second, the Appellate Body has been criticized for addressing issues not raised by the parties or for issuing opinions on matters that were unnecessary for resolving disputes – analogous to obiter dicta in legal terms (Payasova et al., 2018). These practices have contributed to the current impasse, highlighting the need for political consensus to reform the system.

From a delegation perspective, the US's inactivation of the Appellate Body can be seen as a deliberate exercise of "control" over international organizations, particularly through its use of the "veto" power embedded in the consensus-based decision-making process. Delegation theory posits that states, as principals, delegate authority to international organizations, which act as agents managing specific functions on their behalf. To ensure that these agents align with national goals, states design mechanisms to monitor and control them (Hawkins et al., 2006). In the WTO's consensus-based system, states possess formal veto rights, which can

15 "US Continues to Block WTO Appellate Body Appointments." *ABS News Service* (May 28, 2024).

be considered a significant control mechanism for members to block decisions that go against their interests.

In the case of the US, the delegation chain starts with its voters, who are the foundational source of governmental authority. Through the electoral process, voters influence US trade policy. The US Congress, as the representative body, grants authority to the executive branch, which in turn delegates power to international organizations. Interest groups, campaign donors, and party leaders also play a significant role in shaping trade policy, with Congress acting as a key arena where these groups exert influence (Irwin, 2017).[16] The US's frustrations with the WTO have been largely driven by domestic concerns, especially those of the working class and the economic rise of China. Donald Trump's electoral victory is often seen as a reflection of these economic and social grievances. Trump was a vocal critic of the WTO, accusing the organization of unfairly disadvantaging the US He even threatened to withdraw from the WTO unless it reformed to provide more favorable treatment to the US, framing this stance as part of a broader effort to protect American workers and industries.[17]

In recent years, there has been bipartisan consensus in the US to either marginalize the WTO or push for reforms that align with US interests. The inactivation of the WTO Appellate Body has also been used as a tool to pressure other WTO members into negotiating new trade rules that address perceived gaps, particularly those related to China. China's rise has led the US to question the effectiveness of the WTO's multilateral trade system, with policymakers and elites emphasizing that the current system fails to regulate China's economic model, especially its state-owned enterprises controlled by the Chinese Communist Party, which causes concern in the US. As a result, there is growing agreement that the WTO must either be sidelined or reformed to better align with US priorities (Wu, 2019).

The Rise of Trade Protectionism

Trade protectionism has surged globally over the past decade, following a long period of decline throughout much of the 20th century. According to data from Global Trade Alert analyzed by the IMF, new restrictions on goods, services, and investment increased by 14% in 2022 compared to the previous year, reaching a level more than six times higher than in 2013. Investment restrictions experienced

16 The *Reciprocal Trade Agreements Act of 1934* empowered the US President to negotiate trade agreements with foreign nations, allowing the government to transcend the narrow interests of specific producer groups and pursue trade policy from a broader national development perspective. However, Congress still retains significant control over trade and foreign policy and can limit the President's ability to negotiate such agreements. For instance, internal divisions among interest groups once led Congress to refuse ratification of the Havana Charter, which aimed to establish the International Trade Organization. As a result, the USTR, although part of the executive branch, frequently works in close coordination with Congress to ensure that trade agreements align with legislative priorities (Irwin, 2017; Meyer and Sitaraman, 2019).

17 See John Micklethwait et al. "President Trump Threatens to Withdraw US from World Trade Organization 'If They Don't Shape UP'." *Time*. (August 28, 2018)

the sharpest rise, with 239 new measures implemented – more than quadruple the amount imposed in 2021. This trend highlights an escalating geoeconomic fragmentation, a phenomenon driven by policies that reverse economic integration, with international trade at the core of this reversal (Bolhuis et al., 2023).

Most recently, the Biden administration implemented new Section 301 tariffs in May 2024, targeting approximately $18 billion worth of Chinese goods. This action included a significant 100% tariff on all EVs imported from China, aiming to counteract what the administration perceives as unfair trade practices and to support the US EV industry.[18] The EU also launched an ex officio anti-subsidy investigation into the imports of BEVs from China in 2023. Ursula von der Leyen, President of the European Commission, said

> The electric vehicle sector holds huge potential for Europe's future competitiveness and green industrial leadership. EU car manufacturers and related sectors are already investing and innovating to fully develop this potential. Wherever we find evidence that their efforts are being impeded by market distortions and unfair competition, we will act decisively.[19]

In October 2024, the Commission concluded that the BEV value chain in China benefits from unfair subsidization, which is causing a threat of economic injury to EU producers of BEV. The Commission decided to impose countervailing duties on imports of BEVs from China for five years, with tariff rates ranging from 17.0% to 35.3%.[20]

As Irwin notes, the debate over whether the US should engage in open trade with other countries or protect domestic industries from foreign competition has long been a source of intense political conflict (2017). Following the Great Recession, US economic policies have shown a clear trend toward protectionism. Section 1605 of the *American Recovery and Reinvestment Act of 2009*, known as the "Buy American" provision, mandates that all manufactured goods, iron, and steel used in publicly funded infrastructure projects under the Act must be sourced domestically. This measure is widely seen as an act of trade protectionism. Pascal Lamy argues that the surge in protectionism following the Great Recession is driven by structural forces that have steadily altered the political balance in Washington, which had favored trade openness since the 1950s. Among the various factors fueling trade protectionism, US-China rivalry has emerged as a structural and predominant force (2023).

18 The White House, "Fact Sheet: President Biden Takes Action to Protect American Workers and Businesses from China's Unfair Trade Practices" (May 15, 2024).

19 European Commission, "Commission Launches Investigation on Subsidized Electric Cars from China." Available at: <https://ec.europa.eu/commission/presscorner/detail/en/ip_23_4752>

20 European Union, "EU imposes duties on unfairly subsidized electric vehicles from China while discussions on price undertakings continue." Available at: <https://ec.europa.eu/commission/presscorner/detail/en/ip_24_5589>

The Trump administration's "America First" policy signaled an inflection point toward protectionism in US trade policy, stressing that trade must be "fair" and reciprocal in line with Trump's goal of reducing trade imbalances (Chow & Sheldon, 2019). Through this policy, the administration introduced significant tariffs aimed at countering perceived unfair trade practices and imbalances, particularly with China. In 2018 and 2019, tariffs were placed on various goods totaling about $380 billion in value. While the Biden administration has removed tariffs on some EU and Japanese imports, it has largely upheld these trade war tariffs. By March 2024, these tariffs had generated over $233 billion in taxes, with US consumers shouldering the cost. Approximately $89 billion (38%) was collected under Trump, and the remaining $144 billion (62%) has been collected during Biden's term. This policy shift ranks as one of the most substantial tax increases in recent decades, underscoring a strong protectionist stance.[21]

The resurgence of protectionism following the Great Recession has been closely associated with the rise of populist sentiment in the US According to economist Barry Eichengreen, economic hardship, income inequality, and ideology are key drivers behind today's most prominent forms of populism. Poor economic performance naturally breeds dissatisfaction with the status quo, while growing inequality increases the number of people feeling left behind, fueling discontent with economic policies. Furthermore, a nation's unique ideological stance – such as individualism and market fundamentalism – also contributes to the rise of populism. In the US, those negatively affected by globalization and technological changes feel excluded from the benefits of economic growth and are frustrated by the government's inaction. This discontent is amplified by the American ideology of distrust in government and the emphasis on individualism, leading many to see the government as the problem rather than the solution (Eichengreen, 2018).

From Strengthening Interdependence to Managing Risks

For liberals, economic interdependence reduces the likelihood of war by making aggression more costly than trade. States with strong economic ties are less likely to engage in conflict, preferring peaceful relations to safeguard mutual trade benefits. This principle underpins institutions like the GATT and WTO, which promote global cooperation and discourage the use of force. Interdependence is embedded in the WTO's legal framework, shaping its rules on tariffs, services, and intellectual property. By fostering international trade, the WTO seeks to reduce conflict, encouraging interconnected economies to resolve disputes peacefully and promote mutual growth (Keohane & Nye, 2012; Copeland, 1996). However, as the global economic and political landscape evolves, there is a shift from interdependence to de-risking. This new approach focuses on mitigating risks while

21 Data quoted from Erica York, "Tariff Tracker: Tracking the Economic Impact of the Trump-Biden Tariffs." *Tax Foundation*. Available at: <https://taxfoundation.org/research/all/federal/trump-tariffs-biden-tariffs/>

maintaining economic ties, reflecting a change in priorities amid growing concerns over national security and economic vulnerabilities.

The COVID-19 pandemic and the Russia-Ukraine war have accelerated a de-risking trend by exposing weaknesses in global supply chains. Some countries have prioritized national resilience and self-sufficiency over global trade openness. Both the US and the EU have launched reindustrialization initiatives to revitalize domestic manufacturing, driven by the need for more resilient supply chains, the goal of creating and retaining skilled jobs, climate commitments, and a desire to regain a competitive manufacturing edge.[22] In March 2023, European Commission President Ursula von der Leyen proposed a "de-risking" approach, which aims to address the challenges posed by China's commercial and technological power by reducing strategic dependencies and strengthening Europe's autonomy in critical sectors.[23] At the G7 Summit in May 2023, the Biden administration and other leaders embraced the de-risking approach, coordinating their strategies for economic resilience and security by diversifying partnerships and reducing reliance on risky dependencies.

In terms of de-risking, the Biden administration has made it clear that it does not intend to decouple from China's economy. Given China's size and significance, severing the economic ties that sustain the global economy is neither a goal nor considered achievable.[24] In a speech at the Brookings Institution on "Renewing American Economic Leadership," US National Security Advisor Jake Sullivan highlighted four key challenges facing the US: the hollowing out of industries, geopolitical and security competition, the climate crisis, and inequality. To address these issues, Sullivan emphasized that the priority is strengthening domestic capacity through a modern industrial strategy.[25] As part of this effort, the US passed the Inflation Reduction Act (IRA) in 2022, which includes $370 billion for clean energy investments – making it the largest single investment in climate and energy initiatives in US history. The IRA has significantly influenced the US EV market by providing substantial incentives to promote EV adoption and bolster domestic manufacturing. Since its implementation on January 1, 2024, the IRA's clean vehicle advance payment program has delivered over $2 billion in point-of-sale financial benefits to consumers purchasing new and used clean vehicles.[26] These

22 See Capgemini Research Institute, 2024. *The Resurgence of Manufacturing: Reindustrialization Strategies in Europe and the US*. Available at: <https://www.capgemini.com/wp-content/uploads/2024/04/CRI_Reindustrialization_Final_1.pdf>

23 See "Speech by President von der Leyen on EU-China Relations to the Mercator Institute for China Studies and the European Policy Centre." Available at: <https://ec.europa.eu/commission/presscorner/detail/%E2%80%8Cen/speech_23_2063>

24 Mari Yamaguchi, "Trade Envoy Tai Says US not Seeking to 'Decouple' from China." *AP News* (April 20, 2023); Yuka Hayashi, "US Not Seeking Decoupling From China, Commerce Chief Says." *The Wall Street Journal*. (November 20, 2022).

25 The White House, "Remarks by National Security Advisor Jake Sullivan on Renewing American Economic Leadership at the Brookings Institution." (April 27, 2023).

26 Data quoted from the US Department of the Treasury, "US Department of the Treasury Announces More Than $2 Billion in Upfront Savings for Consumers on Electric and Plug-In Hybrid Vehicle Sales Under Biden-Harris Administration's Inflation Reduction Act." (October 1, 2024)

incentives have raised concerns among international trade partners. The European Union has expressed apprehension that the IRA's subsidies, including local content requirements, could distort trade and contravene World Trade Organization rules.

Concluding Remarks

Over the two decades since China's WTO accession, the country has achieved remarkable economic growth by integrating into the global economy. In terms of WTO compliance, China has largely fulfilled its commitments, revising its domestic laws and policies to align with WTO rules and maintaining an exemplary record in implementing Panel reports. China's WTO membership has facilitated its rise as the world's manufacturing powerhouse, leading to significant consequences for Western advanced economies, including job losses, rising income inequality, and concerns over national security. The inactivation of the WTO Appellate Body and the rise of trade protectionism are, in part, responses from advanced economies to these challenges. However, the interplay of consensus-based decision-making, geopolitical competition, and rising protectionism has created a perfect storm, leaving the global trade system struggling to effectively address these issues. Both the US and EU have adopted a firmer stance towards China, developing new policies and tools that culminate in the de-risking approach. This marks a fundamental shift from the post-Cold War model of interdependence to a more strategic rivalry, contributing to a trend of trade fragmentation.

References

Akhtar, S. I., Cimino-Isaacs, C. D., & Sutter, K. M. (2024). U.S. trade policy: Background and current issues. Congressional Research Service, No. IF10156.

Al-Haschimi, A., & Spital, T. (2024). The evolution of China's growth model: Challenges and long-term growth prospects. *ECB Economic Bulletin*, 5. https://www.ecb.europa.eu/press/economic-bulletin/articles/2024/html/ecb.ebart202405_01~a6318ef569.cs.html.

Allison, G. (2017). *Destined for War: Can America and China Escape Thucydides' Trap?* Houghton Mifflin Harcourt.

Autor, D. H., Dorn, D., & Gordon, H. H. (2016). The China shock: Learning from labor-market adjustment to large changes in trade. *Annual Review of Economics*, 8, 205–240.

Baldwin, R. (2024). China is the world's sole manufacturing superpower: A line sketch of the rise. Centre for European Policy Research, Research report, January 17. https://cepr.org/voxeu/columns/china-worlds-sole-manufacturing-superpower-line-sketch-rise.

Bivens, J. (2013). Using standard models to benchmark the costs of globalization for American workers without a college degree. Economic Policy Institute Briefing Paper, No. 354. https://www.epi.org/publication/standard-models-benchmark-costs-globalization/.

Bolhuis, M. A., Chen, J., & Kett, B. (2023). The costs of geoeconomic fragmentation: Disruption in trade threatens losses to global living standards as severe as those from COVID–19. *Finance & Development*, 2.

Chan, S. (1994). Taiwan's application to the GATT: A new urgency with the conclusion of the uruguay round. *Indiana Journal of Global Legal Studies*, 2(1), 275–299.

Chow, D. C. K., & Sheldon, I. (2019). Is strict reciprocity required for fair trade? *Vanderbilt Journal of Transnational Law*, 1, 1–42.

Copeland, D. C. (1996). Economic interdependence and war: A theory of trade expectations. *International Security*, 20(4), 5–41.
Eichengreen, B. (2018). Populism, ideology and materialism. *New Global Studies*, 12(3), 267–275.
Fan, Z., Qin, H., & Zhao, Z. (1996). 论中国古代法中"重农抑商"传统的成因 [On the origin of 'stressing agriculture and neglecting commerce' in ancient Chinese constitution]. *The Journal of Renmin University of China*, 5, 60–65.
Feinerman, J. V. (1996). China's quests to enter the GATT/WTO. *Proceedings of the Annual Meeting (American Society of International Law)*, 90, 401–407.
Grieger, G. (2016). China's WTO accession: 15 years on – Taking, shaking, or shaping WTO rules? European Parliamentary Research Service, PE 593.570. https://www.europarl.europa.eu/thinktank/en/document/EPRS_BRI(2016)593570.
Grossman, G. M., & Helpman, E. (2018). Growth, trade, and inequality. *Econometrica*, 86(1), 37–83.
Hawkins, D. G., Lake, D. A., Nielson, D. L., & Tierney, M. J. (2006). Delegation under anarchy: States, international organizations, and principal-agent theory. In D. G. Hawkins, D. A. Lake, D. L. Nielson & M. J. Tierney (Eds.), *Delegation and Agency in International Organizations* (pp. 3–38). Cambridge University Press.
Huang, H., et al. (2019). 新中国成立70年来的外贸体制变迁：回顾与展望 [The changes of foreign trade system in the 70 years since the founding of new China: Retrospect and prospect]. *Journal of Zhongnan University of Economics and Law*, 5, 19–42.
Irwin, D. A. (2017). *Clashing Over Commerce: A History of US Trade Policy*. The University of Chicago Press.
Kanungo, A. K. (2011). The process of China's accession to the World Trade Organization: Obstacles and implications. *International Studies*, 48(3–4), 305–316.
Keohane, R. O., & Nye, J. (2012). *Power and Interdependence* (4th ed.). Longman.
Kong, Q. (2000). China's WTO accession: Commitments and implications. *Journal of International Economic Law*, 3(4), 655–690.
Jaumotte, F., Lall, S., & Papageorgiou, C. (2013). Rising income inequality: Technology, or trade and financial globalization? *IMF Economic Review*, 2, 271–309.
Lamy, P. (2023). The slow American protectionist turn. *CEPR*, March 27.
Lau, L., Chen, X., Cheng, L. K., & Fung, K. C. (2007). Non-competitive input-output model and its application: An examination of the China-U.S. trade surplus [非竞争型投入占用产出模型及其应用——中美贸易顺差透视]. *Social Sciences in China*, 5, 91–103.
Li, J. (1979). 论清末西方资产阶级经济学的传入中国[On introduction of western bourgeois economic science into China at the end of the Qing Dynasty]. *Economic Research Journal*, 2, 68–75.
Li, J., Liu, Y., & Zhou, Y. (2023). Assessing the impact of WTO accession on China's economic growth: A synthetic control approach. In H. Gao, D. Raess, & K. Zeng (Eds.), *China and the WTO: A Twenty-Year Assessment* (pp. 252–274). Cambridge University Press.
Lim, I. M. (2013). From Haijin to Kaihai: The Jiajing Court's search for a modus operandi along the South-Eastern Coast (1522-1567). *Journal of the British Association for Chinese Studies*, 2, 1–26.
Long, Y. (1998). 中国加入WTO久拖不决的原因及对策 [Reasons and suggestions for China's prolonged delay in WTO accession]. *Qianxian*, 12, 17–22.
Ma, H. (2003). 当代中国外贸思想研究 [The study of contemporary China's foreign trade ideology]. Doctoral Dissertation, Fudan University.
Mavroidis, P. C., & Sapir, A. (2021). *China and the WTO: Why Multilateralism Matters*. Princeton University Press.
Mearsheimer, J. J. (2001 & 2014). *The Tragedy of Great Power Politics*. W. W. Norton.

Mearsheimer, J. J. (2010). The gathering storm: China's challenge to U.S. power in Asia. *The Chinese Journal of International Politics*, 3(4), 381–396.
Mearsheimer, J. J. (2019). *Thucydides' Other 'Traps': The United States, China, and the Prospect of 'Inevitable' War*. National Defense University Press.
Meyer, T., & Sitaraman, G. (2019). Trade and the separation of powers. *California Law Review*, 107(2), 583–672.
Stolper, W. F., & Samuelson, P. A. (1941). Protection and real wages. *The Review of Economic Studies*, 1, 58–73.
Payasova, T., Hufbauer, G. C., & Schott, J. J. (2018). *The Dispute Settlement Crisis in the World Trade Organization: Causes and Cures*. Peterson Institute for International Economics.
Qin, Y. (1993). China and GATT: Accession instead of resumption. *World Trade*, 27, 78–97.
Thorstensen, V., & Ramos, D. (2013). WTO – Market and non-market economies: The hybrid case of China. *Latin American Journal of International Trade Law*, 1(2), 765–798.
Shi, G. (Ed.) (2011). *Handbook on China's Accession to the World Trade Organization* [中国加入世界贸易组织谈判历程]. People's Publishing.
Wu, M. (2019). China's rise and the growing doubts over trade multilateralism. In M. A. Crowley (Ed.), *Trade War: The Clash of Economic Systems Endangering Global Prosperity*. London: CEPR Press.
Wu, X. (2011). No longer outside, not yet equal: Rethinking China's membership in the World Trade Organization. *Chinese Journal of International Law*, 10, 227–270.
Yao, Y. (2019). China's economic growth in retrospect. *China Economic Journal*, 12(1), 2–17.
Yang, G. (2021). Pacta Sunt Servanda: Practices of China as a contracting party to the WTO [条约必须遵守——作为WTO成员的中国实践] *Journal of Administration Reform*, 7, 30–39.
Yang, G., & Cheng, J. (2001). The process of China's accession to the WTO. *Journal of International Economic Law*, 4(2), 297–328.
Yuan, G., & Guo, B. (2001). Foreign trade thoughts in modern China [论近代中国对外贸易思想]. *The Journal of the University of International Business and Economics*, 3, 1–5.
Zhou, W. (2023). The impact of the WTO dispute settlement system on China: Effectiveness, challenges, and broader issues. In H. Gao, D. Raess, & K. Zeng (Eds.), *China and the WTO: A Twenty-Year Assessment* (pp. 252–274). Cambridge University Press.

2 US-China Trade Tensions

A Comparative Analysis with US-Japan Trade Frictions

The US-China Trade Tensions: Causes and Consequences

Until recently, economic and trade ties between the United States and China were often described as a stabilizing force, akin to a ballast stone that helped steady relations and mitigate challenges stemming from US policies and actions. However, since the onset of the US-China trade war in 2018, this stabilizing force has morphed into a metaphorical lit fuse, igniting heightened tensions and uncertainty. Some analysts have even likened the trade war to a Second Cold War. Many Chinese scholars view the US-China trade tensions as an inevitable consequence of shifting global economic power dynamics following the 2008 financial crisis, coupled with the weakening of the WTO's multilateral trading framework. These tensions also reflect broader strategic forces, particularly the logic of containment versus anti-containment, often framed within the Thucydides Trap narrative (Shen, 2019).

The Sweet-and-Sour US-China Trade Relations

In 1979, the United States and China restored diplomatic relations and signed a bilateral trade agreement, paving the way for significant trade growth. Trade between the two countries surged from a combined $4 billion in 1979 to over $690 billion in 2022, reaching a historic high.[1] As of recent data, ASEAN and the European Union collectively surpass the United States as China's largest trading partners when grouped as regional blocs. However, when trade partners are considered individually by country, the United States continues to be China's largest single trading partner.

For decades, economic and trade relations have been regarded in China as the stabilizing ballast of overall US-China bilateral relations. On May 25, 2017, the Ministry of Commerce of the PRC officially released the *Research Report on US-China Economic Trade Relations*. According to the report, the maiden voyage of the American merchant ship "Empress of China" to China over 230 years ago marked the beginning of economic and trade exchanges between China and the US.

1 Data quoted from "China-US Trade Hit Record High of $690 billion in 2022." *CGTN*. (March 11, 2023).

DOI: 10.4324/9781003637110-3

"China and the US are the world's two largest economies, accounting for approximately 40% of the global economic output, a quarter of the goods exports, and 30% of the world's FDI outflows and inflows. The economic cooperation between the two countries has reached an unprecedented depth and breadth, with their economies becoming increasingly interwoven. Sound US-China economic and trade relations are not only in the fundamental interests of the two countries but also vital to the prosperity and stability of the world economy."

US-China bilateral trade relations have faced significant challenges and disruptions since the Trump administration, marked by increased tensions and the imposition of tariffs. In 2017, the Trump administration launched a special 301 review of China's economic practices, focusing on issues such as intellectual property theft, forced technology transfers, and unfair trade practices. In March 2018, the Office of the United States Trade Representative (USTR) released the findings of its Section 301 investigation, highlighting issues of forced technology transfers, intellectual property theft, and discriminatory trade practices. These findings formed the basis for the Trump administration's subsequent imposition of tariffs on Chinese goods.[2]

In July 2018, the United States imposed a 25% tariff on approximately $34 billion worth of imports from China, marking the start of the US-China trade war. In response, China imposed a 25% tariff on 545 US goods, also valued at $34 billion, targeting products such as soybeans, automobiles, and seafood. Over the following months, the United States expanded its tariffs to cover a total of $550 billion worth of Chinese imports, while China imposed tariffs on $185 billion worth of US goods in retaliation. These measures significantly escalated tensions in bilateral trade relations.

After a year and a half of tariff wars and extensive negotiations, the US and China reached a significant milestone with the signing of the US-China Phase One Trade Agreement on January 15, 2020. This agreement comprises eight chapters addressing key areas, including intellectual property protection, technology transfer, agricultural purchases, financial services, currency practices, and the establishment of dispute resolution mechanisms. As part of the agreement, China agreed to increase its purchases of US goods and services by $200 billion over two years, spanning from January 1, 2020, to December 31, 2021.

The Aftermath of the "Phase One" Trade Agreement

However, the Phase One Trade Agreement has fallen short of resolving US-China trade tensions. The outbreak of the COVID-19 pandemic triggered a rapid decline in US-China relations. The Trump administration accused China of mishandling the initial outbreak of the virus in Wuhan, resulting in mutual recriminations and further straining bilateral ties. The Biden administration has largely upheld the tariffs imposed during the Trump era, though there has been some limited relief,

2 USTR. "2018 Special 301 Report." (ustr.gov).

such as tariff exclusions for certain goods to alleviate pressure on US businesses and consumers.[3] As of November 2023, approximately 66.4% of US imports from China are subject to tariffs, with an average tariff rate of 19.3%. This represents a significant increase from pre-trade war levels, where the average tariff was around 3%. Conversely, China has imposed tariffs on about 58.3% of US exports, with an average rate of 21.1%. These elevated tariffs reflect ongoing trade tensions between the two nations.[4] Moreover, in May 2024, the Biden administration announced significant tariff increases on approximately $18 billion worth of Chinese imports. The new tariffs, ranging from 25% to 100%, target a variety of goods, including semiconductors, steel and aluminum products, EVs, batteries and battery parts, natural graphite and other critical materials, medical goods, magnets, cranes, and solar cells.[5] China has also failed to meet its purchasing commitments under the agreement, achieving only 58% of the targets set for the period, falling significantly short of the agreed-upon levels.[6] The ongoing unilateral tariffs have effectively rendered the Phase One Trade Agreement a failure, underscoring the persistent challenges in addressing the fundamental issues in US-China trade relations.

Over the past five years, US-China trade has undergone significant fluctuations driven by escalating trade tensions. The imposition of tariffs resulted in a notable decrease in China's exports to the US, falling from approximately $538.5 billion in 2018 to $449.1 billion in 2019 – a decline of 16.6%. This downward trend continued in 2020, with exports further dropping to $432.5 billion (Table 2.1). In 2022, China's exports of goods rebounded to approximately $536 billion, nearly returning to 2018 levels (Table 2.1). The rebound was largely driven by the COVID-19 pandemic, as American consumers, confined to their homes, increased demand for Chinese-made products, including laptops, toys, and other goods. Despite this temporary recovery, China's exports to the US sharply declined to $426.9 billion in 2023, representing a significant 20.4% drop compared to the previous year. Simultaneously, the US trade deficit with China has been narrowing, declining from $418 billion in 2018 to $279 billion in 2023 (Table 2.1).

The decline in 2023 might signal a fundamental turning point, underscoring the impact of the US strategy to diversify its supply chain, which has adversely affected China's export performance. In 2023, Mexico surpassed China, becoming the US's largest trade partner. In this year, the US imported over $475 billion worth of goods from Mexico, nearly 5% more than in 2022, surpassing imports from China by more than $48 billion. The last time US imports from Mexico exceeded

3 USTR. "USTR Extends Exclusions from China Section 301 Tariffs to Allow for Comments on a Review of the Exclusions and Alignment with Four-Year Review." (December 26, 2023).

4 Data quoted from Lori Ann LaRocco, "As Biden and Xi Meet, Asian Manufacturing Slowdown Returns to a 2020 Low, Led by a Softer China." *State of Freight*. (November 15, 2023).

5 USTR. "Fact Sheet: President Biden Takes Action to Protect American Workers and Businesses from China's Unfair Trade Practices." (September 13, 2024).

6 Data quoted from Chad P. Bown, "US-China Phase One Tracker: China's Purchase of US Goods." *PIIE report* (July 19, 2022).

Table 2.1 China's Trade in Goods with the US from 2018 to 2023

Year	*2017*	*2018*	*2019*	*2020*	*2021*	*2022*	*2023*
Exports of Goods (million USD)	*505,165.1*	*538,514.2*	*449,110.7*	*432,548.0*	*504,246.3*	*536,259.3*	*426,885.0*
Imports of Goods (million USD)	*129,997.2*	*120,281.2*	*106,481.2*	*124,581.5*	*151,439.4*	*154,125.4*	*147,777.8*
Balance	*375,167.9*	*418,232.9*	*342,629.5*	*307,966.5*	*352,806.9*	*382,133.8*	*279,107.2*

Source: United States Census Bureau

those from China was in 2002.[7] This trend shows little indication of reversing, as evidenced by recent statistics. In the first three quarters of 2024, US imports of goods from China amounted to $322 billion, reflecting a modest increase of 2.3% compared to the same period in 2023. [8] In contrast, US imports of goods from Mexico surpassed $378 billion during the same period, marking a more substantial growth of 6.47%. [9] This trend is connected to US efforts to diversify its supply chains through initiatives such as reshoring, which seeks to bring production back to the US, and offshoring to alternative trade partners.[10]

These trends highlight the complex and evolving nature of US-China trade relations amidst heightened tensions and shifting global economic dynamics. Despite the increase in tariffs and restrictions, US-China trade has shown a degree of resilience, with trade volumes remaining substantial. However, trade between the two nations is becoming less interdependent, as reflected in declining shares and slower growth rates on both sides.

Trade Deficit and Its Role in US-China Trade Tensions

The perceived cause of trade tensions between China and the United States has often been attributed to the trade imbalance. Trump has consistently expressed strong opposition to trade deficits, viewing them as a reflection of America's weakness in trade policy. The issue of trade imbalances has transcended economic concerns, becoming a politically sensitive matter with significant implications for domestic and international policymaking.

According to the US Bureau of Economic Analysis and the US Census Bureau, the United States' international trade deficit increased from $504.8 billion in 2016 to $568.4 billion in 2017. This expansion was primarily due to a more substantial rise in imports compared to exports. Notably, the trade deficit with China reached

7 See "Mexico Overtakes China as the Leading Source of Goods by US." *US News* (February 7, 2024)

8 Data quoted from United States Census, "Trade in Goods with China." Available at: <https://www.census.gov/foreign-trade/balance/c5700.html>

9 Data quoted from United States Census, "Trade in Goods with Mexico." Available at: <https://www.census.gov/foreign-trade/balance/c2010.html>

10 Ana Swanson and Simon Romero, "For First Time in Two Decades, US Buys More Than China." The New York Times (February 8, 2024).

a record $375.2 billion in 2017, up $28.2 billion from the previous year's $347 billion, accounting for approximately 66% of the overall US trade deficit.[11]

As a matter of fact, the US has consistently experienced annual trade deficits throughout the majority of the post-World War II era. The trade deficit also triggered the Japan-US trade frictions in the second half of the 20th century, which were exacerbated by their trade imbalance. Japanese economists draw parallels between current China's trade tensions with the US and those Japan previously experienced (Abe 2017). Before World War II, Japanese textiles profoundly influenced the British textile industry. After the war, Japan's textile and heavy industries quickly outpaced their American counterparts. Likewise, as a significant global trading nation, China may encounter the possibility of being surpassed by other developing countries in the future. Historical patterns reveal that trade tensions frequently emerge when an emerging economy is narrowing the gap with the leading economy (Abe, 2017, p. 54). In an effort to address this situation, the US implemented a series of measures, including pressuring Japan to limit its exports to the US, fostering increased imports from the US by "opening" the Japanese market, and participating in the Plaza Accord to appreciate the Japanese yen. Starting in the 1960s, certain perceptions gained traction in the US: that a sizeable fiscal deficit could detrimentally impact the US economy; that the significant US deficit was a consequence of the restricted nature of the Japanese market and Japan's trade surplus; that Japan's trade policies were designed to boost exports and restrict imports; and that dismantling Japanese trade barriers and opening its domestic market could lead to a substantial surge in US exports to Japan, thereby reducing trade deficits and even fiscal deficits significantly (Komiya, 1990, p. 44).

From an economic point of view, the prevailing perspective among most economists is that the US trade deficit is primarily a consequence of US macroeconomic policies and an imbalance between saving and investment in the economy. While trade generates both economic benefits and costs, the overall long-term impact on the economy is positive. However, some still insist that the trade deficit is detrimental to the US economy, as it leads to job losses or unfair trade practices by foreign competitors (Schwarzenberg, 2020). Import-related job losses are driving a populist backlash against trade and globalization that will cause political volatility (McBride & Chatzky, 2019).

According to Irwin, changing political dynamics shaped US trade policy in a historical context. He quotes James Madison to illustrate the difficulty of reconciling the interests of various stakeholders in trade policy in the US: "it is in vain to say that enlightened statesmen will be able to adjust these clashing interests, and render them all subservient to the public good." The goal of US trade policy has changed from revenue to protection, to the recent reciprocal prosperity, as a result of "great political debate" (Irwin, 2017).

11 Data quoted from BEA.gov. "2017 Trade Gap is $568.4 Billion." (March 7, 2018)

Balancing Free Trade and National Security Concerns

The Trump administration adopted a new organizing principle for strategic policy: "Economic security is national security." As Trump proclaimed, "A healthy defense industrial base is a critical element of US power. The ability of the military to surge in response to an emergency depends on our Nation's ability to produce needed parts and systems." He argues that trade deficits pose a threat to national security by making the United States reliant on foreign debt and foreign investment to sustain its economy (McBride & Chatzky, 2019). In emphasizing the connection between economic security and national security, Peter Navarro draws on the principle of "Peace Through Strength," which asserts that a strong military is essential for maintaining peace. This concept, a cornerstone of Ronald Reagan's foreign policy during his first presidency, is widely credited with undermining the core foundations of the Soviet Union without the need for direct military confrontation.[12]

China's rise after the Cold War represents the first instance of a developing nation outside the Western alliance exerting significant spillover effects beyond trade, encompassing military and national security interests. These effects have triggered considerable concerns that China's economic and technological advancements could shift global power dynamics and potentially weaken the Western security alliance. Among industrialized nations, the United States has felt these impacts most acutely, in contrast to other advanced economies that have accepted their diminished roles as mid-sized powers dependent on US security guarantees (Wu, 2019). Consequently, curbing China's economic growth has emerged as a core national strategy for the United States. The Biden administration's *National Security Strategy* also underscores this perspective, identifying China as "the only competitor with both the intent to reshape the international order and, increasingly, the economic, diplomatic, military, and technological power to do so."[13]

The "containment of China" strategy signifies the shift in US policy toward China from defensive realism to offensive realism. In contrast to Kenneth Waltz's defensive realism, which prioritizes achieving a balance of power, offensive realism asserts that "great powers recognize that the best way to ensure their security is to achieve hegemony now, thus eliminating any possibility of a challenge by another great power (Mearsheimer 2001)." Offensive realism is founded on five fundamental assumptions. Mearsheimer's offensive realism is grounded in five core assumptions. First, the international system operates in a state of anarchy, implying the absence of a hierarchically superior, coercive power capable of enforcing constraints on state behavior. Second, all major powers possess offensive military capabilities that can be deployed against other states. Third, there is perpetual uncertainty among states regarding whether others will refrain from utilizing these offensive military capabilities. Fourth, states prioritize the preservation of their survival – specifically, their territorial integrity and domestic autonomy – above all

12 Navarro, Peter. 2018. "Why Economic Security Is National Security." Available at: <https://trumpwhitehouse.archives.gov/articles/economic-security-national-security/>

13 The White House, *National Security Strategy*, (October 2022)

other objectives, as it serves as the means to achieve all their ends. Fifth, states are rational actors, engaging in strategic thinking that considers both immediate and long-term consequences, with a primary focus on survival (Mearsheimer, 2001).

The Legality of Unilateral Trade-related Measures in Global Trade

The United States imposed additional tariffs on Chinese products based on its domestic legal framework, primarily under Section 301 of the *Trade Act of 1974* and Section 232 of the *Trade Expansion Act of 1962*. These unilateral tariff measures have significant implications for the WTO rules-based system.

Unilateral Tariff Measures: Conflicts between US Domestic Law and WTO Rules

After the Second World War, the GATT was established to facilitate international trade by reducing tariffs and eliminating other trade barriers. Together with its successor, the WTO, GATT has played a crucial role in significantly lowering global tariff levels. In 1947, the average tariff rate among major GATT participants was approximately 22%. By the end of the Uruguay Round in 1999, this figure had dropped to just 5%. Analysts attribute much of this reduction to the influence and effectiveness of GATT and the WTO in promoting trade liberalization (Tomz et al., 2007; Goldstein et al., 2007).

The US domestic *law – Trade Act of 1974*, enacted during the GATT period, grants the USTR a set of responsibilities and authorities to investigate and take actions to enforce US rights under trade agreements, as well as address specific foreign trade practices. Section 301 was a frequently used tool in US trade policy from the 1980s to the 1990s. During this period, the statute played a central role, with the USTR conducting nearly 100 investigations into various trade practices. However, since the establishment of the WTO in 1995, the USTR has rarely utilized Section 301. Instead, it has primarily used it as a mechanism to initiate or implement WTO dispute settlement actions. These actions were designed to replace the unilateral trade measures that were previously employed under this statute (Schwarzenberg, 2020; Lincicome, et al., 2022).

During the 1980s and 1990s, US actions under Section 301 played a key role in shaping Article 23 of the WTO Dispute Settlement Understanding (DSU). Article 23 mandates that WTO members resolve disputes related to WTO agreements exclusively through DSU procedures. It also requires members to avoid unilateral measures when: (1) assessing whether another member has breached a WTO Agreement, (2) establishing a deadline for the member to conform to a WTO decision, and (3) implementing any retaliatory measures against a member that fails to comply. Article 23 of the DSU has been considered a significant milestone in the history of the global trading system, as it limits unilateral actions. Departing from this established practice, the Trump administration leveraged the flaws in Section 301 to sidestep the WTO and impose unilateral tariffs on various US trading partners, resulting in substantial economic and geopolitical repercussions (Schwarzenberg, 2020; Lincicome et al., 2022).

To challenge the imposition of additional tariffs, China initiated consultations with the United States concerning certain tariff measures on Chinese goods on April 4, 2018 (DS543). Before the Panel, China challenged two sets of additional duties imposed by the US: (1) a 25% additional duty imposed in June 2018 on a first set of products with an approximate annual trade value of $34 billion; and (2) a second set of duties, initially set at 10% in September 2018 and increased to 25% in May 2019, on products with an estimated annual trade value of $200 billion. China claimed that these additional duties were inconsistent with Articles I:1 and II:1(a) and (b) of the GATT 1994, which provide the most-favored-nation treatment and schedule of concessions.[14]

The US argued that the additional duties were justified under Article XX(a) of the GATT 1994 as measures essential to safeguard US public morals. The United States contended that China's actions, policies, and practices, as outlined in the relevant Section 301 Report, amounted to "state-sanctioned theft" and the improper appropriation of US technology, intellectual property, and commercial secrets, thereby violating the prevailing public morals in the US.

The Panel circulated the Report to Members on September 15, 2020. The Panel analyzed whether the additional measures were necessary to protect public morals invoked by the US in a holistic approach. The holistic approach entailed a comprehensive evaluation based on the Panel's understanding of each component of Article XX(a) and its application to the particular circumstances of this dispute. The Panel noted that the "standards of right and wrong" emphasized by the United States, which included norms against theft, misappropriation, and unfair competition, could, at a conceptual level, fall under the umbrella of the "public morals" concept in Article XX(a). The Panel determined that the United States failed to provide evidence supporting its claim that the products subject to additional duties benefited from practices by China deemed contrary to US public morals. Moreover, there was a lack of evidence demonstrating how the additional duties imposed on specific products contributed to the overall public morals objective as asserted by the United States. The Panel concluded that the challenged measures were *prima facie* inconsistent with Articles I:1, II:1(a), and II:1(b) of the GATT 1994.

This Panel Report confirms that the US' arbitrary imposition of additional tariffs on China violates WTO rules. However, the Panel refrained from addressing China's claim under DSU Article 23, which explicitly prohibits any unilateral retaliatory measures without authorization from the DSB. The unilateral nature of Section 301 is a central issue in this case, yet the Panel chose not to address it. Some commentators argue that, during Trump's presidency, the United States abandoned its traditional leadership role within the global trading system, shifting away from multilateralism in favor of aggressive unilateralism. As one commentator noted, "Under Trump, the United States began behaving as something of a rogue state in

14 Panel Report, United States-Tariff Measures on Certain Goods from China, WT/DS543/R. On 26 October 2020, the United States notified the DSB of its decision to appeal to the Appellate Body certain issues of law and legal interpretations in the panel report.

international trade." This departure from established norms has raised significant concerns about the future of the rules-based global trade order (Hopewell, 2021). Some critics also point out that China undermined WTO rules by implementing retaliatory measures independently, without prior authorization from the DSB. As a result, China's legal victory in this case is seen by some as lacking substantive credibility (Qin, 2020).

National Security Justifications: A Source of Trade Policy Controversy

National security and international trade law share a close connection, and this association has been in existence ever since the birth of GATT in 1947 (Bhala, 1998). The national security exception was built into the GATT in 1947, permitting nations to increase tariffs in response to a potential threat to their domestic security, which highlighted the persistent concerns surrounding the economic and political relations during this period.[15]

The United States has demonstrated a willingness to enact legislation authorizing unilateral trade actions against other countries in the name of national security. The US has always invoked Article XXI to justify its unilateral legislation of highly contentious trade sanctions (Bhala, 1998). Section 232 is one of these national security provisions. It empowers the US President to impose import restrictions when the Department of Commerce conducts an investigation and makes an affirmative determination that specific imports pose a threat to the national security of the US. Prior to the Trump Administration, the Department initiated 26 Section 232 investigations since 1963. Five of the investigations were positive, addressing petroleum products and crude oil. Under the Trump Administration, eight Section 232 investigations were initiated, eventually levying tariffs following two inquiries into steel and aluminum (Fefer & Jones, 2022).

Disputes ruled by the DSB

In the late 1990s, analysts observed that Article XXI of the GATT imposed only limited practical constraints on WTO members when enacting national security sanctions legislation. In practice, national security often overrides international trade law, a relationship that the US has been leveraging to its advantage (Bhala, 1998).

15 Article XXI of Security Exceptions of the GATT reads: Nothing in this Agreement shall be construed (a) to require any contracting party to furnish any information the disclosure of which it considers contrary to its essential security interests; or (b) to prevent any Contracting Party from taking any action which it considers necessary for the protection of its essential security interests (i) relating to fissionable materials or the materials from which they are derived; (ii) relating to the traffic in arms, ammunition and implements of war and to such traffic in other goods and materials as is carried on directly or indirectly for the purpose of supplying a military establishment; (iii) taken in time of war or other emergency in international relations; or (c) to prevent any Contracting Party from taking any action in pursuance of its obligations under the United Nations Charter for the maintenance of international peace and security.

In the DSB, the security exception provision was invoked on a few occasions, but no GATT/WTO panel on this subject was ever adopted until 2019 (Prazeres, 2020).

But in recent years, there has been a surge in trade restrictions justified on national security grounds, and these measures are facing growing scrutiny in WTO dispute settlement. On April 5, 2019, a seminal decision was made by a WTO panel in a case involving Russia and Ukraine (DS 512). Russia asserted that it had implemented trade-restrictive measures under the pretext of safeguarding its national security. The crux of the matter revolved around the "national security exception." In this dispute, Russia invoked this exception to justify measures obstructing trade between Ukraine, Kazakhstan, and the Kyrgyz Republic when transiting through Russia. Russia contended that these measures were a response to the escalating events in Ukraine following political unrest in 2014. The panel decided that the situation between Russia and Ukraine reached the threshold of a "war or other emergency in international relations," satisfying the criteria outlined in section (b)(iii).[16]

In the trade dispute between the US and China (DS 558), the United States imposed a 25% national security tariff on Chinese steel and a 10% tariff on aluminum in 2018 under Section 232 of the Trade Expansion Act of 1962. These tariffs, established through Proclamations 9704 and 9705 issued by the Trump administration in March 2018, were justified on national security grounds. The proclamations asserted that imports of steel and aluminum were occurring "in such quantities and under such circumstances as to threaten to impair the national security of the United States." In retaliation, China imposed additional import duties on 128 US products valued at $3 billion, including agricultural commodities. The United States subsequently challenged China's retaliatory measures before a WTO Panel.

In this dispute (DS 558), the US invoked Article XXI of the GATT 1994, which allows for "Security Exceptions," as the legal basis for these measures. The US maintained that its tariffs were essential to address the national security threat posed by imports of Chinese products, emphasizing the importance of protecting domestic industries to uphold its broader national security interests.[17] After examining the Section 232 measures, the WTO Panel found merit in the US national security argument. The Panel ruled that "the United States' determination of a threat to its national security under Section 232 is a central aspect of the measures with respect to their legal characterization as being sought, taken, or maintained according to Article XXI of the GATT 1994."[18]

The recent rulings by two WTO Panels on the national security exception appear to be transforming the global trading system into a "black hole" of exceptions. Some argue that the misuse of national security provisions is undermining the integrity of the world trading system (Lester & Zhu, 2019; Prazeres, 2020).

16 Panel Report, Russia – Measures Concerning Traffic in Transit, WT/DS512/R.

17 Panel Report, Russia – Measures Concerning Traffic in Transit, WT/DS512/R.

18 Panel Report, China-Additional Duties on Certain Products from the United States, WT/DS558/R

Achieving an appropriate balance in the application of the national security exception is essential; otherwise, there is a risk of reverting to a system dominated by power dynamics, undermining the rule of law in international trade (Bacchus, 2022).

Japan's Gaiatsu Model: Lessons for US-China Relations

The US has triggered two trade conflicts against the second-largest economies, Japan and China, post-World War II. Studies show that both trade tensions shared some common factors, involving trade imbalance, "competition between political-economic systems", and "a struggle for hegemony" reflected in viewing the opponent as a threat (Kwan, 2021). The trade tensions differ in size and scale, organizational structure, and geopolitics (Wu, 2019). Also, the Japanese and Chinese governments exhibit markedly distinct attitudes and approaches in dealing with the trade tensions with US trade hegemonism. For instance, by the 1970s, Japan had emerged as a formidable competitor in the automobile industry. From 1970 to 1976, Japanese car sales in the United States tripled to over 1 million units, capturing an 8% market share. By 1980, Japanese automakers had further increased their market share to 21%. The surge in Japanese car imports and significant losses in Detroit led the Reagan Administration to negotiate a "voluntary export restraint (VER)" agreement with Japan in 1981. Japan agreed to limit its auto exports to the US to 1.68 million units, the 1979 level, for three years starting in 1981. To circumvent quota restrictions and avoid potential new protectionist measures, Japanese producers established auto plants in the US. These protectionist measures benefited the US national interest by encouraging investment and boosting long-term production.[19] Both China and Japan are East Asian countries facing similar situations. Could China adopt the Japanese approach to address trade tensions with the US?

Political and Economic Factors Influencing Trade Policies

According to Ryutaro Komiya, a prominent Japanese economist who made substantial contributions to the development of economics in Japan and its economic policy, Japan consistently yielded to US demands during trade negotiations. Komiya observed that Japan accepted nearly all of the US's requests, with the primary focus of negotiations being the timing and extent of Japan's concessions. In contrast, the US offered little, if anything, in return for these compromises (Komiya, 1990, p. 34).

In the post-World War II era, Japan adopted a comprehensive "bandwagoning" strategy, aligning closely with the US in military and security matters, though this alignment has come at the expense of some political independence. This

19 King, Wells, & Vaughn, Dan Jr. 2022. "The Import Quota that Remade the Auto Industry." American Compass.

inherent dependence on the US is a key factor driving Japan's inclination to compromise in trade negotiations with the US Security relations are the cornerstone of the Japan-US alliance. Japanese officials sensed a debt of gratitude to the US for ensuring national security in Japan. Concurrently, the US acknowledged that safeguarding Japan and leading the Western bloc posed a substantial burden. In this scenario, Japan consistently made concessions in trade negotiations with the US, while the US exerted pressure on Japan to increase military expenditures. Although Japan made modest concessions in response, the Japanese government, mindful of domestic politics, refrained from extensive involvement in military cooperation with the US Therefore, when juxtaposed with military concessions, Japan's compromises in trade and economic matters appear more necessary and feasible. (Komiya, 1990).

In addition to relying on US military security, Japanese government officials also struggled with a sense of guilt over the trade surplus with the US Japan, so they tried to prevent the passage of protectionist legislation by the US through diplomatic compromises. There was a genuine concern in Japan that failure to compromise might trigger retaliatory measures from the US The act of making compromises served to assuage protectionist sentiments within the US While there are factions in Japan advocating for trade protectionism, political figures and business leaders have increasingly embraced the principles of free trade. Moreover, a growing number of Japanese citizens now believe that maintaining a global free-trade regime is crucial for Japan's economic well-being. They contend that Japan should exert every effort to collaborate with the US in eliminating trade imbalances that could undermine the global free trade system (Komiya, 1990).

The Decline of Japanese Nationalism

Japan's compromises have created a negative impression among government officials and the general public in the US, who perceive Tokyo as playing a waiting game to evade its responsibilities (Komiya, 1990). However, the Japanese public displayed minimal criticism or protest against their country's compromises, owing to the waning influence of Japanese nationalism during the Cold War.

Following World War II, reflections on war responsibility led to the severance of the intertwined relationship between statism and militarism. Japan's ideological sphere commenced a process of exposing and scrutinizing the nation's turbulent history of warfare. In 1946, Masao Maruyama, a leading Japanese political scientist of the post-war era, examined Japan's wartime ideology in his seminal work, "The Logic and Psychology of Ultranationalism," which delves into the contemporary ideological landscape of Japan. Maruyama asserted that the trinity of "ultranationalism," comprised of the Japanese emperor system, military, and bureaucracy, resulted in a lack of self-awareness among the Japanese populace. According to Maruyama, the fusion of ultranationalism and fascism drove Japan irreversibly toward a path of aggression.[20] In the aftermath, the US guided Japan toward democracy through the implementation of the "Yoshida Doctrine." This strategy emphasized minimizing military expenditures and prioritizing economic development, albeit at the cost of some sovereignty. This approach enabled Japan to achieve rapid economic revitalization.[21]

In the 1960s, Japan experienced nationalist social movements, most notably the "Anpo struggle," which revolved around opposition to the US-Japan Security Treaty (*Anpo*, short for *Anzen Hosho Joyaku*, or Security Treaty). Despite this significant movement, Japanese society largely avoided open discussions on nationalism. The Anpo struggle resulted in the resignation of Prime Minister Nobusuke Kishi but ultimately failed to block the renewal of the Security Treaty between the United States and Japan. Subsequent Prime Minister Hayato Ikeda ushered in the "Income Doubling Plan," transitioning Japan from a "season of politics" to a "season of economy."[22] As Gaven McCormack observes, Japan shifted its priorities away from national pride, glory, and identity. Instead, the nation directed its efforts towards producing affordable, high-quality goods for the global market, aiming to achieve economic prosperity (McCormack, 2000). Gradually, Japan has developed a complex yet fragile form of "Client State" nationalism, characterized by a paradoxical combination of dependency and self-assertion – unquestioning submission to the United States alongside a strong emphasis on a pure and proud Japanese identity. This duality is aptly described by oxymoronic terms such as "Dependent Shinto" or "Zokkoku Nationalism" (Shinto, Japanese religion; Zokkoku meaning dependent) (McCormack, 2009).[23]

Japan's National Culture and Trade Relations

The inferiority complex, "Gaijin Complex," also contributes to Japanese concession, a prominent feature of Japanese national identity. The inferiority complex has originated from the hierarchical mentality in Japanese history and the value of "everyone should be properly placed." For a long time, Japan has been isolated

20 Sasaki, Fumiko (2012). *Democracy in Japan: The Thought of Masao Maruyama*. Routledge.

21 The Yoshida Doctrine, introduced by Japan's first post-war Prime Minister, Shigeru Yoshida, outlines a strategic framework shaped by the post-war context. This Doctrine emphasizes reliance on the United States to address Japan's security concerns, allowing the Japanese government to focus its efforts on economic recovery and revitalization, which became the cornerstone of its foreign policy.

22 Hayato Ikeda's policies are widely regarded as an extension of the "Yoshida Doctrine," as Ikeda, a disciple of Shigeru Yoshida, carried forward his mentor's vision. Under Ikeda's leadership, Japan experienced rapid economic growth, marked by several milestone achievements.

23 With the collapse of the bubble economy and the end of the Cold War, Japanese intellectuals began reassessing the advantages and shortcomings of the Yoshida Doctrine. During the 1990s, this policy faced significant criticism, driven by Japan's diplomatic and economic challenges during that period. Critics argued that the doctrine had contributed to Japan's diminished global influence and self-image, prompting calls for a reevaluation of its post-war strategies.

from mainstream international economic affairs. The Japanese social, legal, and administrative systems are legacies of the past Japan as a backward nation, which do not fit the country with its present economic status in the international community. The Japanese still regard Japan as a small country and agree that Japan has introduced and utilized technologies and liberalized markets from foreign countries, especially from the developed world. In a word, Japanese people always keep a low profile and they seldom exchange opinions and views with foreigners, making them difficult to understand. This is the biggest weakness in Japan's diplomacy (Komiya, 1990).

In a popular book on Japanese national culture by Tatsuru Uchida, a particular incident is recounted. Following US President Obama's inaugural address, some individuals inquired about the Japanese Prime Minister's thoughts. In response, the Japanese Prime Minister replied, "The US requires assistance from a world-leading economy (Uchida, 2012)." Following their defeat in World War II, many Japanese held deep admiration for their victorious foe. "The US excels in numerous domains, including politics, economy, and military strength, among others, and we are in dire need of such a nation' (Uchida, 2012). Japan has consistently followed advanced models throughout its history. Initially influenced by Chinese civilization, Japan later looked to Western Europe during the Meiji Era, followed by Germany in WWII, and the United States in the post-war period. Uchida contends that Japan tends to adopt others' proposals without articulating its own ideas based on inherent experiences. Nationalists in Japan often harbor a deep sense of shame regarding their country's perceived differences from others. They believe that Japan's primary focus should be emulating other nations and adhering to established "global standards." Both the left and right wings in Japan share a common trait – they are not considered "utopian" or "idealistic" enough. Rather than aspiring to be a global model, the Japanese are preoccupied with their perceived comparative disadvantages, frequently selecting a "model country" to emulate but refraining from envisioning themselves as a global exemplar. The prevailing sentiment in Japan is a reluctance to acknowledge the possibility of achieving such a lofty goal.

Shaped by its hierarchical culture and distinct national identity, Japan's foreign policy evaluation is profoundly influenced by perceptions of national power. In the 2019 trade conflict with South Korea, Japan adopted a firm stance by implementing export controls on crucial semiconductor chemicals, dealing a substantial blow to South Korea's economy. The roots of the trade dispute trace back to October 2018 when South Korea's Supreme Court ruled that Japanese companies must compensate forced laborers from South Korea. Tokyo contested the verdict, and Seoul, refusing direct negotiations, called for third-party arbitration. On July 1, 2019, the Japanese government announced heightened export controls on three semiconductor materials to South Korea, removing it from its "white list" of trusted trade partners. Given South Korea's significant economic reliance on key chips from Japan, the export controls on semiconductor chemicals were viewed as a strategic strike targeting the country's vulnerable points.

China's Approach to Managing Foreign Trade Pressures

Unlike Japan's full concession, the Chinese government strongly condemned and retaliated against what it described as "trade protectionism," "trade bullying," and "trade hegemonism." China's official position accuses the US of violating WTO rules and undermining the multilateral trade system. The Chinese government has emphasized a firm yet balanced approach to trade conflicts, stating that "China will act rationally... However, China will not bow under pressure and will rise to any challenge." Officials have reiterated that while "China does not want a trade war, it is not afraid of one and will fight if necessary." In response to US unilateralism and trade protectionism, China has justified its countermeasures by asserting, "If some American politicians insist on a zero-sum game, China will fight to the end."[24] These statements reflect China's resolute stance in protecting its national interests while remaining open to dialogue.

Critics have pointed to several reasons behind China's resolute stance. Firstly, China emphasizes its independence from the US, asserting its autonomy in managing trade disputes. There is also concern that making concessions could weaken the government's authority and reputation, potentially compromising China's standing on the global stage. Some argue that only by adopting a firm approach to the trade war can China effectively counter US pressure. Furthermore, certain officials suggest that the trade war might compel domestic interest groups to make necessary concessions, paving the way for deeper reforms and greater economic openness. In this view, the trade war is not entirely detrimental to China.[25]

Concerns about Entering into a Modern Plaza Accord

Chinese officials and think tanks do not endorse Japan's compromise with the US They strive to avoid signing any document resembling the Plaza Accord and advocate for a hard-line stance. Chinese media often links Japan's economic recession with pressure from the US Some public opinions contend that the Plaza Accord was an international conspiracy by America to suppress the Japanese economy, resulting in a prolonged economic downturn in Japan. In "Guard against the Second Conspiracy of America," the author considers America's clampdown on Japan's economy as the first conspiracy. Faced with Japan's flourishing economy, American media initially spread the theory of the "Japan Menace" to instigate extreme fear of the Japanese among Americans. This became the foundation of public opinion for the US government to confront Japan. In the guise of addressing the trade deficit, the US imposed trade barriers against Japanese goods and compelled Japan to sign

24 See "The Facts and China's Position on US-China Trade Friction," issued by the State Council Information Office of the People's Republic of China on September 24, 2018, and "China's Position on the US-China Economic and Trade Consultations" on June 2, 2019. These two white papers highlight the comprehension of US-China trade frictions by the Chinese intellectual community.

25 See "Perspective: Why is China's Attitude Toward the Trade War so Firm?" [观点：中国对贸易战的态度为何如此强硬?]*BBC News*. (April 9, 2018)

the Plaza Accord. This led to a decline in export competitiveness and economic bubbles in Japan, contributing to its economic recession (Wang, 2003).

In China, numerous studies indicate that Japan's economic bubbles emerged before the Plaza Accord. Although the Plaza Accord did result in a significant appreciation of the yen, strictly speaking, it is not the direct cause of Japan's long-term economic recession. It was the expansionary financial and monetary policies at that time, rather than the yen's appreciation, that had a detrimental impact on Japan's economy (Wang, 2004). Another signatory of the Plaza Accord, Germany, also experienced an appreciation of the D-mark but did not face the "Lost Two Decades" afterward. Nonetheless, public opinion in China widely believes that Japan's "Lost Two Decades" are closely linked to the Plaza Accord. Therefore, Chinese think tanks and scholars consistently urge the government not to compromise with the US by signing international agreements similar to the Plaza Accord, as Japan did (Wang, 2004).

Shortly after the US announced its first tariff hikes in 2018, the *People's Daily* published an article by former Japanese Prime Minister Yasuo Fukuda titled "A Painful Lesson from the Trade War: China Ought to Learn from Japan" (translated). In the article, Fukuda reflected on Japan's experience in the 1980s when it was pressured into signing the Plaza Accord with the US, leading to a rapid appreciation of the yen and significant economic repercussions for Japan. Drawing from this painful lesson, he advised China to act vigilantly and prudently. On May 24, 2019, *China Daily* responded with an article titled "US's Futile Quest for a Yuan Plaza Accord," asserting that China is not Japan and dismissing the idea as a fantasy of US trade hawks aiming to suppress China through a similar agreement involving the yuan.[26]

The Emphasis on Respect and the Rise of Modern Chinese Nationalism

The Chinese government has stressed that the US-China trade friction should be addressed based on equality and mutual respect. Saying no to hegemonism has been the unswerving diplomatic stance and attitude taken by the Communist Party of China. Opposing hegemonism, China sticks to the philosophy of "equality in diplomacy," which guides China's diplomatic practices since the reform and opening up (Liu, 2019). The Chinese government and its high-ranking officials have consistently underscored the importance of respect and equal treatment in the context of trade tensions with the US. In terms of equality, they declare that all countries, regardless of size or strength, should respect each other and engage in equal dialogue. China expresses readiness to resume bilateral investment agreement negotiations and promptly initiate discussions on a bilateral free trade agreement, all based on the principles of equality and mutual benefits. China's Foreign Minister Wang Yi highlighted China's longstanding advocacy for addressing trade and economic issues through negotiations held on equal terms. On October 26,

26 Dan Steinbock, "US's Quest for Yuan Plaza Accord." *China Daily* (May 21, 2019).

2019, the official newspaper the *People's Daily* featured an editorial titled "The Development of China-US Relations Can't Do Without Mutual Respect," emphasizing that only through equality and mutual respect can China and the US effectively address their core concerns and create a conducive environment for mutually beneficial cooperation.

The emphasis on equality, resistance, and mutual respect mirrors the rise of nationalism in contemporary China. The concept of "rising nationalism" has been widely discussed in the analysis of China's growing material power since the early 1990s. Many analysts argue that the increasing nationalism, particularly among China's youth, plays a crucial role in compelling the Chinese leadership to adopt a more assertive stance on various foreign policy issues, especially maritime disputes in East Asia (Johnston, 2017). Entering the 21st century, China assumed a proactive role as a leader and contributor to diplomacy, propelled by its growing economic prowess. Since the 18th National Congress of the CPC, Chinese state leaders have attached great importance to "cultural confidence." The "Belt and Road" initiative, the principles of "consultation, contribution and shared benefits," and the notion of "building a community with a shared future for mankind" have been documented in UN resolutions, showcasing China's sense of responsibility as a major country (Liu, 2019). On May 13, 2019, China submitted *China's Proposal on WTO Reform*, a "Chinese plan" credited by the Chinese media, declaring its stand of firmly defending the WTO. The document suggests tightening disciplines to curb the abuse of the national security exception, which is regarded as a fightback against the US's trade protectionism in the name of national security. The term "Chinese plan" has been frequent in China's political discourse in recent years, and the Chinese state leaders have elaborated on China's ways of global governance on major diplomatic occasions.

The Resistance Politics

As the sole superpower since World War II, the United States exhibits a strong sense of superiority regarding its social, legal, and administrative systems, frequently advocating that other nations adopt its approaches. This confidence and ideology often manifest in imperialistic tendencies during trade negotiations, particularly with countries that possess distinct historical and cultural traditions (Komiya, 1990).

In the writings of Takeuchi Yoshimi, one of the leading intellectual figures of postwar Japan, he utilized Lu Xun's concept of "resistance" to elucidate the subjectivity of Japan and China, which in Chinese means "to endure, bear, risk one's life, and live through"[27]. Being a nation focused on learning, Japan embraced the European model without encountering any "resistance" during its pursuit of modernization. Japan consistently imitated Europe without undergoing structural reform. In contrast, China adopts a resistant approach. When influenced by

27 Quoted from Calichman, 2010; Sun, 2019.

a foreign culture, it actively struggles against and resists that culture, engaging in self-adjustment and renewal to transform into an independent entity. According to Yoshimi, China establishes its subjectivity through the process of "struggle," while Japan lacks subjectivity due to the absence of "resistance."[28] Yoshimi's observations of Japan and China remain pertinent, offering insights into the two countries' approaches to addressing trade friction. China's modern history is characterized by aggression and resistance against aggression. Consequently, resistance politics becomes the primary political solution for China in managing its relations with the West.

Since the founding of the People's Republic of China, the Chinese government has consistently emphasized the principle of "equality" in shaping its foreign relations. This focus stems not only from the historical experience of the "century of humiliation" but also serves important instrumental purposes. Emphasizing "equality" helps to mitigate the adverse effects of prolonged ideological struggles, secure additional rights and interests in an international system dominated by superpowers, and facilitate the country's self-development (Liu, 2019).

The Chinese government characterizes American unilateral trade actions as "trade hegemonism." In China's discourse, "hegemony" carries a strongly derogatory sense, and "hegemonism" is even more egregious. Given China's historical suppression by Western hegemony and its Cold War-era threat from Soviet Union hegemony, the Chinese people instinctively harbor antipathy toward hegemony in global politics (Wang, 2003). President Xi Jinping emphasized that cultural confidence is crucial for a nation's destiny, cultural security, and the independence of national spirit. This reflects China's aspiration to move away from Western-centered theories after achieving economic growth. A Chinese scholar in international relations pointed out that "Breaking away from the West-centered theory is a breakthrough, reshaping discourse power in economic globalization, and asserting oneself. Soft power is a significant constraint on the great rejuvenation of the Chinese nation. To achieve this goal, China must overcome such a hindrance by transcending the logic of catching up with the West and presenting a historical vision with common concerns for all humanity" (2016). Xi Jinping emphasized that achieving the Chinese dream requires following the Chinese path, promoting the Chinese spirit, and uniting Chinese strength. Emphasizing China's subjectivity is the core of China's opposition to Western hegemony. In the trade friction with the US, China's resistance to US trade hegemonism aims to steadfastly adhere to the economic development path of the China model.

Concluding Remarks

The contrasting responses of Tokyo and Beijing to Washington's trade policies underscore significant differences in national culture and nationalism at various developmental stages. Grounded in political realism, Japan views the US as the

28 Quoted from Calichman, 2010; Sun, 2019.

global leader and prioritizes collaboration to sustain a liberal and multilateral economic order. Recognizing that challenging the US would yield more losses than gains, Japan has historically made significant concessions to address trade tensions, guided by its reliance on US security assurances. In contrast, China has taken a more assertive approach to US trade frictions, emerging during a period of heightened nationalism in both nations. Cautious of agreements like the Plaza Accord, China rejects Japan's perceived compromises and labels US actions as "trade hegemonism." China has responded with countermeasures, including increased tariffs, reflecting its principles of equality, respect, and independence. These differing strategies stem not only from contrasting international relations with the US but also from the unique cultural and historical contexts of Japan and China.

In conclusion, Japan's approach, shaped by external pressures, leans toward compromise with dominant powers, while China emphasizes resistance to establish its self-identity, rooted in its history of foreign invasion. Despite predictions of nationalism's decline post-Cold War, both Chinese and American nationalism have resurged in recent years. "America First" nationalism opposes any perceived compromises on sovereignty, while Chinese nationalism, centered on national rejuvenation, champions the "China model." These opposing forces have transformed the once interdependent US-China economic relationship into a competitive and increasingly decoupled dynamic. Resolving these frictions requires both nations to seek common ground despite their ideological divides.

References

Abe, T. (2017). The history and significance of Japan's trade and industrial policy: A case study of trade friction at the end of the 20th century. *Japan Spotlight*, 2017(6), 50–54.

Bacchus, J. (2022). The Black hole of national security: Striking the right balance for the national security exception in international trade. Policy Analysis, Cato Institute, No. 936. https://www.cato.org/sites/cato.org/files/2022-11/policy-analysis-936.pdf.

Bhala, R. (1998). National security and international trade law: What the GATT says and what the United States does. *Pennsylvania Journal of International Economic Law*, 19(2), 263–317.

Calichman, R. F. (2010). *Takeuchi Yoshimi: Displacing the West*. Cornell Press.

"Cultural Confidence: An Epochal Issue Proposed by Xi Jinping"[文化自信——习近平提出的时代课题]. *Xinhua*. August 5, 2016.

Fefer, R. F., & Jones, V. C. (2022). Section 232 of the Trade Expansion Act of 1962. CRS Report, No. IF10667.

Goldstein, J. L., Rivers, D., & Tomz, M. (2007). Institutions in international relations: Understanding the effects of the GATT and the WTO on World Trade. *International Organization*, 1, 37–67.

Hopewell, K. (2021). When the Hegemon goes Rogue: Leadership amid the US assault on the liberal trading order. *International Affairs*, 4, 1025–1043.

Irwin, D. A. (2017). *Clashing Over Commerce: A History of US Trade Policy*. The University of Chicago Press.

Johnston, A. I. (2017). Is Chinese nationalism rising? Evidence from Beijing. *International Security*, 3, 7–43.

Komiya, R. (1990). *The Japanese Economy: Trade, Industry, and Government*. University of Tokyo Press.

Kwan, C. H. (2021). *Deep-rooted causes behind the China-US friction: Similarities to and differences from the Japan-US friction*. RIETI Report. https://www.rieti.go.jp/en/china/21010701.html.

Lester, S., & Zhu, H. (2019). A proposal for 'rebalancing' to deal with 'national security' trade restrictions. *Fordham International Law Journal*, 42(5), 1451–1474.

Lincicome, S., et al. (2022). Unfair trade or unfair protection? Cato Policy Analysis, No. 930. https://www.cato.org/policy-analysis/unfair-trade-or-unfair-protection-evolution-abuse-section-301.

Liu, Z. (2019). 新中国70年外交哲学进路 [Philosophical revolution in Chinese diplomacy: Revolution, equality, and leadership]. *Global Review*, 5, 33–53.

McBride, J., & Chatzky, A. (2019). The trade deficit: How much does it matter. *Council on Foreign Relations*. https://www.cfr.org/backgrounder/us-trade-deficit-how-much-does-it-matter.

McCormack, G. (2000). Nationalism and identity in post-Cold War Japan. *Pacifica Review: Peace, Security & Global Change*, 7(3), 247–263.

McCormack, G. (2009). History too long denied: Japan's unresolved colonial past and today's North Korea problem. *The Asia-Pacific Journal*, 7(29), 1–7.

Mearsheimer, J. J. (2001). *The Tragedy of Great Power Politics*. W.W. Norton.

Prazeres, T. L. (2020). Trade and national security: Rising risks for the WTO. *World Trade Review*, 137–148.

Qin, J. (2020). The elephant in the room: The missing claim in DS53. *International Economic Law and Policy Blog*. https://ielp.worldtradelaw.net/2020/09/the-elephant-in-the-room-the-missing-claim-in-ds543.html.

Schwarzenberg, A. (2020). The US trade deficit: An overview. CRS Report, No. IF10619. https://sgp.fas.org/crs/row/IF10619.pdf.

Shen, W. (2019). 修昔底德"逻辑和规则遏制与反遏制——中美贸易摩擦背后的深层次动因 [The 'thucydides' logic and containment and anti-containment through rule-making: The underlying reason behind the Sino-US trade friction]. *Frontiers*, 1, 40–59.

Sun, G. (2019). Takeuchi Yoshimi's study on Asianism. *Open Times*, 8(1), 115–137.

Tomz, M., Goldstein, J. L., & Rivers, D. (2007). Do we really know that the WTO increases trade? Comment. *American Economic Review*, 5, 98–114.

Uchida, T. (2012). 日本边境论 [Japan as Marginal]. Shanghai Art and Literature Publishing House.

Wang, J. S. (2003). 美国霸权的逻辑 [The logic of American hegemony]. *American Studies Quarterly*, 17(3), 7–29.

Wang, Y. G. (2004). 广场协议"对日本经济的影响及启示 [Influence and enlightenment of the plaza accord on Japan's economy]. *International Economic Review*, 1, 47–50.

Wu, M. (2019). China's rise and the growing doubts over trade multilateralism. In *Trade War: The Clash of Economic Systems Endangering Global Prosperity*. London: CEPR Press.

3 Challenges in the Interaction of Trade and Competition Policies

China's State-owned Enterprises Issues in Foreign Trade

China's socialist market economy, referred to as "China, Inc." by Mark Wu, is widely regarded as a key factor driving trade tensions between the US and China (Yu, 2019; Wu, 2019). While the US-China Phase One Trade Agreement addresses trade imbalances to ease these tensions, it falls short of tackling deeper structural issues within the Chinese economy. These include industrial subsidies, the behavior of state-owned enterprises (SOEs), and the overarching role of the state in economic activities. Concerns about the "China, Inc." model are not limited to the US; other nations have also expressed similar grievances. For example, Sabine Weyand, the European Commission's Director-General for Trade, has called on China to align its economic practices with international norms. Specific areas of concern include state subsidies, forced technology transfer, the dominance of SOEs, and the broader influence of the state in shaping economic outcomes. These issues remain central to ongoing debates about global trade and economic fairness.[1]

Pressures from Confronting "China, Inc."

"China, Inc.," also known as the Chinese economic model or the Beijing Consensus, has emerged as a prominent alternative to the "Washington Consensus" and its (neo-)liberal market approach, particularly in the aftermath of the 2008–2009 financial crisis (Breslin, 2011). In November 2008, the US National Intelligence Estimate observed that

> wealth is shifting not just from West to East but is increasingly concentrating under state control. In the wake of the 2008–2010 global financial crisis, the State's role in the economy is gaining broader appeal worldwide. These states are not adopting the Western liberal model for development but are instead following a different path – 'state capitalism.'[2]

1 See Weyand, Sabine. "Reports of Globalization's Death Are Greatly Exaggerated," International Politik Quarterly, (Jan 04,2023).

2 Quoted from US Department of State, "Ensuring a Sound Basis for Global Competition: Competitive Neutrality." (Remarks by Rober D. Hormats, May 5, 2011)

DOI: 10.4324/9781003637110-4

China is widely regarded as the most successful example of this "state capitalism" approach.

In a seminal article published in 2016, Mark Wu introduces the shorthand term "China, Inc." to describe the Chinese economic structure, which is a unique product of China's economic and political history (Wu, 2016). Wu argues that "China, Inc." poses a significant challenge to global trade governance. While the WTO can serve as an effective forum for resolving certain trade disputes, it has proven unable to address the complexities associated with "China, Inc." effectively. First, WTO rules are incomplete because they were established before the emergence of the current form of "China, Inc." Second, these rules were designed to regulate actions taken by governments or entities acting on behalf of governments. However, in the context of "China, Inc.," the problematic actions often stem from informal agreements that are neither documented nor explicitly verbalized. Third, the nature of WTO remedies presents another limitation, as the organization lacks the authority to issue retrospective remedies for past harms (Wu, 2019).

China's economic structure is defined by some distinctive features. The Chinese state functions as a corporate holding entity, with the State-owned Assets Supervision and Administration Commission of the State Council (SASAC) as the controlling shareholder. The state maintains control over financial institutions, ensuring they align with national priorities. Economic planning and resource allocation are centrally directed by national and local development and reform commissions. Nested corporate group structures enable state-owned and state-affiliated entities to form interconnected networks, leveraging complementary resources to advance state interests. Also, the Communist of China (CPC) plays a crucial role in overseeing appointments and managing the Chinese economy. However, despite the substantial control exerted by the Chinese state, it allows the market to determine winners and losers in numerous sectors (Wu, 2016). Some have metaphorically likened the CPC to the management of "China, Inc.," with the Politburo Standing Committee serving as the board of directors and the party's General Secretary acting as the CEO. The various ministries function as the organization's operational departments, while Chinese residents are seen as employees, often needing the party's approval for decisions related to residence, employment, and investments. SOEs are viewed as business units or subsidiaries, private companies operate as joint ventures under the party's guidance, and foreign companies are treated as franchisees operating within the framework of party influence (Li, 2022).

In effect, China's "dual tracks" economic model merges substantial state control with market-oriented reforms. By striking a balance between government intervention, state ownership, and market-driven policies, this approach allows China to maintain its ideological commitment to socialism while leveraging the practical advantages of market dynamics. As China's economic influence has grown, so too has its prominence in global trade discussions, attracting increasing scrutiny from its trade partners. The success of China's foreign trade is often attributed to its unique economic model, particularly the state-controlled elements such as industrial planning, subsidies, and SOEs. Ambassador Katherine Tai emphasized this challenge, stating that, "China remains the biggest challenge to the international trading system established by the World Trade Organization." Despite 22 years of WTO membership, China continues to embrace "a state-controlled, non-market approach to the economy and trade, which runs counter to the norma and principles embodied by the WTO."[3] The US and the EU have adopted a de-risking approach in supply chain management, signaling that strategic competition and security concerns are increasingly taking precedence over economic interests in the relationship between China and the West, particularly in the China-US dynamic.

The Role of SOEs in China's Foreign Trade

The classic theory of Marxist political economy asserts that the forces of production determine the relations of production, and the economic base shapes the superstructure. In China, SOEs are regarded as material and political foundations for socialism with Chinese characteristics. They serve as crucial pillars and reliable forces for the governance of the country by the CPC. The strengthening of the Party's leadership within SOEs is viewed as fundamental to defining the core essence of Chinese SOEs.[4]

Recent empirical research suggests that the involvement of SOEs in China's economy is on the rise. While official statistics that precisely quantify the contribution of China's SOEs to the country's gross domestic product (GDP) and employment are unavailable, empirical research has been conducted to shed light on the role of SOEs in China. Zhang Chunlin's widely referenced analysis suggests that the proportion of SOEs in China's GDP ranged from 23 to 28% , while their contribution to employment could vary from 5 to 16% in 2017(Zhang, 2019). In capital terms, the total capital of firms with some level of state ownership in China has risen to roughly 68% of the total capital of all firms (40 million) in the economy in 2017.[5] Analysis by the Peterson Institute for International Economics revealed that the proportion of China's state sector, including both mixed-ownership enterprises, in which the state owns between 10 and 50%, and majority-owned SOEs, among China's 100 largest listed companies increased from less than 60% a year earlier to over 63% at the end of 2023 (Huang & Verson, 2024).

To what extent do China's SOEs contribute to its foreign trade? In 2001, foreign-invested enterprises accounted for nearly 50.8% of China's total foreign trade, with SOEs in second place at around 42.5%. Private enterprises, by contrast, contributed less than 7%. However, following the decentralization of foreign trade management in 2004, as part of China's commitment upon joining the WTO, the share of foreign-invested and private enterprises began to rise, while the share of SOEs steadily declined. By 2004, the contribution of SOEs dropped to 28.6% (Table 3.1).

3 USTR, "USTR Releases Annual Report on China's WTO Compliance." (February 23, 2024).

4 See "Xi Stresses CPC Leadership of State-owned Enterprises." <http://www.xinhuanet.com//english/2016-10/11/c_135746608.htm>

5 Allen, Franklin and Cai, Junhui and Gu, Xian and Qian, Jun and Zhao, Linda and Zhu, Wu, "Centralization or Decentralization? The Evolution of State-Ownership in China," working paper, <SSRN: https://ssrn.com/abstract=4283197 or http://dx.doi.org/10.2139/ssrn.4283197>

Table 3.1 Share of Foreign Trade Value of the Three Types of Companies in China

Year	*2022*	*2019*	*2004*	*2001*
Private Enterprises	50.9%	42.7%	14%	6.6%
Foreign-invested Enterprises	32.9%	39.9%	57.4%	50.8%
State-owned Enterprises	16.1%	16.9%	28.6%	42.5%

Source: Chinese Customs Statistics

According to 2022 statistics on China's foreign trade, there were 598,000 enterprises engaged in imports and exports, with 510,000 of them being private enterprises, making up over 85% of the total. The import and export volume of private enterprises reached 21.4 trillion *yuan*, accounting for 50.9% of the total import and export value, marking the first time their annual share exceeded 50% (see Table 3.1).[6] In contrast, China's SOEs accounted for only about 16% of the country's foreign trade in 2022.

As a result of China's accession to the WTO, private enterprises have played an increasingly important role in China's foreign trade performance, gradually eroding the market share of both foreign-invested enterprises and SOEs. This shift is evident not only in the number of enterprises but also in their share of total trade. It is clear that the rise of China's private enterprises – rather than the expansion of SOEs – has been the primary driver behind China's growing prominence in global foreign trade, with private enterprises often referred to as a "stabilizer" in the foreign trade sector.

Competitive Neutrality Policy

A commitment to competitive neutrality has been identified as a solution to address competition issues arising from SOEs. Competitive neutrality ensures that state-owned and private businesses compete on a level playing field. According to the OECD, which adopted its *Recommendation on Competitive Neutrality* in 2021, this principle is vital for fostering fair competition.[7] Globally, Australia is recognized as a pioneer in establishing a regulatory framework for competitive neutrality. In 2012, the OECD described Australia's competitive neutrality as "the most complete competitive neutrality implemented today."

6 Data quoted from The State Council Information Office of the PRC, "SCIO Briefing on China's Import and Export of 2022." (January 13, 2023)

7 This recommendation aims to ensure a level playing field for enterprises, irrespective of their ownership, location, or legal framework. It recommends both members and non-members ensure competitive neutrality in the legal framework and prevent any undue hindrance, limitation, or distortion of competition. Furthermore, it advises against providing selective advantages or implementing measures that could unjustly boost an enterprise's market performance and disrupt competition. Additionally, it suggests establishing accountability mechanisms to support and oversee the implementation of the principles outlined in this recommendation. OECD, Recommendation of the Council on Competitive Neutrality.

The Australian Experience

Australia first adopted a competitive neutrality policy in the *Competition Principles Agreement* on 11 April 1995. The objective of the Agreement was "the elimination of resource allocation distortions arising out of the public ownership of entities engaged in significant business activities." Competitive neutrality requires that "Government business activities should not enjoy any competitive advantages simply as a result of their public sector ownership." The Australian Commonwealth Competitive Neutrality Policy Statement, issued in June 1996, outlines the requirements and implementation framework for achieving competitive neutrality. This includes specifications regarding organizational structure, taxation neutrality, debt neutrality, rate of return requirements, regulatory neutrality, and adherence to full-cost pricing principles. The Australian Government Competitive Neutrality Complaints Office was established within the Productivity Commission in 1998 to administer the complaints mechanism. In December 2016, the Commonwealth and five other jurisdictions signed the *Intergovernmental Agreement on Competition and Productivity-Enhancing Reforms*, reaffirming their dedication to competitive neutrality in the previous instruments.

Australia remains the only country with an operational competitive neutrality complaint-handling mechanism. However, its competitive neutrality regime, being policy-based rather than explicitly codified in competition law or other laws, poses specific limitations. One significant limitation is the lack of uniformity across jurisdictions, as each region may interpret and implement the policy differently. Furthermore, breaches of the competitive neutrality policy do not constitute violations of competition law, resulting in a lack of penalties and remedies for non-compliance. The absence of legal frameworks makes it challenging to hold government entities accountable for breaches of competitive neutrality, potentially undermining the regime's effectiveness and eroding public trust in the fairness of government business practices (Smith, 2023).

Integrating Competitive Neutrality Policy in (CP)TPP

The SOE chapter in the Trans-Pacific Partnership (TPP) and its successor, the *Comprehensive and Progressive Agreement for Trans-Pacific Partnership* (CPTTP), is widely regarded as a significant milestone in the development of international rules on SOEs. This chapter prohibits SOEs from discriminating against other firms when purchasing or selling goods or services. Some experts propose using the CPTTP as a model to reform multilateral disciplines on China's SOEs as these rules are seen as capable of addressing the concerns expressed by China's trading partners (Mavroidis & Sapir, 2021). In effect, the TPP SOE chapter was written with China's potential entry into the deal, giving the original members some leverage when negotiating China's entry. During the TPP negotiations, the application of SOE disciplines to Vietnam was regarded as a potential litmus test for handling similar challenges posed by China in the future (Kawase & Ambashi, 2018). The USA has played the role of a normative leader in shaping the SOE disciplines in TPP (Zhou, 2021; Sylvestre-Fleury & Marcoux, 2016). Robert D.

Hormats, the US former Under Secretary of State for Economic, Business, and Agricultural Affairs, stressed the significance of integrating a competitive neutrality framework into bilateral, regional, and multilateral engagements as essential for the US to address the challenges posed by state capitalism.[8] A joint proposal by the Coalition of Services Industries and the US Chamber of Commerce advocated for the inclusion of provisions in the TPP commitments aimed at effectively addressing issues such as market access and distortions caused by government intervention favoring SOEs. Central to this proposal was the insistence on ensuring competitive neutrality within the commercial market (Kawase & Ambashi, 2018).

In Vietnam, SOEs also play significant economic and social roles, however, under CPTPP, these roles are increasingly constrained by new regulations that limit SOEs from receiving financing or preferential treatment from the Vietnamese government. Moreover, all SOEs within CPTPP member states are required to ensure transparency in their operations and disclose information publicly. In May 2017, Vietnam formally acknowledged the need to restructure and enhance the efficiency of SOEs while, for the first time, emphasizing the importance of promoting the private sector. To align further with the CPTPP, Vietnam amended its *Law on Enterprises* in 2020.[9] The revised law expands the definition of SOEs to comply with Article 17.1 of the CPTPP, which defines SOEs as entities "principally engaged in commercial activities" that meet one of the following criteria: (a) the government directly owns more than 50% of the share capital; (b) the government, through ownership interests, controls more than 50% of the voting rights; or (c) the government has the power to appoint a majority of the board of directors or an equivalent management body.In addition to implementing legislative reforms, the Vietnamese government launched initiatives to equitize and divest SOEs. However, progress in reforming the SOE sector has remained limited and insufficient as of 2022. For example, Vietnam planned to equitize 127 SOEs between 2017 and 2020 but fell short by 54. While some equitized SOEs showed improvements in operational efficiency, the overall reform of the SOE sector has seen limited material progress.[10]

Some legal experts have argued that the SOE chapter of the CPTPP does not provide more rigorous or effective rules than those already required under China's existing WTO obligations. Instead, it has a narrower scope of application and includes additional exemptions, making it less comprehensive. A key criticism lies in the CPTPP's definition of SOEs, which creates significant loopholes when addressing Chinese state-owned enterprises. Specifically, this definition excludes enterprises that are effectively controlled by the government but do not meet the

8 Hormats, Robert D. "Ensuring a Sound Basis for Global Competition: Competitive Neutrality" <https://2009-2017.state.gov/e/rls/rmk/20092013/2011/163472.htm>

9 "OECD Review of Corporate Governance of Stated-Owned Enterprises in Vietnam," OECD iLibrary.

10 Data quoted from Nguyen Anh Duong, "Time for Vietnam to get Cracking on CPTTP Reform." *East Asia Forum*. (January 13, 2022).

prescribed thresholds. These limitations undermine the chapter's effectiveness in tackling the challenges posed by Chinese SOEs (Zhou, 2021).

Industrial Policies and Subsidies

Industrial policy has long been a central topic in economics, despite the absence of a universally accepted definition. In general terms, it refers to state-driven measures aimed at influencing economic activity, as opposed to outcomes shaped purely by market forces. Debates about industrial policy often center on the "state *versus* market" dichotomy, with two distinct schools of thought emerging on its significance. One school, rooted in conservative neoclassical economic theory, minimizes the importance of industrial policy, particularly in relation to the productive sectors of the economy. On the other hand, proponents of industrial policy view it as a critical instrument for promoting industrial development, arguing that such progress would be unlikely without active government intervention (Strunz, 2018).

The Role of Industrial Policies for Developing Countries

In China, the government has played an active role in influencing its economic development by shaping the conditions for industrialization and implementing industrial policies. However, a longstanding debate in Chinese economic circles revolves on the role of industrial policy, particularly between economists Justin Yifu Lin and Weiying Zhang. Lin, a national political advisor and a leading figure in development economics, stresses the significance of industrial policy and the government's role in the economy. In contrast, Zhang, a proponent of free-market principles and market-oriented reforms, contends that industrial policy posed significant obstacles to economic development. [11]

Perspective from Development Economics

China and other successful Asian economies have frequently been labelled as developmental states. This term refers to a state formation, often nationalistic, that is capable of intervening in the economy with long-term goals and plans, while still accommodating the presence of economic incentives typical of market economies (Woo, 2021). According to Knight, for a country to be called a developmental state two conditions must be met. One is that the government tops priority to economic growth, and the other is that governance should be incentivized to achieve that objective. By these two criteria, China is a developmental state (Knight, 2014).

Japan is renowned as one of the most successful examples of a developmental state. The economic prosperity Japan achieved after the war is credited to substantial government engagement in economic activities (Sakoh, 1984; Johnson, 1982).

11 See "Industrial Policy: Catalyst or Hindrance?" <https://newsen.pku.edu.cn/news_events/news/focus/5167.html>

In his seminal work, *MITI and the Japanese Miracle: The Growth of Industrial Policy, 1925–1975*, Johnson initially introduced the term "developmental government" to describe Japan's postwar growth strategy. Johnson argued that rather than merely acting as an impartial regulator of the market, Japan's developmental government actively supported and led the nation's economic expansion. Significantly, Japan's economic growth strategy was crafted and executed by a select group of high-ranking bureaucrats within central agencies, notably the Japanese Ministry of International Trade and Industry, which is considered instrumental in Japan's modern economic and political history (Johnson, 1982). The model established by Japan has been replicated by South Korea, Taiwan, and Singapore throughout the 21st century, and its influence is evident in China's current economic development strategies (Woo, 2021).

From a development economics perspective, Lin advocates for industrial policy for developing countries to achieve industrialization and modernization. Modern economic growth entails a continual cycle of technological innovation, which raises labor productivity and industrial upgrading, and moves an economy from low-value-added industries to higher-value-added ones, consequently boosting labour productivity (Lin, 2017, 2020). In Lin's perspective, successful catching-up cases like Japan and the four Asian Tigers-South Korea, Taiwan, Singapore, and Hong Kong, along with China, are referenced for their economic development strategies. To elucidate the economic growth experienced by these economies, Lin introduces the third generation of development economics, known as "new structural economics."[12] This framework advises governments in developing countries to adopt a facilitating role in advancing industries within a market economy framework, leveraging the nation's comparative advantages (Lin, 2017, 2020). Industrial policy serves as a valuable tool for the state to facilitate economic development. By strategically allocating limited resources, industrial policy enables effective support for technological innovation and industrial upgrading. This approach tackles inherent challenges such as externalities and coordination issues, thereby aiding structural transformation (Lin, 2017, 2020). China's success is credited to the implementation of a dual-track transition strategy. This strategy entailed maintaining protection and subsidies for nonviable state-owned firms in traditional

12 The first generation of development economics, known as structuralism, focused on addressing market failures in developing countries. It advocated for governments to adopt import-substitution strategies to develop modern advanced industries. The second generation, neoliberalism, centered on identifying government failures in developing countries and recommended implementing Washington Consensus reforms through shock therapy. However, both structuralism and neoliberalism were deemed unsuccessful. From the perspective of new structural economics, structuralism failed because it disregarded the endogeneity of a developing country's economic structure and overlooked the comparative advantages determined by its factor endowment. Neoliberalism faltered because it failed to recognize that the distortions in a developing country's economy were designed to protect nonviable firms in existing industries, which were established by previous strategies defying comparative advantage. Additionally, the shock therapy approach disregarded the costs associated with transition. For details, see Lin (2020).

capital-intensive sectors, while concurrently liberalizing market entry for previously restricted labor-intensive industries (Lin, 2017, 2020).

The Evolution of Chinese Industrial Policies

Chinese industrial policies have undergone significant changes throughout the reform era. During the 1970s and 1980s, the focus was on rectifying imbalances in the industrial structure. Following Deng Xiaoping's visit to the South in 1992, China gradually established a socialist market economy system. Direct intervention methods in industrial policies decreased, while indirect intervention methods using a combination of economic, legal, administrative, and other measures increased steadily. Since China acceded to the WTO in 2001, China has embraced the concept of free trade and adjusted its domestic policies in line with WTO requirements (Wei, 2020). The global financial crisis of 2008 brought about significant changes in both international and domestic circumstances for China. In December 2008, the Central Economic Working Conference emphasized the importance of maintaining growth, expanding domestic demand, and restructuring the economy organically. This led to the implementation of initiatives to revitalize key industries and nurture strategic emerging industries (Wei, 2020).

In 2010 the State Council initiated the strategic emerging industries policy, subsequently emphasizing these industries as key focuses for industrial development in each new five-year plan. In 2015, the State Council launched the "Made in China 2025" initiative, aiming to transform China from being the "world's factory" to a global leader in high-tech manufacturing. The strategic emerging industries policy and the "Made in China 2025" initiative indicate that China has pivoted its industrial policies towards the objective of achieving industrial strength, fostering high-quality development, and constructing a modern industrial system. It reflects the Chinese government's efforts to transform the country from a low-value-added, labor-intensive manufacturing hub into a significant global player at the higher end of the value chain, particularly in high-tech and advanced manufacturing sectors.

However, China's ambition in high-tech industries and advanced manufacturing has garnered significant attention both domestically and internationally. Chinese policymakers see it as a strategic roadmap for China's economic future, while others raise concerns about its potential impacts on global trade dynamics and intellectual property rights. Regarding the "Made in China 2025" initiative, policymakers and security officials in developed economies have expressed hostility towards the initiative. The European Union Chamber of Commerce in China has labeled the plan as a regression to "top-down decision-making." Former President Trump and other leaders have considered this initiative a threat. Critics argue that China is distorting global markets by prioritizing political considerations over economic incentives. The US Chamber of Commerce has suggested it represents a "strategy to utilize state resources to manipulate and establish comparative advantage in these sectors on a global scale"(ISDP, 2018; McBride & Chatzky, 2019).

The Reform of WTO Subsidy Rules

Subsidies are frequently employed as a conventional instrument in both industrial and trade policies.[13] Studies show that governments across the world not only implement measures to define and uphold competitive rules but also enact policies aimed at promoting structural change (Bianchi & Labory, 2006). State support for welfare and development presents a dilemma for the WTO, as delineating the boundaries of trade concessions permitted for developing nations remains ambiguous in the *Agreement on Subsidies and Countervailing Measures* ("ASCM") (Singh, 2017).

The Effectiveness of WTO Subsidy Disciplines

The ASCM categorizes subsidy practices into three classes: prohibited (red light) subsidies, permitted yet actionable (yellow light) subsidies, and permitted non-actionable (green light) subsidies.[14] Export subsidies and import substitution subsidies are classified as prohibited. Vice-Minister of Financial Zou Jiayi emphasized that China's subsidies are strictly under WTO rules and have not caused market distortion or unfair competition. Zou noted that China has eliminated all prohibited subsidies since joining the WTO. The majority of Chinese subsidies fall under the category of non-actionable subsidies, with a small portion classified as actionable subsidies.[15]

The ASCM offers two forms of remedy: imposing countervailing duties and via formal dispute settlement through the WTO. However, China's increasing presence in sectors such as steel, aluminum, and solar panels has raised concerns about the effectiveness of the remedies of the ASCM in addressing Chinese subsidies. One problem is that the definition of subsidy outlined in the ASCM is insufficient to tackle the diverse forms of subsidization existing in China. A contentious issue arises as to whether a Chinese SOE constitutes a "public body." In the landmark case concerning US-Anti-Definitive Anti-Dumping and Countervailing Duties on Certain Products from China (DS379), the Appellate Body introduced a standard, known as the "governmental authority approach" to address this matter.[16]

13 Traditional industrial policy is commonly defined by its selective strategies, often involving subsidies and trade protection. However, the dynamics of globalization and technological advancements have instigated revisions to industrial policies at national and international levels. New approaches to industrial policy have been tried out in many countries, in particular the formulation and implementation of policies 'from the bottom' (local or regional) (Bianchi & Labory, 2006).

14 The definition of "subsidy" as outlined in the ASCM encompasses three fundamental components: (a) a financial contribution, (b) provided by a government or any public body, (c) resulting in a conferred benefit. All these three elements must be met for a subsidy to be identified.

15 See "China's Subsidy Policies Strictly Follow WTO Rules," <https://english.www.gov.cn/news/video/2018/09/25/content_281476317804792.htm>

16 This dispute concerns countervailing and anti-dumping duties imposed by the US on specific products from China. China challenged these measures through the WTO's dispute settlement mechanism. The Appellate Body overturned the Panel's interpretation of the term "public body," defining it as an entity possessing, exercising, or vested with governmental authority. Following its analysis, the Appellate Body determined that the United States had acted inconsistently with the ASCM

WTO members have expressed two different approaches: the government control approach and the governmental function approach. The US and the Panel support the government approach and hold that an entity is a public body if the majority of its shares are owned by the government. China argues for the government approach, under which an entity is a public body if it exercises delegated powers to perform functions of a governmental character (Ding, 2018; Chiang, 2018). However, the Appellate Body did not endorse either approach. Instead, it established the "governmental authority approach," a nuanced standard incorporating elements of both approaches above (Ding, 2018; Chiang, 2018). The "governmental authority approach" established by the Appellate Body is criticized for effectively excluding contributions by Chinese SOEs from being classified as subsidies.

Additionally, subsidies provided through other policies, such as export taxes, are not effectively addressed. Moreover, several aspects of the ASCM pose challenges for complainant countries in meeting their burden of proof to demonstrate the provision of prohibited or actionable subsidies. Problems with notifications and the inability to provide sufficient remedies are also alleged shortcomings of the ASCM (Bown & Hillman, 2019).

The US-EU-Japan Trilateral Cooperation

The US, EU, and Japan initiated a trilateral process aimed at addressing China's utilization of industrial subsidies and the deployment of SOEs in 2017. The trilateral cooperation has been reported as an "anti-China" alliance.[17] The trilateral cooperation has its roots in the 1970s when Columbia University professor Zbigniew Brzezinski proposed cooperation among Western Europe, Japan, and the United States to address global economic challenges. Brzezinski saw this approach as a viable alternative to depending solely on the United Nations, which encountered difficulties due to ongoing North-South divisions.[18] To counter Chinese trade practices, US think tanks have proposed that the US, EU, and Japan band together in strong partnership to exert pressure on China. They argue that without concerted and aggressive action, leading economies across Europe, Asia, and North America could face overwhelming unfair competition, leading to job losses across diverse industries such as aerospace, automobiles, biopharmaceuticals, chemicals, electronics, digital media, internet services, machine tools, semiconductors, and more.[19]

---

regarding certain SOEs being classified as public bodies. Also, it found that China did not establish that the US had acted inconsistently with the ASCM in its assessment of certain State-owned commercial banks as public bodies.

17 See Jenny Leonard, Alberto Nardelli, and Bryce Baschuk, "US, EU, Japan to Renew Alliance Against China," Bloomberg.

18 See "Trilateral Diplomacy: the United States, Western Europe and Japan," Archive, US Department of State, <https://2001-2009.state.gov/r/pa/ho/time/qfp/103525.htm>

19 See "US, EU, Japan Must Strengthen Trilateral Effort to Confront China's Mercantilist Trade Practices, Leading Think Tank Advises," <https://itif.org/publications/2020/01/13/us-eu-japan-must-strengthen-trilateral-effort-confront-chinas-mercantilist/>

The Ministers released a joint statement on industrial subsidies on January 14, 2020. Acknowledging the limitations of the narrow definition of subsidy outlined in the ASCM, the Ministers agreed to broaden the scope of prohibited subsidies and establish new rules to determine subsidies. New types of unconditionally prohibited subsidies, such as unlimited guarantees and certain forms of direct debt forgiveness are proposed to add to ASCM. The Ministers criticized the "governmental authority approach" adopted by the WTO Appellate Body for undermining the effectiveness of WTO subsidy rules. Furthermore, the Ministers agreed to reverse the burden of proof, requiring the subsidizing Member to demonstrate that there are no significant negative trade or capacity effects and ensuring effective transparency about the subsidy in question. Finally, they proposed adding a strong incentive to properly notify subsidies. This would render any non-notified subsidies prohibited if counter-notified by another Member unless the subsidizing Member provides the required information within specified timeframes.[20]

The Impacts of EU Foreign Subsidies Regulation on China

In 2022, the EU adopted the Foreign Subsidies Regulation (FSR).[21] The FSR aims to address limitations in the existing WTO Agreement on Subsidies and Countervailing Measures (ASCM), which only empowers the Commission to intervene when subsidized goods enter the Union, but not in cases involving subsidized investments, services, or financial transactions. As indicated in the FSR, by introducing the regulation, the EU complements its existing regulatory framework with a new mechanism to address market distortions caused by foreign subsidies. It has been widely acknowledged that the formulation of the FSR aims to tackle Chinese state-backed economic activities within the EU by enhancing the powers and regulatory toolkit of the European Commission (Stas & Geisel, 2023).

Similarities Between the State Aid Control System and the FSR

Lawyers have observed a remarkable resemblance between the FSR and the EU State aid law, despite the terminological differences.[22] Given the absence of EU case law on foreign subsidy, State aid law and practice will serve as a guide for assessing what constitutes a foreign subsidy (Stas & Geisel, 2023). Under the FSR,

20 See "Joint Statement of the Trilateral Meeting of the Trade Ministers of Japan, the United States and the European Union," Office of the United States Trade Representative.

21 The FSR entered into force on January 12 2023 and applies from July 12 2023. On July 10, 2023, the Commission adopted the long-awaited FSR Implementing Regulation along with two annexes including the notification forms, detailing the reporting obligations of notifying parties.

22 According to Article 107(1) of the Treaty on the Functioning of the European Union, any aid granted by a Member State or through State resources in any form whatsoever that distorts or threatens to distort competition by favoring certain undertakings or the production of certain goods shall, in so far as it affects trade between Member States, be incompatible with the internal market.

a foreign subsidy exists when a non-EU country provides, either directly or indirectly, a financial contribution that benefits an undertaking engaged in economic activity within the EU and is limited, either in law or in practice, to one or more undertakings or industries (art. 3). Unlike the ASCM, the FSR specifies that a foreign subsidy can originate from a private entity whose actions can be attributed to a non-EU country, which is in line with the EU's established case law on state aid. The Court of Justice has expressed that

> there is no necessity to draw any distinction according to whether the aid is granted by the State or by public or private bodies established or appointed by it to administer the aid. In applying Article 92 [now Article 107] regard must primarily be had to the effects of the aid on the undertakings or producers favored and not on the status of the institutions entrusted with the distribution and administration of the aid.[23]

The FSR employs an attributability or imputability approach rooted in the European case law of state aid. Initially, the attributability approach appeared to involve little more than identifying indicators of institutional public control. In the *Van der Kooy* case, the Court established criteria including 50% of shares being held by the State, half of the members of the supervisory board appointed by the State, and the Minister having discretion to approve the tariffs set (Sauter & Schepel, 2009).[24] However, in the *Stardust* case, the Court recognized that "the mere fact that a public undertaking is under State control is not sufficient for measures taken by that undertaking to be imputed to the State." According to the Court, imputing an aid measure to the State based on actions of a public undertaking may depend on various indicators derived from the specific circumstances and context of the case.[25] Signifying a shift away from the prior emphasis solely on institutional public control, the Stardust case ruling holds particular significance for the operations of publicly owned controlled enterprises. It expressly acknowledges the importance of the "attributability" or "imputability" of these enterprises' actions to the State (Hancher, 2003).

Investigations under the FSR and their Impact

Under the FSR, companies involved in concentrations or public procurement procedures in the EU market triggering thresholds must notify the Commission from October 12, 2023. For example, participants in public procurement must notify the Commission if the value of public procurement exceeds €250 million and if they have received at least €4 million in foreign subsidies in the three years prior

23 Judgment of the Court of March 1977, Steinnike and Weinlig v. Federal Republic of Germany, ECLI: EU: 1977: 52, para 21.

24 Joined Cases 67, 68 and 70/85 Van der Kooy [1988] ECR 219, paras. 35–38.

25 Judgment of the Court of 16 May, 2002, France v. Commission (State aid), [2002] EUECJ C-482/99, paras. 51–52, 55–56.

to notification. The Commission will conduct a preliminary review of the notification and may decide to initiate an in-depth investigation. In addition to the notification-based procedures, the Commission is empowered to launch ex officio investigations into all other market situations, enabling it to initiate reviews on its own initiative. As of May 2024, the Commission has launched three in-depth investigations and one ex officio investigation. Notably, all of the investigations have focused on Chinese companies.Top of Form

The Commission initiated its inaugural in-depth investigation into a Chinese train manufacturer's bid for public procurement in the EU in February 2024. The company in question, Qingdao Sifang Locomotive, is a subsidiary of China's railway giant CRRC Corp., and it bid for a €610 million Bulgarian public procurement contract. Following the investigation, the Chinese train manufacturer withdrew its bid in March 2024. Thierry Breton, the Commissioner for the Internal Market, remarked that the Commission's investigation under the FSR yielded outcomes within a few weeks. He stressed the Commission's commitment to taking all necessary measures to safeguard Europe's economic security and competitiveness swiftly and decisively.[26] After the initial successful probe, the Commission launched two in-depth investigations targeting two consortia in the solar industry in March 2024. These two investigated consortia, including three leading Chinese solar photovoltaic suppliers and a domestic manufacturer in Romania, participated in a public tender for the design, construction, and operation of a photovoltaic park in Romania, financed by the EU Modernisation Fund.[27]

In April 2024, the Commission initiated its first ex officio investigation into Chinese wind turbine suppliers under the FSR. Wind parks located in five EU member states – Spain, Greece, France, Romania, and Bulgaria – are under scrutiny to ascertain whether illegal subsidies have been provided to Chinese wind turbine suppliers. According to Margrethe Vestager, the Commission's Executive Vice-President, China achieved dominance in the solar panel industry by attracting foreign investment, acquiring technology, and providing "massive subsidies" to domestic suppliers. "We can't afford to see what happened on solar panels happening again on electric vehicles, wind or essential chips."[28]

China has voiced strong opposition to the EU's subsidy probes, which have exacerbated tensions in EU-China trade relations. A spokesperson for the Chinese Ministry of Commerce described the subsidy investigations as "typical protectionism." He emphasized that these investigations disrupt the mutually beneficial cooperation between China and Europe. Chinese business groups accused the EU of using the FSR as a form of economic coercion against Chinese firms. The China Chamber of Commerce to the European Union, representing over 1000 Chinese

26 "CRRC Drops Bulgarian Train Bid following EU investigation," <https://www.railwaygazette.com/crrc-drops-bulgarian-train-bid-following-eu-investigation/66206.article>

27 "Commission opens two in-depth investigations under the Foreign Subsidies Regulation in the solar photovoltaic sector" <https://ec.europa.eu/commission/presscorner/detail/en/ip_24_1803>

28 Hanna Ziady, "Europe Launches Subsidies Probe into Chinese Wind Turbine Suppliers," CNN, <https://edition.cnn.com/2024/04/09/business/europe-wind-turbine-probe-china/index.html>

companies operating across the EU, stated that the FSR has led to discrimination against foreign enterprises and "distort the level playing field for Chinese enterprises operating in the EU."[29]

Reforming Domestic Industrial Policy and SOEs

In recent years, discussions surrounding Chinese industrial policy and subsidies have evolved into "difficult conversations" between China and its trading counterparts, prompting a re-evaluation of international trade competition rules. The US and the EU have voiced concerns about overcapacity in Chinese industries resulting from industrial policies and subsidies, particularly in sectors such as electric vehicles, lithium-ion batteries, and solar panels. They argue that China's industrial development heavily relies on state support, including extensive subsidies, leading to overcapacity and market distortions. This argument is supported by statistics showing that industrial subsidies in China are significantly higher, ranging from three to four times, and in some cases up to nine times, compared to major EU and OECD countries (Bickenbach et al, 2024).

Reforming Subsidies Rules and Practices

Subsidies have been a contentious tool in economic development, often used to support key industries, stimulate growth, or maintain competitiveness. Opinions on providing subsidies to enterprises vary even among developed economies. For example, the Boeing-Airbus dispute underscores how subsidies can become a point of contention between major economies, particularly in strategic industries where innovation and market dominance are crucial.

Reflections on the Boeing-Airbus Dispute

The Boeing-Airbus dispute over subsidies primarily stems from the rivalry between the two in the aerospace industry, particularly in the large civil aircraft (LCA) sector. As the birthplace of flight, the US had long held dominance in the LCA sector until the emergence of Airbus. In the late 1960s, the governments of France, Spain, Germany, and the UK collaborated to establish Airbus as a consortium to strengthen aircraft production in Europe. Initially, the US did not view Airbus as a significant threat to its dominant position in the sector, as it boasted up to 90% of global production (Levick, 1992). Realizing its rapid loss of the world market of civil aircraft in the 1970s, concerns arose in the US about European competition and the subsidies provided by European governments to support research, production, and export assistance. To address complaints and disputes regarding subsidies, the two blocs signed the *EC-US Agreement on Trade in Large Civil*

29 See Ralph Jennings, "China Protests Europe's New Wind-Turbine Probe and Report Alleging 'Distortions in the Economy'," South China Morning Post (April 11, 2024).

Aircraft in 1992. This agreement stipulates that direct government support for new aircraft programs should not exceed 33% of total development costs, and indirect support should be limited to 3% of the nation's large civil aircraft industry turnover. The production of the 1992 Agreement has been considered a major compromise between the two world giants (Levick, 1992).

The compromise in 1992 aimed to resolve the subsidy dispute, but it failed to eliminate tensions between the two blocs. The dominance of Airbus and Boeing in the aviation industry has solidified into a duopoly, with each maintaining a significant market share. Despite fluctuations, Airbus has consistently held a substantial portion of the market since the 1990s, intensifying competition between the two giants. In October 2004, the US abrogated the 1992 Agreement unilaterally and initiated the WTO dispute settlement process. The US alleged that the EC and the member states provide subsidies to Airbus, inconsistent with their obligations under the ASCM and GATT (DS316).[30] In response, the EC launched its own WTO case against subsidies given to Boeing on the same day, and a second complaint in 2006 (DS317 & DS353).[31] Both the EC and the US accused each other's aircraft manufacturers of receiving unfair subsidies. The WTO determined that both sides provided illegal subsidies to their respective aircraft makers, yet neither side fully complied with the WTO rulings. In 2019, the WTO authorized the US to impose countermeasures on European exports valued at up to $7.5 billion. Similarly, in 2020, the WTO authorized the EU to impose similar countermeasures on $4 billion worth of US products exported to the EU. On June 15, 2021, the EU and the US agreed to suspend all retaliatory tariffs authorized by the WTO for five years, effectively signaling a ceasefire in a 17-year-long conflict. The cessation of hostilities between the US and EU aims to "counter China's non-market practices in this sector in specific ways," as stated in the official release.[32]

State Support in Strategic Industries

The Boeing-Airbus dispute represents an international competition in strategic industries between the two blocs. State support for strategic sectors like aerospace is deemed necessary due to the industry's high capital intensity, which demands high costs for research and development, and skilled workforce wages.

30 The dispute was filed against the governments of Germany, France, the United Kingdom, Spain and the European Community. The measures at issue are more 300 separate instances of alleged subsidization over a period of almost forty years. See Appellate Body Report, European Communities and Certain Member States- Measures Affecting Trade in Large Civil Aircraft, WTO Doc. WT/DS316/R (adopted 18 May, 2011).

31 On October 6, 2004, the EC requested consultations with the US. On December 4, 2006, the EC filed a second complaint in 2006. See Appellate Body Report, United States – Measures Affecting Trade in Large Civil Aircraft, WTO Doc. WT/DS353/R (adopted 12 March 2012)

32 The White House, "Fact Sheet: US-EU Understanding on a Cooperative Framework for Large Civil Aircraft" (June 15, 2021).

In the US, while the economy typically operates on free market principles, the US also offers government support to strategic industries. The WTO ruling and various studies confirm the existence of industrial policies supporting strategic industries like aerospace. The US's state support for the aerospace sector has been deemed crucial due to the significant role aerospace technologies play in national security systems (Lawrence & Braddon, 2001). Moreover, aerospace exports have significantly bolstered the US trade balance, with around $124.91 billion worth of aerospace products exported in 2023.[33] The US's commercial aerospace dominance relies heavily on defense technology funded by the government, leading to lower transparency compared to the European Commission's support for Airbus. US support includes initiatives such as NASA research assistance and military spending. According to the EU, US federal, state, and local governments have granted subsidies benefiting Boeing, amounting to USD 23.7 billion. This includes approximately USD 16.6 billion provided through federal research programs to Boeing between 1986 and 2006.[34]

In Europe's history, the formation of the Airbus Consortium has often been praised as a model of effective government intervention in the economy, challenging Boeing's global dominance. This initiative has been facilitated by government subsidies, commitments to absorb losses, and funding for fixed development costs since its inception (Agarwal, 2023). For instance, to launch the A380 program, the governments of France, Germany, and the UK loaned Airbus €3.5 billion, with refundable advances reaching €5.9 billion ($7.3 billion). The financial scale of the A380 program grew significantly, leading Airbus to cease releasing figures altogether in 2016. According to estimation, the development costs for the A380 program reached around $25–30 billion.[35]

Recent years have seen a notable increase in trade interventions in strategic industries. These interventions are motivated by a combination of factors such as national security, environmental concerns, and geopolitical competition. Governments are increasingly resorting to measures like industrial policies, subsidies, and import/export controls. The US's implementation of acts like the Inflation Reduction Act (IRA) and the CHIPS and Science Act (CHIPS) in 2022 reflects this trend, with significant financial support directed towards specific industries such as green energy and semiconductors.

Harmonizing Subsidies Practices

"Local corporatism" has been identified as a major factor in China's rapid economic development since the open-door policy. Political scientist Jean C. Oi introduces

33 Data quoted from "United States Exports of Aircraft, Spacecraft," Trading Economics, <https://tradingeconomics.com/united-states/exports/aircraft-spacecraft>

34 European Commission, "The WTO Boeing-Airbus Dispute," (March 22, 2007). <https://ec.europa.eu/commission/presscorner/detail/en/MEMO_07_112>

35 Jake Hardiman, "How Much Did the Airbus A380 Cost," <https://simpleflying.com/airbus-a380-cost/>

the concept of "local state corporatism" to depict China's unique approach to state-driven economic expansion. Oi suggests that China's growth is primarily fueled by the significant rise of rural industry, for which local governments bear responsibility. Within their administrative jurisdiction, local governments view enterprises as integral components of a larger corporate entity. Local officials often function akin to a board of directors and occasionally even assume direct roles akin to chief executive officers (Oi, 1992). This concept has wielded considerable influence in the field of China studies, offering a robust framework to elucidate the phenomenon of rural development in China. Recent research indicates that China's unique decentralized structure of both central and local governments has fostered internal competition among local administrations. This dynamic is identified as the most direct factor contributing to China's economic growth (Abbasi et al., 2022; Fang et al., 2022) In practice, local governments in China often attract capital inflows and suppress the outflow of local enterprises through subsidies, tax incentives, and other supportive measures to promote local economic development. However, these subsidy measures, to some extent, have promoted local economic development but have also undermined the fairness of the market competition environment and reduced the efficiency of market operation.

In 2016, the State Council of the PRC established the fair competition review system in the construction of the market system, clearly stipulating that "discriminatory pricing and discriminatory subsidy policies shall not be implemented for foreign and imported goods and services" and "specific operators shall not be illegally given preferential policies." It shows the central government's intention to prohibit the local implementation of discriminatory subsidy measures and preferential policies for specific operators. In November 2018, Xi Jinping pointed out at a private enterprise symposium that industrial policies should be transformed from differentiation and selectivity to universality and functionality, and policies violating fair, open, and transparent market rules should be cleaned up. It indicates that the reform of industrial subsidy should shift towards universality, functionality, and transparency.

Reforming State-owned Enterprises in China

After the foundation of the PRC, China operated under a centralized socialist planning system. Each SOE was a production unit responding to the production plans of the central government. In addition to undertaking all the nation-building tasks, Chinese SOEs also played a crucial role in sustaining the livelihoods of numerous individuals, providing employment and various social services, including education, healthcare, medical care, and retirement protection.[36] Since the reform and

36 See Fan, Gang et.al, "The Role of State-Owned Enterprises in the Chinese Economy," https://www.chinausfocus.com/2022/wp-content/uploads/Part+02-Chapter+16.pdf (accessed on 12 March 2024); Lin, Karen Jingrong et.al, "State-owned Enterprises in China: A Review of 40 years of Research and Practice," China Journal of Accounting Research, iss.1, 2020.

opening-up policy in 1978, the reform of SOEs has undergone a gradual and progressive transformation.

SOE Reform Process in China

The first phase (1978–1992) of SOE reform focused on "delegating power and sharing profits." This phase sought to explore effective methods of separating ownership and management, including separating taxes and profits, contracting operations, leasing operations, and implementing joint-stock operations to enhance enterprise vitality. For example, in 1985, the long-standing "factory director responsibility system under the leadership of the Party committee" in SOEs was transformed into the "factory director responsibility system." Although this period of reform modestly expanded the operating autonomy of SOEs, the planned economy largely remained intact, and SOEs continued to exhibit low efficiency. By the end of 1991, one-third of SOEs were openly losing money, one-third were secretly losing money, and one-third were profitable (Gao & Zhou, 2023; Xiang, 2018).

During the second phase (1993–2002), more radical reforms were introduced. In December 1993, the Company Law was enacted, providing the legal foundation for establishing a modern enterprise system and subsequent corporate reforms. In response to the widespread losses and general operational difficulties faced by SOEs in the 1990s, the reform focused on consolidating and strengthening major enterprises, while allowing small and medium-sized SOEs to exit the market and permitting insolvent enterprises to go bankrupt. The achievements of this stage of SOE reform were notable. SOEs made progress in establishing and improving a modern enterprise system. The goal of overcoming difficulties for large and medium-sized SOEs within three years was essentially achieved by the end of 2000 (Xiang, 2018).

In the third phase (2003–2012), the focus of reform shifted to the asset management mechanism for SOEs, a crucial and core component of SOE reform. This involves administrative system reform, government institutional reform, interest adjustment, and power redistribution. In 2003, the SASAC was established, marking an important step forward in clarifying and modernizing the administration of government property rights and improving the oversight of government managers. The new SASAC system has yielded significant results, but some issues have also emerged in practice. For example, SASAC combines the roles of public management and investor representative, becoming a tool for the government to achieve various policy objectives and issue directives to SOEs, acting as both "boss and overseer." This dual role has caused it to deviate from its function as an investor (Xiang, 2018).

The ongoing round of SOE reforms since 2013, initiated under Xi Jinping's administration, is regarded as a pivotal step in the structural transformation of China's economy. Consistent with previous policies, the Xi administration has emphasized transforming SOEs into modern corporations and shifting the government's role from managing state enterprises to managing state capital. In November 2013, the Third Plenary Session of the 18th Central Committee of the

Communist Party of China proposed enhancing the state-owned asset management system, focusing on capital management. In 2015, the Central Committee and State Council released a major SOE reform policy document, the Guiding Opinions on Deepening the Reform of SOEs, further elaborating on the 2013 plans. Compared to the previous state-owned asset supervision system, which focused on managing personnel, operations, and assets, the "managing capital" approach deepens the separation of ownership from management rights.

Mixed Ownership and Managing Capital Reform

Singapore's Temasek Holdings Private Limited has served as a significant model for China's SOE reform. It has been frequently proposed that China's state sector should be restructured similarly to Temasek. Founded in 1974, Temasek was established to take over the government-held shareholdings of numerous businesses, thereby separating the government's roles as a business owner and regulator. Over the past five decades, Temasek has grown its net portfolio value to S$389 billion (US$288 billion) as of 31 March, 2024. However, while Temasek's model is often cited as a benchmark, some studies suggest that China cannot fully replicate its key features. Certain Chinese institutional characteristics hinder the adoption of Temasek's principles of non-intervention and non-preference. Despite these differences, Temasek remains an influential example in discussions about the future of China's SOE reforms.

For a long time, SOEs have struggled with a low degree of specialization and division of labor. The lack of separation between ownership and management has led to excessive supervision by a dominant single shareholder, resulting in undue interference. Additionally, there is insufficient oversight and inadequate incentives due to a lengthy principal-agent chain, leading to neglect in necessary areas. These two issues have prevented SOEs from escaping "family workshop-style" interference, hindering the use of specialized social division of labor to improve efficiency. Moreover, unresolved principal-agent problems, which do not exist in family workshops, make state-owned enterprises resemble "new classical capitalist enterprises" with apparent "agency problems."

To address these issues, the ongoing SOE reform highlights mixed ownership and managing capital. Managing capital is a strategy to prevent government over-interference by drawing a clear line between the government and the market. To implement this mechanism, the SASAC launched the State Capital Investing and Operating Company pilot reform (Hu, 2024).[37] The State Capital Investing and

37 Between 2013 and 2021, 21 pilot State Capital Investment and Operating Companies were established at the central enterprise level, following a "function-based classification" approach. This approach clearly distinguishes between state-owned capital investment companies and capital operating companies. At the regional level, over 30 provincial SASACs restructured and established more than 150 state-owned capital investment and operation companies. In certain localities, a "function-combined" approach was implemented, integrating state-owned capital investment and operation functions into a single entity to enable unified operation.

Operating Company pilot reform serves as an important tool for optimizing the layout of the state capital and reducing government intervention. This process is expected to revitalize inferior assets, prevent state asset loss, reduce the fiscal burden on the state (Zheng, 2015), and improve the efficiency of state capital operations. Mixed ownership is expected to share control between SOEs and private enterprises, creating competition among shareholders and fostering a rational decision-making mechanism.

Concluding Remarks

China's rise in foreign trade has raised concerns about its economic structure, often referred to as "China Inc.," which is characterized by substantial state control over the economy. However, an analysis of the share of trade value across various types of enterprises by ownership reveals that China's post-WTO accession rise in foreign trade is largely driven by the expansion and effectiveness of private enterprises, rather than SOEs. While SOEs continue to play a prominent role in China's economy, particularly in strategic sectors, their contribution to foreign trade is comparatively smaller. Incorporating competitive neutrality policies into high-standard preferential trade agreements is an attempt to address the challenges posed by state-led economic models, but the effects remain uncertain.

Among the issues at the center of debate, industrial policies – particularly those involving subsidies – stand as the most contentious point of China's industrial development. From the perspective of development economists, industrial policies are vital for enabling developing economies to catch up with advanced nations in technology and high-value industries. China's success in its manufacturing sector and strategic industries demonstrates the effectiveness of industrial policies in fostering growth. However, these policies have also created distortive effects, such as the well-documented issue of overcapacity. The prolonged subsidy dispute between Boeing and Airbus highlights that even advanced economies rely on subsidies to support their strategic sectors. Despite this, Western economies have formed alliances to push for reforms in competition rules within international trade law, creating significant challenges for China's foreign trade practices.

In response, China has begun reforming its domestic industrial policies by harmonizing local subsidy practices to establish a unified national market. It is also reforming its SOEs by introducing mixed ownership models and exploring innovative capital management approaches. However, as a socialist economy, it is evident that China is unlikely to relinquish state control over its SOEs entirely. Instead, the focus is on improving the methods of state management while maintaining substantive state influence over the economy.

References

Abbasi, K. R., et al. (2022). Analyze the environmental sustainability factors of China: The role of fossil fuel energy and renewable energy. *Renewable Energy*, 187, 390–402.

Agarwal, R. (2023). Industrial policy and the growth strategy trilemma. *Finance & Development*, 3, 50–53.

Bianchi, P., & Labory, S. (Eds.). (2006). *International Handbook of Industrial Policy*. Edward Elgar.

Bickenbach, F., Dohse, D., Langhammer, R. J., & Liu, W. -H. (2024). Foul play? On the scale and scope of industrial subsidies in China. *Kiel Policy Brief*, 173, 1–28. https://www.ifw-kiel.de/fileadmin/Dateiverwaltung/IfW-Publications/fis-import/bc6aff38-abfc-424a-b631-6d789e992cf9-KPB173_en.pdf.

Bown, C. P., & Hillman, J. A. (2019). WTO'ing a resolution to the China subsidy problem. *Journal of International Economic Law*, 4, 557–578.

Breslin, S. (2011). The 'China model' and the global crisis: From Friedrich list to a Chinese mode of governance? *International Affairs*, 6, 1323–1343.

Chiang, T. W. (2018). Chinese state-owned enterprises and WTO's anti-subsidy regime. *Georgetown Journal of International Law*, 2, 845–886.

Ding, R. (2018). *The 'Public Body' Issue in the WTO: Proposing a Comparative Institutional Approach to International Issues on State-Owned Enterprises (SOEs)*. S.J.D. Thesis, Georgetown University Law Center.

Fang, Z., et al. (2022). Spatial spillovers and threshold effects of internet development and entrepreneurship on Green innovation efficiency in China. *Technology in Society*, 68.

Gao, H., & Zhou, W. (2023). *China's State-Owned Enterprises and the World Trading*. Cambridge University Press.

Hancher, L. (2003). Case C-482/99, French Republic v. Commission ('stardust marine') judgment of the full court of 16 May 2002. *Common Market Review*, 40, 739–751.

Huang, T., & Verson, N. (2024). Share of China's top companies in the private sector continued to steadily decline in 2023. PIIE Report. https://www.piie.com/research/piie-charts/2024/share-chinas-top-companies-private-sector-continued-steadily-decline-2023.

Hu, C. (2024). 健全以管资本为主国资监管体制 优化调整国有资本布局结构——国有资本投资运营公司十年改革成效分析[Improving the capital management-oriented state-owned asset supervision system and optimizing the structure of state]. *State-Owned Enterprise Management*, 1, 11–25.

ISDP. (2018). *Made in China 2005.. Backgrounder* Institute for Security & Development Policy.

Johnson, C. (1982). *MITI and the Japanese Miracle: The Growth of Industrial Policy, 1925–1975*. Princeton University Press.

Kawase, T., & Ambashi, M. (2018). Disciplines on state-owned enterprises under the trans-Pacific partnership agreement: Overview and assessment. ERIA Discussion Paper Series (ERIA-DP-2017-13). https://www.eria.org/ERIA-DP-2017-13.pdf.

Knight, J. B. (2014). China as a developmental state. *The World Economy*, 10, 1335–1347.

Lawrence, P. K., & Braddon, D. (2001). *Aerospace Strategic Trade: How the US Subsidizes the Large Commercial Aircraft Industry*. Routledge.

Levick, M. J. (1992). The production of civil aircraft: A compromise of two world giants. *Transportation Law Journal*, 2(2), 433–467.

Li, S. (2022). *China, Inc.: How the Chinese Communist Party Transformed China into a Giant Corporation*. Cambridge University Press.

Lin, J. Y. (2017). New structural economics and industrial policies for catching-up economies. *Journal of Chinese Economic and Business Studies*, 1, 5–18.

Lin, J. Y. (2020). New structural economics: The third generation of development economics. *Asian Education and Development Studies*, 9(3), 279–286.

Mavroidis, P. C., & Sapir, A. (2021). *China and the WTO: Why Multilateralism Still Matters*. Princeton University Press.

McBride, J., & Chatzky, A. (2019). *Is 'Made in China 2025' a Threat to Global Trade? Backgrounder*. Council on Foreign Relations.

Oi, J. C. (1992). Fiscal reform and the economic foundations of local state corporatism in China. *World Politics*, 45(1), 99–126.

Sakoh, K. (1984). Japanese economic success: Industrial policy or free market? *Cato Journal*, 4, 521–543.
Sauter, W., & Schepel, H. (2009). *State and Market in European Union Law: The Public and Private Spheres of the Internal Market before the EU Courts*. Cambridge University Press.
Singh, G. (2017). *Subsidies in the Context of the WTO's Free Trade System*. Springer.
Smith, R. L., Healey, D., Bai, X. (2023). Competitive neutrality: OECD recommendations and the Australian experience. *Journal of Competition Law & Economics* 19(2), 250–276.
Stas, K., & Geisel, B. (2023). The foreign subsidies regulation of the European Union: A new instrument levelling the playing field? *Global Trade and Customs Journal*, 10, 360–371.
Strunz, B. (2018). *The Interface of Competition Law, Industrial Policy and Development Concerns: The Case of South Africa*. Springer.
Sylvestre-Fleury, J., & Marcoux, J. M. (2016). The US shaping of state-owned enterprise disciplines in the trans-Pacific partnership. *Journal of International Economic Law*, 19(2), 445–465.
Wei, J. (2020). China's industrial policy: Evolution and experience. ECIDC Project Paper, No. 11. (UNCTAD/BRI PROJECT/RP11). https://unctad.org/system/files/official-document/BRI-Project_RP11_en.pdf.
Woo, M. (2021). The developmental state. In J. H. Han, R. Pacheco Pardo, & Y. Cho (Eds.), *The Oxford Handbook of South Korean Politics*. Oxford Handbooks. https://doi.org/10.1093/oxfordhb/9780192894045.013.7.
Wu, M. (2016). The 'China, Inc.' Challenge to global trade governance. *Harvard International Law Journal*, 2, 261–324.
Wu, M. (2019). China's rise and the growing doubts over trade multilateralism. In M. A. Crowley (Ed.), *Trade War: The Clash of Economic Systems Endangering Global Prosperity* (pp. 101–110). CEPR Press.
Xiang, A. (2018). Restarting a new round of substantial and robust state-owned enterprise reforms – Commemorating 40 years of state-owned enterprise reforms [重启新一轮实质性、有力度的国企改革——纪念国企改革40年]. *Management World*, 34(10), 95–104.
Yu, M. (2019). The status of China's market economy and structural reforms: The issues behind the US–China Trade War. *Asian Economic Papers*, 18(3), 34–51.
Zhang, C. (2019). How much do state-owned enterprises contribute to China's GDP and employment. *World Bank Document*, July 15, 2019.
Zheng, Z. (2015). 国企公司治理与混合所有制改革的逻辑和路径 [The logic of governance and mixed-ownership reform of state-owned enterprises]. *Securities Market Herald*, 6, 4–12.
Zhou, W. (2021). Rethinking the (CP)TPP as a model for regulation of Chinese state-owned enterprises. *Journal of International Economic Law*, 24(3), 572–590.

4 Trade Sanctions and Non-tariff Barriers

The establishment of GATT and WTO has significantly reduced global tariff rates. In 1995, the simple average tariff across all products was 11.61%, which dropped to 5.47% by 2022. This tariff reduction has contributed to a global increase in trade, with the total value rising from 9,421,718 million in 1995 to 49,978,519 million in 2022, a growth rate of approximately 430.76%.[1] At the same time, however, trade sanctions and non-tariff barriers have become increasingly significant in shaping international trade patterns. Traditionally, sanctions have been viewed as tools to induce policy changes by inflicting harm on target nations (Kaempfer & Lowenberg, 1988). Human rights sanctions, in particular, have long served as a tool to pressure nations, including China, over various policy issues. In the case of the US-China rivalry, US sanctions are understood as measures intended to curb China's technological and economic ascent. According to UNCTAD, non-tariff measures include technical measures (such as sanitary or environmental protection), commercial policy tools (such as quotas, price controls, and export restrictions), and behind-the-border measures (such as competition rules).[2] With growing environmental awareness, many countries, especially the EU, have adopted green trade policies. These sanctions and non-tariff barriers have placed significant pressure on China's foreign trade.

Export Controls on Technology

Intellectual property trade tensions have been a longstanding issue between the US and China. US threats to impose sanctions under the so-called "Super 301 Provision" garnered significant attention throughout the 1990s.[3] After China's WTO accession, IP-related trade tensions continued to be a source of conflict in

1 Data quoted from: World Integrated Trade Solution (wits.worldbank.org).

2 See *International Classification of Non-tariff Measures – 2019 version* (UNCTAD/DITC/TAB/2019/5).

3 During the 1990s, the USTR initiated multiple investigations against China under Section 301 of the Trade Act of 1974, primarily focusing on inadequacies in China's IP rights protection, market access barriers, and trade practices deemed unfair or damaging to US economic interests. China was designated as a "priority foreign country" under the "Special 301" provisions in 1991, 1994, and 1996. See USTR. 2000. Monitoring and Enforcing Trade Laws and Agreements. *Fact Sheet.* (May 1, 2000)

DOI: 10.4324/9781003637110-5

US-China relations. In April 2007, the US launched two complaints against China at the WTO (DS362, DS363), seeking to eliminate significant structural barriers in China's enforcement of IP rights. These complaints focused on three key issues: the thresholds for criminal prosecution of IP violations, inadequate civil and administrative enforcement mechanisms, and restrictions on the importation and distribution of US goods.[4] In the years that followed, the US introduced a series of measures to limit China's access to technology, with Huawei Technologies Co., Ltd. – a leading Chinese telecommunications company – and its affiliates at the center of these efforts.

US Technology Export Controls on China

Under US law, export controls are primarily justified on national security and foreign policy grounds. The Department of Commerce follows a general licensing policy for China, typically approving items intended for civil end use by civil end users. However, distinguishing between civil and military (or dual-use) applications in China is often challenging. Additionally, the concept of 'national security' in US policy extends to economic considerations, particularly regarding technologies that could enhance China's strategic capabilities (Bateman, 2022).

Policy Tools

Huawei's rapid rise since the early 2010s raised concerns in the US The Trump administration argued that Huawei's products pose a significant security risk, asserting that the Chinese government could force Huawei to share sensitive information or install 'backdoors' for access to its systems. While Huawei denied these allegations, the US Congress and executive branch initiated various legal actions to curb the company's involvement in international supply chains and telecommunications networks. What started as restrictions on federal spending evolved into a broader campaign to remove Huawei equipment from both domestic and international telecommunications infrastructure (Mulligan & Linebaugh, 2021).

One of the primary tools is the 'Entity List' used by the Bureau of Industry and Security (BIS), a division of the US Department of Commerce, which has been frequently used to target Chinese high-tech companies. Between 2018 and 2022, the US revised the list 30 times, adding a total of 668 Chinese entities, with few

4 The panel report for DS362 recommended that China bring its Copyright Law and the Customs measures into conformity with its obligations under the TRIPS Agreement. The panel report for DS363 concluded that several Chinese measures were inconsistent with China's obligation to grant "trading rights" under its Accession Protocol. China appealed certain issues of law and legal interpretations of the panel report to the Appellate Body, but the Appellate Body largely upheld the panel's findings. See *China – Measures Affecting the Protection and Enforcement of Intellectual Property Rights* – Report of the Panel, WT/DS362/R; *China – Measures Affecting Trading Rights and Distribution Services for Certain Publications and Audiovisual Entertainment Products* – AB-2009-3 – Report of the Appellate Body, WT/DS363/AB/R.

being removed (Hu et al., 2024). Prominent Chinese companies in sectors like AI and telecommunications, including Huawei, have been included. In 2019 and 2022, Huawei and over 150 of its non-US affiliates were added to the Entity List, triggering *Export Administration Regulations* (EAR) that require licenses for the export, re-export, and in-country transfer of items to these entities.[5]

In addition to export controls, the US employs measures such as divestment orders, licensing denials, and other means to strengthen its tech controls. In 2022, President Biden signed the *Creating Helpful Incentives to Produce Semiconductors Act* into law, known as the CHIPS Act, to implement incentives for semiconductor research, development, and manufacturing in the US This Act, along with export controls, is designed to curtail China's capacity to develop advanced technologies with potential military applications and to curb its challenge to US technological leadership. Further escalating these efforts, on August 9, 2023, President Biden signed an executive order to restrict outbound investment in critical sectors such as semiconductors, quantum information, and AI in foreign "countries of concern," including China. In May 2024, the US revoked licenses allowing chip companies to sell semiconductors used in laptops and handsets to Huawei, tightening the restrictions on its access to crucial technology.

The Forced Technology Transfer Dispute

As China's economy grew and its technological capabilities advanced, allegations of forced technology transfer practices became a major point of contention in US-China trade relations. The 2018 Special 301 Report published by the USTR identified various mechanisms – such as foreign investment restrictions, joint venture requirements, licensing constraints, administrative pressure, and state-backed acquisitions – as methods for China to compel foreign companies to transfer technology.[6] Based on this investigation, the US filed a WTO complaint (DS542) on March 26, 2018, accusing China of depriving foreign IP rights holders of the ability to protect their intellectual property and hindering their ability to negotiate market-based terms for licensing and technology contracts. However, the US did not pursue the case to a conclusion, as the authority to establish a WTO panel lapsed.

5 The BIS added Huawei and 68 of its non-US affiliates to the Entity List in May 2019. In August 2019, an additional 46 non-US affiliates were added to the list. These actions were taken due to concerns that Huawei was engaged in activities that threatened national security or conflicted with US foreign policy interests. In August 2020, the BIS further tightened restrictions by revising the foreign-produced direct product rule, expanding the scope of export controls on foreign products. The BIS added 38 more non-US affiliated entities of Huawei to the Entity List. See BIS, *Addition of Huawei Non-US Affiliates to the Entity List, the Removal of Temporary General License, and Amendments to General Prohibition Three (Foreign-Produced Direct Product Rule)* (August 20, 2020).

6 See USTR. 2018. *Report on China's Acts, Policies, and Practices Related to Technology Transfer, Intellectual Property, and Innovation.*

This likely resulted from a shift in US strategy towards bilateral negotiations and alternative methods of addressing these issues.[7]

The Phase One Trade Agreement between the US and China begins with chapters focused on intellectual property and technology transfer. For intellectual property, the agreement emphasizes procedural changes aimed at aligning China's intellectual property administration with the norms of developed countries. These changes include improvements in the protection and enforcement of patents, trademarks, copyrights, and trade secrets. A separate chapter on technology transfer addresses broader concerns raised in the 2018 Special 301 Report. Specifically, it prohibits China from conditioning market access on the transfer of technology and restricts Chinese government entities from directing or supporting overseas investments aimed at acquiring technology to fulfill industrial policy objectives (Bisio et al., 2020). Before the Phase One Trade Agreement was finalized, China enacted the *Foreign Investment Law* of the PRC, which replaced and consolidated earlier foreign investment regulations. This new law explicitly prohibits the Chinese government from compelling foreign investors to transfer technology to China, responding directly to longstanding US complaints that foreign companies were pressured to share their technology as a condition for market access in China.[8]

The Phase One Trade Agreement made significant strides in addressing some aspects of intellectual property protection, but it has not fully resolved the broader issues related to intellectual property rights in the context of US-China relations. Many experts argue that while the agreement included some positive changes, the moderate adjustments it introduced did not tackle the deeper structural issues, such as the Chinese economic model and enforcement challenges that have long troubled US-China trade relations (Bisio et al., 2020). As noted by Jyh-An Lee (2020), the forced technology transfer dispute not only exemplifies the economic and technological competition between the two powers but also marks a critical juncture in China's economic trajectory.

Long Arm Jurisdiction

The EAR not only governs US-origin items but also applies to certain foreign-origin goods that have a connection to controlled US technology or materials. Under the *Foreign Direct Product Rule* (FDPR), foreign-produced items located outside the US are subject to the EAR if they are a 'direct product' of specified 'technology' or 'software,' or if they are produced by a plant or 'major component' of a plant that is itself is a 'direct product' of specified 'technology' or 'software' (§ 734.9 of the EAR).

7 *China – Certain Measures Concerning the Protection of Intellectual Property Rights – Request for consultations by the United States*, WT/DS542/15.

8 The *Foreign Investment Law* consolidates the *Sino-Foreign Equity Joint Ventures Law*, the *Wholly Foreign-Owned Enterprises Law*, and the *Sino-Foreign Cooperative Joint Ventures Law*, which came into effect on January 1, 2020. Article 22 of this law explicitly prohibits the use of administrative means to compel foreign investors or enterprises to transfer technology

Initially established during the Cold War to prevent the Soviet Union and its allies from acquiring advanced US technologies, the FDPR has progressively expanded. In August 2020, the BIS revised the rule to extend US export controls to cover foreign-made items destined for Huawei and its affiliates on the BIS Entity List.[9] In October 2022, BIS extended the FDPR to include advanced computing and semiconductor manufacturing technologies. This extension targeted entities on the Entity List, particularly those in China, and was part of a broader strategy previously employed against Huawei.[10]

Due to the US's long-arm jurisdiction in export controls and its technological dominance, foreign governments and companies often face significant pressure to comply with US regulations to retain access to critical technologies and markets. For instance, in 2018, ASML, a leading Dutch semiconductor equipment manufacturer, agreed to supply EUV lithography machines to SMIC, a Chinese semiconductor manufacturing company. EUV machines are essential for producing advanced semiconductors, and ASML is the sole company globally capable of manufacturing them. However, under US pressure, the Dutch government intervened. In January 2024, the Netherlands officially revoked export licenses for the shipment of certain chip-making systems produced by ASML to China.[11] This situation highlights the global reach of US export controls and their impact on international business decisions, particularly in the highly sensitive semiconductor sector.

The Politics of Technology Controls: Kicking Away the Ladder

The US technology controls on China serve as a key indicator of the broader US-China technological decoupling, described as "one of the most consequential global trends of the early twenty-first century" (Bateman, 2022). This trend is expected to have significant implications for global trade and geopolitical dynamics, as technological advancements are central to US competition with its geopolitical rivals. US technology controls have not only disrupted China's global trade supply chain but also complicated its efforts to advance its technological capabilities.

Ha-Joon Chang, a South Korean economist based at Cambridge University, has adopted Friedrich List's phrase "kicking away the ladder" to describe the policies of today's developed countries, such as the UK and the US, towards developing nations. Chang argues that these now-developed countries initially relied on protectionist policies – such as tariffs, subsidies, and government intervention – to nurture and protect their emerging industries during the early stages of their economic development. Through such state intervention, they were able to build their

9 BIS. *Foreign-Direct Product Rules: Organization, Clarification, and Correction. Federal Register* [Docket No. 220127-0035] (March 2, 2002)

10 BIS. Commerce Implements New Export Controls on Advanced Computing and Semiconductor Manufacturing Items to the People's Republic of China (PRC). (October 7, 2022)

11 See Ma Jingjing, "Netherlands May Lose Top Chip Market Amid Crackdown on China: analysts." *Global Times* (February 20, 2024)

industrial capacity and technological base. However, once these countries became economically powerful, they shifted to promoting free trade and liberal economic policies on a global scale (Chang, 2002).

Chang's argument has sparked significant debate among economists and policy-makers about the best strategies for economic development and the role of global institutions in shaping these strategies. As reviewed by Douglas Irwin, Chang's book contrasts the free-market orthodoxy of Adam Smith with the managed interventionist approach of Friedrich List, ultimately siding with List's perspective. However, Irwin critiques Chang's work for not convincingly addressing specific questions, such as the extent to which protectionist policies were responsible for the success of today's developed countries. Despite this shortcoming, Chang's book has gained recognition as an important and iconoclastic critique of the neo-liberal "market fundamentalism" advocated by mainstream economics and international institutions (Irwin, 2004).

Marking the End of Exchanging Market Access for Technology

China has long sought to adopt advanced Western technology as part of its modernization efforts. Chinese elites began to realize the power of technology after the Opium Wars, which exposed China's vulnerabilities to foreign powers. During the late Qing period, the Qing court initiated the Self-Strengthening Movement to learn from the West and modernize China's military, industry, and infrastructure. In the 1910s, Chen Duxiu, a leading Chinese intellectual and founder of the Chinese Communist Party, observed that modern European nations had achieved their dominance not only through the advancement of democratic ideas but also through the flourishing of science. He famously contended that China required both "Mr. Democracy" and "Mr. Science" to eliminate the darkness in its politics, morals, academics, and thought. Over the past century, Chen's argument has resonated powerfully, becoming a significant and influential idea among intellectuals of the May Fourth era and continuing to impact discourse to this day (Schmalzer, 2021).

In the late 1970s, the CPC adopted the "Four Modernizations" (agriculture, industry, national defense, and science and technology) as a central strategy to rejuvenate China's economy.[12] To modernize the country, the CPC recognized the urgent need for advanced technology. Deng Xiaoping's plans for modernizing Chinese science and technology involved a significant redirection of resources into this sector. Deng stressed the importance of acquiring knowledge from abroad, whether through importing advanced technology or through the exchange of

12 Originally proposed by Zhou Enlai in 1963 and formally articulated at the Third National People's Congress in 1964, the Four Modernization initiative was later emphasized by Deng Xiaoping in the late 1970s as a key component of China's reform and opening-up policy. The essence of this policy has been described as "a quest for accelerated economic development through import and absorption of foreign technology."

human expertise (Xiong, 2021). And the government adopted a strategy known as "exchanging market access for technology," where China leveraged its growing market to acquire advanced technology from foreign firms. This approach was formally codified in the 1979 *Law of the PRC on Sino-Foreign Equity Joint Ventures*, which was the first significant legal framework allowing foreign companies to invest in China through partnerships with Chinese firms. This law specifically required that the technology and equipment provided by foreign partners be genuinely advanced and tailored to China's specific needs, as outlined in Article 5. If a foreign partner failed to meet these standards and caused losses by supplying outdated or inadequate technology, they were obligated to compensate for the damages. This law was a key component of China's broader strategy to accelerate its industrial development by acquiring cutting-edge technology from more developed countries (Xia & Zhao, 2012).[13]

Initially, to protect China's domestic market, most products manufactured by joint ventures were required to be exported. However, this restriction was gradually relaxed to attract foreign investment.[14] Despite the relaxation, the introduction of advanced technology remained a consistent goal linked to expanding market access. Article 3 of the 1986 Law on Wholly Foreign-Owned Enterprises of the PRC reiterated this by stating that "the establishment of foreign enterprises must benefit the development of China's national economy and must utilize advanced technology and equipment, or ensure that all or most of their products are exported" (Xia & Zhao, 2012).

The strategy of exchanging market access for technology remained in place until the late 1990s. During the negotiations for China's accession to the WTO, several members of the Working Party raised concerns about China's laws, regulations, and practices related to technology transfer, particularly in the context of investment decisions. They argued that the terms and conditions of technology transfer, especially in investment situations, should be freely negotiated between the parties without government interference. In response, the representative of China assured that the Chinese government would not intervene in voluntary technology transfers between foreign and Chinese parties. The Working Party acknowledged these

13 The 1979 Law of the People's Republic of China on Sino-Foreign Equity Joint Ventures underwent three amendments – in 1990, 2001, and 2016 – while retaining the provisions of Article 5 until it was repealed in 2020.

14 The policy began to shift in 1982 within the Shenzhen Special Economic Zone, where some products made with foreign technology and equipment were allowed to be sold domestically. On September 3, 1983, the Central Committee of the CPC and the State Council issued the "Directive on Strengthening and Utilizing Foreign Investment," which further expanded market access for joint ventures in China. The directive established that joint ventures would no longer be required to export all or part of their products. It recognized that, while it had previously been necessary to mandate that Sino-foreign joint ventures export a significant portion of their products to protect national industries and conserve foreign exchange, this requirement could discourage foreign investment. As a result, the directive called for more flexible measures moving forward.

commitments.[15] These commitments were laid out in Article 7 of China's WTO Accession Protocol. It mandates that China must ensure that the distribution of import licenses, quotas, tariff-rate quotas, or any other forms of approval for importation, as well as the right of importation or investment by national and subnational authorities, is not conditioned on "the transfer of technology" or the conduct of research and development in China. To comply with these requirements, China subsequently amended its foreign-related investment laws and regulations, particularly those related to technology transfer and foreign investment.[16]

Although the Chinese government did not force foreign companies to transfer technology, Chinese companies and entities have benefited from international technology exchange through international trade, talent mobility, and joint ventures with foreign companies. However, as China has evolved from a developing country to a major global economic power, its development strategies, including exchanging market access for technology, have come under increased scrutiny by its trading partners, even though this policy is not uncommon among developing countries. This scrutiny has compelled China to begin limiting these practices, albeit with some reluctance, as they have been crucial to China's past economic success. Nevertheless, this shift also presents China with an opportunity to pivot towards independent innovation, facilitating a transition from a model of rapid catch-up growth to one focused on sustained, innovation-driven development (Lee, 2020). The US comprehensive technology controls have almost ended China's practices of exchanging market access for technology, posing a challenge to the country's innovation-driven development.

Seeking Self-reliance When the Ladder is Kicked Away

Before the US implemented comprehensive technology controls, China's export-driven growth had already encountered challenges during the global financial crisis, resulting in a decline in international trade and heightened global competition (Guo, 2011).[17] In response, China began exploring alternative drivers for its economic development. By 2012, the country shifted its focus towards optimizing its economic structure and improving the quality of growth, with technological innovation emerging as a crucial factor in sustaining steady economic progress. China's

15 See Paragraphs of 48 and 49 of the *Report of the Working Party on the Accession of China*. WT/MIN/CHN/49/Corr.1, October 5, 2001.

16 For instance, Article 3 of the Law on Wholly Foreign-Owned Enterprises was amended in 2001 and states: "The establishment of a foreign enterprise must benefit the development of China's national economy. The state encourages the establishment of foreign-invested enterprises that either export products or employ advanced technology."

17 To promote exports, significant measures were implemented, including substantial tariff reductions – particularly on intermediate goods – and the introduction of incentives, such as tariff exemptions for the import of technologically advanced capital goods. As a result of this export-led strategy, by 1995, China had established an international trade model dominated by the import and export of industrial manufacturing goods, solidifying its position as a global manufacturing hub (Guo, 2011).

current goal is to transition the primary driver of GDP growth from expanding investment to advancing technology.

The US technology controls are effectively "kicking away the ladder" for China, a notion that has significantly impacted the field of development economics, especially in China, where it has influenced discussions on industrial policy and the application of comparative advantage theory in economic development. In a debate between Justin Lin Yifu and Ha-Joon Chang, organized by the *Development Policy Review* journal, Chang criticizes the rigid adherence to comparative advantage theory, arguing that it can confine developing countries to low-value-added industries. He asserts that if countries like South Korea had solely relied on their existing comparative advantages, they would not have advanced into high-tech industries such as electronics and automobiles (Chang & Lin, 2009). This debate underscores the critical challenge of global economic integration while avoiding dependence on low-value-added sectors. It also offers valuable insights for Chinese policymakers in determining how China can successfully integrate into the global economy without becoming reliant on low-value-added industries.

The US technology controls have made China acutely aware of its vulnerability due to its reliance on foreign advanced technology. The CPC has emphasized the importance of independent innovation with Chinese characteristics, the greatest advantage of which lies in the ability of the socialist system to concentrate resources to accomplish major tasks.[18] China has faced significant challenges in narrowing the gap with the US and other leading nations in semiconductor technology, particularly in the production of the most advanced chips. To tackle this, China has established the National Integrated Circuit Industry Investment Fund, widely known as the Big Fund. In 2024, six major state-owned commercial banks made the largest investment to date, contributing 344 billion yuan to the fund's third phase. This move is viewed as a key part of China's broader strategy to boost self-reliance in science and technology.[19]

Human Rights Sanctions

Human rights have long been a contentious issue in the relationship between China and the Western world. In recent years, human rights concerns have been increasingly employed by states and non-state actors as a tool to achieve various policy objectives. Trade liberalization and the protection of human rights are both highly topical issues in today's global discourse. Most prominently, the impact of trade liberalization on human rights remains a contentious issue without consensus. Proponents of trade liberalization argue that free trade has the potential to foster economic growth and increase welfare, so trade liberalization can be seen as a means to support the protection of human rights. On the contrary, free trade

18 "Xi Stresses sci-tech modernization, innovation." *The State Council of the PRC*. (June 24, 2024).
19 "Six Banks to Invest in Big Way in IC fund," *The State Council of the PRC*. (May 29, 2024).

opponents argue that trade liberalization can also pose threats to human rights in certain situations (OHCHR, 2005; Bartels, 2009).

In theory, trade liberalization enhances economic welfare, while the protection of human rights ensures individual dignity (Cottier et al., 2006). Thus, there is no inherent conflict between trade liberalization and human rights norms, and both strive to achieve a shared objective: the enhancement of human well-being. This is in line with Article 55 of the United Nations Charter, which mandates the organization to promote "higher standards of living, full employment, and conditions of economic and social progress and development" as well as "universal respect for, and observance of, human rights and fundamental freedoms for all without distinction as to race, sex, language, or religion" (Bartels, 2009). In practice, while trade liberalization can lead to economic growth and development, it can also have negative effects on human rights, particularly when trade liberalization leads to exploitation, environmental degradation, or the erosion of labor rights. Conversely, human rights concerns can sometimes be used as justification for imposing trade barriers.

The Link Between Trade and Social Values in the GATT/ WTO Regime

The GATT/WTO regulatory framework addresses the relationship between trade and civil society issues; however, for the first four decades of GATT history, members generally resolved conflicts between human rights and trade in an ad hoc, country- or sector specific manner (Aaronson & Zimmerman, 2006). The text of the GATT does not explicitly list human rights as grounds for the exclusion of products, but Article XX acknowledges the "linkages" between trade and civil society issues. Article XX of the GATT, known as the general exceptions provision, acknowledges the potential "linkages" between trade and civil society concerns. Article XX plays a crucial role by providing a legal basis for restricting trade when it poses harm to civil society, reflecting a balance between various human interests and international trade regimes (Chow, 2013; Howse & Mutua, 2000). However, justifying trade restrictions based solely on a member's human rights record under GATT/WTO remains challenging. The GATT framework has primarily focused on trade barriers and is mainly concerned with how states treat non-citizens engaged in trade, rather than how they treat their own citizens. This focus contrasts with the human rights law regime, which transcends national sovereignty and aims to incorporate international norms into national law (Finlayson & Zacher, 1981; Aaronson & Zimmerman, 2006).

In the 1999 WTO protests in Seattle, commonly referred to as the 'Battle of Seattle', activists argued that the push for trade liberalization often ignored or undermined labor rights, environmental protections, and economic equality.[20] The

20 The WTO planned to convene its third ministerial conference in Seattle from November 30 to December 4, 1999, marking the first WTO assembly in the US An estimated 40,000 to 60,000 protesters gathered in Seattle to protest globalization and the WTO (Gibson, 2024). Also see Gene

Battle of Seattle marked a significant moment in the anti-globalization movement, described by some as 'one week to change the world' (Gibson, 2024). While many of the issues raised by the protesters remain unresolved two decades later, the 'Battle of Seattle' is credited with demonstrating that mass demonstrations and civil disobedience can effect change (Smith, 2001). Moreover, it reawakened the connection between trade liberalization and other non-trade normative values, raising concerns that the WTO regime imposes a deregulatory, laissez-faire model on states, which impairs their ability to pursue human rights objectives. Since then, a wide array of issues has been addressed, including the imposition of trade sanctions for human rights abuses, the inclusion of human rights conditionality in trade agreements, and the effects of trade liberalization on human rights (Van Hees, 2004).

Human Rights as a Condition of China's Most-Favoured-Nation Status

In the 1970s, the Chinese viewed the human rights debate as a hypocritical farce. During this period, human rights in China were not prominently discussed in American foreign policy, probably due to the positive atmosphere in US-Chinese relations following the Ping-Pong diplomacy of 1971–1972 (Shirk, 1977). Since the late 1980s, human rights concerns have entered the debate of trade liberalization, and the UN human rights institutions are increasingly addressing aspects of international trade (Grant, 2006).

Restoring the Most-Favoured-Nation (MFN) status with the US was a priority for the Chinese government during the normalization of US-China relations. China's MFN status with the US was conditionally restored in 1980 under Title IV of the Trade Act of 1974.[21] In the 1980s, annual extension of MFN to China was nearly automatic; however, in July 1989, the US Congress passed the so-called Tiananmen Sanctions as part of a foreign aid authorization bill, which banned military sales to China, suspended high-level military talks, and strengthened US export controls on dual-use goods (CRS, 1998).

In the 1990s, unusual congressional coalitions formed and regrouped around the specific issue of China's MFN status, highlighting the complex attitudes and interests toward free trade and human rights in the US American business groups, several major American corporations, PRC leadership and the "China lobby" all played vital roles in the extension of MFN status to China (Levine, 2000). Congress passed joint legislation that would have placed further conditions on China's MFN

Johnson, "WTO Protests in Seattle 20 years ago Helped Change Progressive Politics," *Los Angeles Times*, November 29, 2019.

21 The Trade Act of 1974 requires the US to grant MFN status to trading partners, except where specified otherwise. Title IV outlines conditions for MFN status, including compliance with the Jackson-Vanik Amendment (Sections 402 and 409) and a bilateral commercial agreement with the US MFN status allows imports to be subject to lower Column One tariff rates under the Harmonized Tariff Schedule (HTS). Without MFN status, imports face higher Column Two rates, raising tariffs on Chinese goods from an average of 6% in 1997 to around 44%. (Source: US Department of State, Fact Sheet on MFN Treatment, June 17, 1997).

status in both 1991 and 1992, but President Bush vetoed the legislation (CRS, 1998). On May 28, 1993, newly elected President Clinton issued Executive Order 12850, stating that he would consider human rights issues in making future recommendations for China's MFN status (CRS, 1998). He linked the 1994 renewal of MFN for China to Beijing's adherence to the Universal Declaration of Human Rights and other human rights conditions (Saunders, 1995; CRS, 1998). On May 26, 1994, Clinton announced that he would renew MFN status for China but delinked the extension from human rights issues that had been imposed a year earlier (CRS, 1998). Despite this, a bipartisan congressional coalition objected to the President's "de-linkage" decision, leading Congress to consider the United-China Act of 1994, H.R. 4590. In the second vote, the House endorsed the President's position on MFN status for China, effectively ending the MFN debate for the year. The Senate took no action on H.R. 4590 or several related bills introduced by its members (CRS, 1998).

On May 24, 2000, the US House of Representatives voted to grant Permanent Normal Trade Relations to China, ending the need for annual reviews and paving the way for China's entry into the WTO. Chow has commented that throughout the 1990s, "China was made to endure over a decade of a humiliating annual lecture and review of its human rights record as a condition for renewal of its MFN trading rights under the Jackson-Vanik amendment." (Chow, 2013).

Recent Legislative Development and China's Response

Recent legislative developments and practices reflect a growing trend to integrate human rights and environmental standards into trade policies. In recent years, there have been significant legislative developments at the intersection of trade and human rights. The UK Modern Slavery Act 2015 was one of the first laws globally designed to increase transparency in supply chains and hold businesses accountable for preventing modern slavery. This legislation addresses the issue by placing obligations on businesses to ensure that their operations and supply chains are free from these abuses. The UK Modern Slavery Act set a precedent that, along with other international initiatives, has influenced several European countries, such as France, the Netherlands, Norway, and Germany, to implement or consider legislation focused on human rights and environmental due diligence in supply chains.[22] After years of legislative development at both the national and EU levels, the European Parliament formally adopted the Corporate Sustainability Due Diligence Directive (CSDDD), which entered into force on July 25, 2024, marking a significant milestone in EU corporate regulation. The CSDDD aims to

22 France enacted the Duty of Vigilance Law (Loi de Vigilance) in 2017, requiring companies to create a vigilance plan to identify and address risks related to human rights violations, health and safety, and environmental damage. Similarly, the Netherlands introduced the Child Labor Due Diligence Law in 2019. Germany's Corporate Due Diligence Obligations in Supply Chains Act, effective January 1, 2023, mandates that large companies ensure human rights and environmental standards are upheld throughout their supply chains.

enhance corporate responsibility regarding human rights and environmental standards by setting minimum requirements for companies to develop and implement appropriate measures for conducting due diligence. The adoption of the CSDDD represents a major advancement in the legal regulation of corporate human rights and environmental due diligence.

The US, EU, and other countries have implemented sanctions to hold accountable those responsible for human rights abuses. The human rights situation in Xinjiang has become a major focal point of Western criticism against China. This, along with geopolitical and economic factors, led to the suspension of the *EU-China Comprehensive Agreement on Investment.* The agreement, which had been negotiated for seven years, was frozen by the European Parliament in response to mutual sanctions imposed by the EU and China over human rights abuses in Xinjiang.[23] Despite China's denial of human rights abuses, President Biden signed the Uyghur Forced Labor Prevention Act (UFLPA) into law on December 23, 2021, which took effect on June 21, 2022. Before the UFLPA, the US Customs and Border Protection had issued 11 "Withhold Release Orders" on products produced in Xinjiang, including all cotton, tomato, and silica-based products.[24]

The official newspaper of the CCP, the People's Daily, has characterized the UFLPA as a form of trade protectionism disguised as human rights protection. Some US politicians have openly expressed their intent to compete with China in the clean energy sector. Xinjiang is crucial to the global photovoltaic industry, producing nearly half of the world's polysilicon. The ban on polysilicon from Xinjiang is seen as a move to protect US photovoltaic manufacturers from Chinese competition. Regarding cotton production, China highlights that Xinjiang has developed a highly mechanized and industrialized system, with comprehensive mechanization levels exceeding 98% in most areas. The boycott of products made in Xinjiang represents a politicization of trade issues.[25] China has consistently criticized the United States for employing long-arm jurisdiction to impose sanctions and other measures on foreign entities. In China, the US long-arm jurisdiction is regarded as "a hegemonic tool to maintain US hegemony, suppress foreign competitors, interfere in the internal affairs of other countries, and even subvert the governments of

23 China imposed sanctions on five members of the European Parliament's human rights subcommittee after 27 EU countries sanctioned four Chinese officials involved in the mass internment of Uyghur people in Xinjiang. The European Parliament subsequently froze any consideration or ratification of the Comprehensive Agreement on Investment (CAI) until China lifts these sanctions. For details, see Stuart Lau, "European Parliament Votes to 'Freeze' Investment Deal until China Lifts Sanctions," *Politico*, (May 20, 2021).

24 China exports nearly a quarter of the world's cotton and 40% of its tomato paste. Of these exports, 84% of cotton and 70% of tomato paste originate from the Xinjiang Uyghur Autonomous Region. The region also produces about half of the world's polysilicon, which is used in solar panels globally. Data quoted from: Marti Flacks & Madeleine Songy. "The Uyghur Forced Labor Prevention Act Goes into Effect," *CSIS*, (July 27, 2022).

25 "The Politicization of Economic Issues Severely Hinders Fair Competition – America's Sinister Plot to Use Xinjiang to Contain China will Never Succeed" [经济问题政治化严重阻碍公平竞争——美国"以疆制华"的险恶图谋不会得逞]. *The People's Daily*, (July 19, 2022).

other countries."[26] In response, China has established a robust legal framework to counter and block the extraterritorial application of US laws, including the *Law on Countering Foreign Sanctions*, the *Export Control Law*, the *Measures for Blocking the Improper Extraterritorial Application of Foreign Laws and Measures*, and the *Provisions on the Unreliable Entity List.*

Green Tariffs: The Carbon Border Tax

In 2020, European Commission President Ursula von der Leyen introduced plans for the Carbon Border Adjustment Mechanism (CBAM) as part of the European Green Deal. By 2023, the EU formally established the CBAM, becoming the first region in the world to implement a multi-sectoral mechanism that addresses carbon leakage by imposing a carbon price on specific imported goods.[27] The preamble to the Marrakesh Agreement Establishing the World Trade Organization also acknowledges the importance of sustainable development and environmental objectives. GATT Article XX could provide the legal foundation for climate-related trade measures, with paragraphs (b) and (g) offering justifications for environmental protection. However, the integration of trade measures with climate policies through the CBAM has faced criticism from developing countries, which view it as a form of trade protectionism.

The EU Carbon Border Tax and Its Impacts on China

Efforts to mitigate climate change have been a significant part of the international agenda since the 1990s, largely propelled by the UN Framework Convention on Climate Change (UNFCCC) and subsequent agreements like the Kyoto Protocol and Paris Agreement. The UNFCCC now has near-universal membership, making it one of the most widely supported international agreements under the UN. Since the negotiations of the UNFCCC, the EU has played a significant role in shaping international norms and mechanisms to address climate change. It has consistently pushed for climate targets and was instrumental in the negotiation and adoption of landmark agreements such as the Kyoto Protocol and the Paris Agreement (Kilian & Elgström, 2010).

The European Approach to Climate Change

The EU's green leadership has been driven largely by its member states, particularly France, alongside increasing global cooperation in tackling climate change.

26 In February 2023, China's Foreign Ministry released a report titled "*The US Willful Practice of Long-arm Jurisdiction and its* Perils," outlining its official stance on the US use of long-arm jurisdiction. Also see: Gao Yang, "US' 'long-arm jurisdiction' inflicts hardships on the global community," *Global Times*, (August 30, 2023); "US should renounce long-arm jurisdiction measures," *China Daily*. (February 9, 2023).

27 Regulation (EU) 2023/956 establishing a carbon adjustment mechanism.

The idea of CBAM was first introduced by French President Jacques Chirac in 1995, proposing a tax at the EU border on goods from countries that were not making equal contributions to combating climate change. However, Chirac's proposal was perceived as a form of pressure or even a threat to the negotiations surrounding the Kyoto Protocol (Roginko, 2022).

To implement the Kyoto Protocol, the EU launched the world's first Emissions Trading System (ETS) in 2005, which became a cornerstone of its climate policy and a key tool for reducing emissions. Due to carbon pricing, changes in fuel prices, and other climate policies, greenhouse gas emissions covered by the EU ETS have significantly decreased, with emissions in 2022 being 37% lower than in 2005. The new ETS target for 2030 aims for a 62% reduction in emissions compared to 2005 levels across the entire ETS scope.[28] When Nicolas Sarkozy became president, the push for a cross-border carbon tax gained significant momentum. In 2009, France proposed a "carbon inclusion" mechanism aimed at taxing imports from countries with less stringent climate policies. However, these proposals were swiftly rejected at the European level.

Making use of the failure of the Copenhagen Climate Change Conference, Sarkozy submitted a new proposal to Brussels in January 2010. To strengthen his position, he enlisted the support of Italian Prime Minister Silvio Berlusconi. Despite this alliance, the European Commission, aware of the tax's unpopularity, attempted to slow down the French-Italian initiative. Nevertheless, the French proposal gradually gained recognition, receiving support from environmental NGOs and economists, marking a turning point in the broader acceptance of the CBAM across Europe (Roginko, 2022; Leturcq, 2022).

In 2016, following the global adoption of the Paris Agreement, France submitted an informal proposal for a CBAM to the European Commission, focusing on carbon-intensive sectors such as cement. With the political change, the EU introduced the European Green Deal in 2019, which was approved in 2020. Von der Leyen described the Green Deal as Europe's "man on the moon moment," with the central goal of making the EU climate-neutral by 2050. To achieve this, the "Fit for 55" legislative package was introduced in July 2021 as part of the Green Deal, aiming to align existing EU laws with its ambitious climate targets. These goals are enshrined in the European Climate Law, which also sets an intermediate target of reducing net greenhouse gas emissions by at least 55% by 2030,

28 Data quoted from: European Environment Agency. *Greenhouse gas emissions under the EU Emissions Trading System*. The legislative framework of the EU ETS is outlined in Directive 2003/87/EC. The legislative framework of the EU ETS is outlined in Directive 2003/87/EC. The EU ETS operates on a "cap and trade" principle, where the cap sets the maximum permissible amount of specific greenhouse gases that installations within the system can emit. Companies can trade emission allowances within this cap, providing them with flexibility in meeting their reduction targets. The Directive has been revised multiple times to align with the EU's broader climate goals. In 2023, the Directive was amended to set a new target of a 62% reduction compared to 2005 levels for the entire ETS scope.

compared to 1990 levels.[29] The EU officially adopted Regulation (EU) 2023/956 of the European Parliament and of the Council of 10 May 2023, establishing a carbon border adjustment mechanism, which has sparked significant global attention. On October 1, 2023, the CBAM entered its transitional phase, during which importers must report the emissions embedded in their goods but are not yet required to make any financial payments. Full implementation of the CBAM is expected to begin on January 1, 2026, when importers will be required to purchase certificates to account for the carbon emissions embedded in their imported goods. The CBAM applies to imports of certain carbon-intensive goods and selected precursors at significant risk of carbon leakage, including cement, iron and steel, aluminum, fertilizers, electricity, and hydrogen.

Potential Trade Impact of the CBAM

The legislative history of the CBAM in the EU reflects a significant evolution in EU policy and attitudes towards carbon emissions. Early resistance within the EU was driven by concerns that it might violate WTO rules, leading to retaliatory tariffs from trading partners. Lamy et al. have suggested that CBAM should be compliant with international trade law and widely accepted on a global scale. To avoid trade conflicts, the EU must reassure its trading partners that the CBAM would not create an exclusive "rich club" that benefits wealthier nations at the expense of poorer ones. Failing to do so could lead to a "first mover disadvantage" for the EU (Lamy et al., 2021). While the EU has managed to adopt the CBAM, ongoing concerns about its potential trade impact and compatibility with WTO rules remain a source of tension in international trade relations.[30]

Over the past few decades, China has been a major driver of global urbanization and manufacturing, accounting for more than half of the world's production of steel, cement, and aluminium.[31] China has pledged to peak its greenhouse emissions before 2030 and achieve carbon neutrality by 2060, and it established its own domestic ETS in 2021. However, China has openly criticized the EU's CBAM, largely due to its potential trade impact. Chinese officials have repeatedly expressed strong opposition to the CBAM, viewing it as a unilateral measure that

29 Regulation (EU) 2021/1119 of the European Parliament and of the Council, dated 30 June 2021, establishes the framework for achieving climate neutrality and amends Regulations (EC) No 401/2009 and (EU) 2018/1999 (European Climate Law).

30 The United States, China, India, Brazil, South Africa, and several others have expressed concerns that the CBAM will further complicate trade and raise export costs for non-EU manufacturers. For instance, the Indian think tank Center for Science and Environment issued a report criticizing the CBAM. See Nandita Banerji, "EU's Carbon Border Tax Mechanism Unfair to Developing Countries: CSE," *Down to Earth.* (19 July, 2024); Ewa Manthey and Warren Patterson. "How the EU's carbon border tax will affect the global metals trade." *Think.ing.com* (May 2, 2023).

31 Emissions figures are calculated based upon Carbon Emission Accounts & Datasets. 2023. *Annual Report 2023 for Carbon Dioxide Emission Accounts of Global Economies*. "China Dominates Global Aluminum Production with Nearly 60% Share," "China Produces More Than Half the World's Steel," *Voronoi.*

unfairly targets countries with different levels of economic development. Chinese exporters regard the CBAM as "a new trade barrier."[32]

The increased costs associated with the carbon pricing system may reduce the appeal of Chinese goods in the European market, reshaping trade dynamics between the two regions. In 2022, China's exports from industries covered by the CBAM totaled around €20 billion. China's ETS currently only covers power generators, the scope of which is narrower compared to the EU ETS. Additionally, the carbon price within China's ETS remains significantly lower than that in the EU. By the end of 2023, the carbon price in China's ETS stood at 79.42 yuan (approximately €10) per metric ton of CO^2, while the price under the EU ETS reached about €100 per metric ton – a tenfold difference. This carbon pricing gap contributes to a competitive advantage for Chinese carbon-intensive goods in the global market.[33]According to estimates, the implementation of the CBAM could lead to a significant rise in import costs for Chinese products entering the EU. Specifically, the cost of importing Chinese aluminum into the EU could increase by around 17%, while export costs for China's steel industry could see a rise of 4-6%.[34]

Justifications for and Controversy surrounding the CBAM

The North-South divide is a central issue in international climate negotiations. Developing countries, primarily in the Global South, contend that the responsibilities of addressing climate change should be differentiated between them and developed nations (Ülgen, 2021). Striking a balance between the need for global emissions reductions and the unequal starting points of various countries continues to pose a challenge. While the EU's CBAM aims to lower global emissions, its one-size-fits-all approach has generated controversy, especially due to its perceived neglect of these differences.

Justifications for the CBAM

Research by Peters et al. shows that from 1990 to 2008, CO_2 emissions stabilized in developed countries, while they doubled in developing countries. A key factor driving these changes is international trade. The transfer of emissions through international trade has become a significant and growing component of national, regional, and global emissions. They have proposed that policies affecting international trade should be closely aligned with climate policy to more effectively tackle global emissions (2011).

32 *Ibid.*

33 Data quoted from Ouyang, Yan et al. 2024. "What is the Extent of the Impact of the EU Carbon Tariffs on China's Export Trade?" [欧盟碳关税对中国出口贸易影响几何]. *Petroleum Business News.* (April 25, 2024).

34 Data quoted from: Ewa Manthey and Warren Patterson. "How the EU's Carbon Border Tax Will Affect the Global Metals Trade." *Think.ing.com* (02 May 2023); "China Briefing 15 June 2023: CBAM Fight: New Energy Milestone: Extreme Heat." *Carbon Brief* (June 15, 2023).

Due to variations in carbon pricing across countries, production of carbon-intensive goods often shifts to nations with lower environmental standards or cheaper carbon pricing, to avoid higher carbon costs. A CBAM is a measure aimed at preventing such carbon leakage by imposing tariffs on imports (Fontagne & Schubert, 2023). Some economists have argued that not pricing carbon acts as a de facto subsidy for domestic production, which should raise concerns for trade defense measures. They suggest that an import tax should be levied to offset this implicit subsidy (Stiglitz, 2006).

There are multiple justifications for implementing a carbon tax. The first is the level-playing-field argument: carbon embedded in imports should be taxed similarly to carbon emitted by domestic industries. By imposing costs based on the carbon content of imported goods, the CBAM aims to preserve the competitiveness of EU industries, preventing foreign competitors from gaining an economic edge due to less stringent environmental standards. Another argument involves incentivizing nonparticipating countries; taxing carbon at the coalition border reduces market opportunities for exporting countries that do not impose a carbon tax (Fontagne & Schubert, 2023). Thus, the design of a carbon tax has been described as a compromise between environmental effectiveness (in preventing carbon leakage), economic effectiveness (in preserving competitiveness), ensuring public acceptability, technical feasibility, and WTO compatibility (Fontagne & Schubert, 2023). In addition to the EU's CBAM, the UK plans to implement a new import carbon pricing mechanism by 2027 to support its decarbonization efforts. Several countries, including the US, Canada, and Australia, are considering adopting similar measures to the CBAM.[35]

The Equity Concern

The controversy surrounding the CBAM largely stems from its apparent disregard for the principle of "common but differentiated responsibilities" (CBDR), a cornerstone of international climate agreements. Since the announcement of the CBAM, it has faced critiques of developmentalism and concerns that it may deepen the North-South divide (Venzke & Vidigal, 2022). Developing countries, often relying on heavier industries, have argued that the CBAM limits their capacity to decarbonize effectively.

Globally, there is a broad consensus on the need to address climate change, but there remains a divide over which countries – developed or developing – should bear more responsibility. Developing countries argue that industrialized nations, having historically emitted more greenhouse gases, should take on a larger share of the responsibility for mitigating climate change(Ülgen, 2021). The CBDR

35 Sources quoted from: HM Treasury and The Rt Hon Jeremy Hunt MP. "The UK is to implement a new import carbon pricing mechanism by 2027 to support the decarbonisation drive." *GOV.UK.* (December 19, 2023); Kimberly Clausing and Catherine Wolfram. "Putting Progress over Protectionism in Climate Policy." *Peterson Institute for International Economics* (December 19, 2023).

principle recognizes this historical responsibility, serving as the foundation for climate equity by acknowledging that developed nations should carry a greater burden in reducing emissions.

The Kyoto Protocol establishes legally binding emission reduction targets specifically for industrialized countries. Under the Kyoto Protocol, only 37 industrialized nations and the European Community were obligated to reduce their greenhouse gas emissions by an average of 5% below 1990 levels during the 2008-2012 commitment period.[36] However, given the fact that emerging countries, such as China and India, are among the world's top emitters, developed countries argued that these emerging countries should do more to address climate change. This concern led the Bush Administration to withdraw from the Protocol in 2001, citing potential economic harm and lack of obligations for major emitters.[37] Consequently, both the US and China – who together account for approximately 40% of global CO2 emissions – were not bound by the Protocol, contributing to its limited effectiveness in curbing global emissions (Rosen, 2015). The Paris Agreement, being the most significant global climate accord to date, also upholds the CBDR principle. However, it requires all nations to establish emissions targets, referred to as nationally determined contributions (NDCs). This decentralized and voluntary approach has fostered global participation, but it has also faced criticism for limiting its effectiveness (Nordhaus, 2019).

The unilateral nature of the CBAM could potentially weaken global cooperation on climate change efforts. William Nordhaus, the Nobel Prize-winning American economist, emphasizes the need for global, rather than merely national or local, actions to combat climate change. According to Nordhaus, the most promising path to effective coordination is through the establishment of a "climate club" – a coalition of nations committed to robust emissions reduction efforts, paired with mechanisms to penalize non-participating countries (2019). Many have argued that the CBAM alone cannot effectively reduce global emissions in a climate-just manner. They suggest that a unilateral, one-size-fits-all approach may not adequately address the diverse needs and circumstances of different countries, particularly those with varying levels of economic development and climate vulnerability.[38]

36 The Protocol entered into force on February 16, 2005, and has been ratified by 192 Parties. See UNFCCC. *Fact Sheet: The Kyoto Protocol.*

37 The US cited concerns that the Protocol would harm the US economy, leading to higher energy prices and allowing other countries to take advantage of an agreement with limited enforcement capabilities. The last time a US president withdrew from a global climate deal was when President George W. Bush opposed the Kyoto Protocol (ABC News, June 2, 2017).

38 See Hanh (Minh) Duong et al. "Unveiling Carbon Border Adjustment Mechanism (CBAM) Challenges: The Potential Dispute Between China and EU." *The SAIS Review of International Affairs* (July 24, 2023).

Concluding Remarks

Market access and technology have been two key drivers of China's economic development, with market access serving as the tool and technology as the ultimate goal. The strategy of exchanging market access for technology was central to China's reform and opening-up process, as enshrined in Chinese policy. However, this tactic has been largely abandoned due to increasing international pressures. In light of these pressures, particularly after the US imposed comprehensive technology bans, China has shifted its focus toward achieving technological self-reliance. With the "ladder" of technology transfer now effectively removed, China's development strategy is centered on building indigenous technological capabilities. Beyond technology restrictions, human rights have emerged as a significant basis for trade sanctions, reflecting the growing integration of moral considerations, such as human rights and environmental protection, into trade policies. While these trends seek to promote normative values by using free trade as a tool for non-trade goals, they also present challenges for developing economies, raising concerns about equity and fairness. The challenge of balancing trade and non-trade values has become an increasingly important issue in international trade law, particularly as it seeks to reconcile the interests of advanced economies with those of developing nations.

References

Aaronson, S. A., & Zimmerman, J. M. (2006). Fair trade? How Oxfam presented a systemic approach to poverty, development, human rights, and trade. *Human Rights Quarterly, 28*(4), 998–1030.

Bartels, L. (2009). Trade and human rights. In D. Bethlehem et al. (Eds.), *The Oxford handbook of international trade law* (pp. 571–596). Oxford University Press.

Bateman, J. (2022). *US-China Technological 'Decoupling': A Strategy and Policy Framework*. Carnegie Endowment for International Peace.

Bisio, V., Horne, C., Listerud, A., Malden, K., Nelson, L., Salidjanova, N., & Stephens, S. (2020). *The US-China 'Phase One' Deal: A Backgrounder*. US-China Economic and Security Review Commission.

Chang, H.-J. (2002). *Kicking Away the Ladder: Development Strategy in Historical Perspective*. Anthem Press.

Chang, H.-J., & Lin, J. Y. (2009). Should industrial policy in developing countries conform to comparative advantage or defy it? A debate between Justin Lin and Ha-Joon Chang. *Development Policy Review, 27*(5), 493–509.

Chow, D. C. K. (2013). Why China opposes human rights in the World Trade Organization. *University of Pennsylvania Journal of International Law, 34*(1), 1–39.

Congressional Research Service (CSR). (1998). *China's Most-Favored-Nation (MFN) status: Congressional consideration, 1989–1998*. CRS Report for Congress, 98-603F. https://www.everycrsreport.com/reports/98-603.html.

Cottier, T., Pauwelyn, J., & Bürgi, E. (Eds.). (2006). *Human Rights and International Trade*. Oxford University Press.

Finlayson, J. A., & Zacher, M. W. (1981). The GATT and the regulation of trade barriers: Regime dynamics and functions. *International Organization, 35*(4), 561–602.

Fontagné, L., & Schubert, K. (2023). The economics of border carbon adjustment: Rationale and impacts of compensating for carbon at the border. *Annual Review of Economics, 15*, 389–424.

Gibson, D. W. (2024). *One Week to Change the World: An Oral History of the 1999 WTO Protests*. Simon & Schuster.
Grant, S. (2006). Function distinction or bilingualism? Human rights and trade: The UN human rights system. In F. M. Abbott et al. (Eds.), *International Trade and Human Rights* (pp. 221–245). University of Michigan Press.
Guo, K. (2011). Is China's export-oriented growth sustainable? In V. B. Arora & R. Cardarelli (Eds.), *Rebalancing Growth in Asia: Economic Dimensions for China* (pp. 139–161). International Monetary Fund.
Hu, H., Yang, S., Zeng, L., & Zhang, X. (2024). US–China trade conflicts and R&D investment: Evidence from the BIS entity lists. *Humanity Social Science Communication, 11*, 829.
Irwin, D. A. (2004). Review of Ha-Joon Chang, *Kicking away the ladder: Development strategy in historical perspective. The Economic History Review, 57*(2), 411–412.
Kaempfer, W. H., & Lowenberg, A. D. (1988). The theory of international economic sanctions: A public choice approach. *The American Economic Review, 78*(4), 786–793.
Kilian, B., & Elgström, O. (2010). Still a green leader? The European Union's role in international climate negotiations. *Cooperation and Conflict, 45*(3), 255–273.
Lamy, P., Pons, G., & Leturcq, P. (2020). *GT6- towards a European carbon border adjustment mechanism*. Europe Jacques Delors Policy Paper, July. https://doi.org/10.4337/relp.2020.01.03.
Lee, J.-A. (2020). Forced technology transfer in the case of China. *Boston University Journal of Science & Technology Law, 26*, 324–352.
Leturcq, P. (2022). The European Carbon Border Adjustment Mechanism and the path to sustainable trade policies: From 'coexistence' to 'cooperation'. *Cambridge Yearbook of European Legal Studies, 24*, 67–87.
Levine, R. (2000). *Complex interactions: Why President Clinton de-links human rights conditions from the criteria for China's Most Favored Nation Status*. https://apps.dtic.mil/sti/tr/pdf/ADA431700.pdf
Mulligan, S. P., & Linebaugh, C. D. (2021). Huawei and US law. *Congressional Research Service, R46693*, February 2023.
Mutua, M., & Howse, R. (2001). Protecting human rights in a global economy: Challenges for the World Trade Organization. In H. Stokke & A. Tostensen (Eds.), *Human rights in development yearbook 1999/2000: The millennium edition* (pp. 51–82). Martinus Nijhoff Publishers.
Nordhaus, W. D. (2019). Climate change: The ultimate challenge for economics. *American Economic Review, 109*(6), 1991–2014.
Office of the United Nations High Commissioner for Human Rights (OHCHR). (2005). *Human rights and world trade agreements: Using general exception clauses to protect human rights*. HR/PUB/05/5. https://www.ohchr.org/sites/default/files/Documents/Publications/WTOen.pdf.
Peters, G. P., Minx, J. C., Weber, C. L., & Edenhofer, O. (2011). Growth in emission transfers via international trade from 1990 to 2008. *Proceedings of the National Academy of Sciences (PNAS), 108*(21), 8903–8908.
Roginko, S. A. (2022). French tax for the European Union: The genesis of cross-border carbon adjustment. *Herald of Russian Academy of Sciences, 92*(Suppl. 6), S521–S528.
Rosen, A. M. (2015). The wrong solution at the right time: The failure of the Kyoto protocol on climate. *Politics & Policy, 43*(1), 30–58.
Saunders, P. (1995). *Most-favored-nation status and China*. Princeton Open Access Repository. https://oar.princeton.edu/bitstream/88435/pr15h7bt3n/1/Saunders.pdf
Schmalzer, S. (2021). The global comrades of Mr. Democracy and Mr. Science: Placing May Fourth in a transnational history of science activism. *East Asian Science, Technology and Society: An International Journal, 16*(3), 305–326.
Shirk, S. L. (1977). Human rights: What about China? *Foreign Policy, 29*, 109–127.

Smith, J. (2001). Globalizing resistance: The battle of Seattle and the future of social movements. *Mobilization, 6*(1), 1–20.

Stiglitz, J. E. (2006). A new agenda for global warming. *The Economists' Voice, 3*(3), 22–27.

Ülgen, S. (2021). How deep is the North-South divide on climate negotiations?. *Carnegie Europe,* October 6.

Van Hees, F. (2004). Protection v. protectionism: The use of human rights arguments in the debate for and against the liberalisation of trade. https://www.abo.fi/wp-content/uploads/2018/03/2004-van-Hees-Use-of-HR-arguments.pdf

Venzke, I., & Vidigal, G. (2022). Are unilateral trade measures in the climate crisis the end of differentiated responsibilities? The case of the EU Carbon Border Adjustment Mechanism(CBAM). In M. den Heijer & H. van der Wilt (Eds.), *Netherlands Yearbook of International Law 2020* (Vol. 51, pp. 121–139). T.M.C. Asser Press.

Xia, L., & Zhao, L. (2012). 以市场换技术"方针的历史演变 [The historical evolution of the strategy of exchanging market access for technology]. *Contemporary China History Studies, 19*(2), 105–130.

Xiong, C. (2021). Deng Xiaoping's views on science and technology: Origins of the Sino-US science and technology cooperation, 1977–1979. *The Journal of American-East Asian Relations, 28*(2), 159–185.

5 China's Solar Photovoltaic Industry

A Case Study on Development, Policy, and Global Impact

Photovoltaics (PV) is a technology that directly converts solar energy into electricity through the PV effect at a semiconductor interface. The PV industry value chain consists of several stages: ranging from the production of raw silicon material and silicon wafers to the manufacturing of solar cells, and ultimately to the construction and operation of solar power plants (or solar power stations). Silicon material and wafers are the upstream components, while solar power stations represent the downstream application. Research indicates a significant transition in global solar PV manufacturing capacity from Europe, Japan, and the United States to China over the past two decades (IEA, 2022; Wen et al., 2021). The rise of China in the solar PV industry has become a concern for policymakers in many countries.

Development of the Solar Photovoltaic Industry in China

In 1954, Bell Labs invented the first PV device in the US, initially used in space satellites. The oil crisis of the 1970s shifted the focus to renewable energy, inspiring new science and technology policies, as well as innovations in alternative nuclear, solar, wind, and other renewable energy sources. Among these, PV technology stands out due to its safety, cleanliness, and efficiency, making it a key component of sustainable development strategies worldwide (Sen & Ganguly, 2017). Before 2000, the development of PV power generation was slow due to high costs. In 1975, the global PV module price was \$125.83 per watt, with total production reaching just 2 megawatts.[1] The US led PV technology development from the 1960s to the 1990s, while Germany and Japan emerged as the leading nations in solar PV development from the 1990s through the early 2000s.

China's Emergence as a Global Leader in Solar Energy

In 2001, China's solar cell production accounted for just about 1% of the global output. However, within six years, China became the world's largest producer of solar cells by 2007. By this year, five of the world's top 16 solar cell manufacturers were from China. Large PV industrial parks rapidly emerged in regions such as

1 Data quoted from: "Solar Photovoltaic Module Price," Our World in Data,

DOI: 10.4324/9781003637110-6

Jiangsu and Baoding, forming a relatively complete PV industry chain, including silicon materials, silicon wafers, silicon ingots, solar cell components, and PV system applications. The rapid development of China's PV industry was largely driven by soaring international market demand, especially from Europe. In 2007, newly installed PV capacity in China accounted for only 1.84% of total production, with over 98% of solar cell components exported (Zhao et al., 2008).

The 2008 global financial crisis led to a decline in demand for solar panels. In response, the Chinese government shifted focus to the domestic market and initiated a two-year stimulus package worth 4 trillion yuan (about $586 billion) – equivalent to 13.3% of China's 2008 GDP. This package included substantial subsidies for solar energy deployment, which resulted in a significant increase in the production of solar PV products. Between 2009 and 2011, solar cell and polysilicon production increased eightfold, and wafer production grew tenfold (Zhang et al., 2021). Figure 5.1 shows the exponential growth of China's solar cell output in the past two decades, especially during the periods of 2009-2011 and 2019-2023.

By 2011, China's PV products accounted for over 66% of global production (Wen et al., 2021). By then, China controlled more than 80% of the market share in all stages of solar panel manufacturing, including polysilicon, wafers, cells, and modules. China also became home to the world's top 10 suppliers of solar PV manufacturing equipment. It is expected that China will remain a key player in the global solar PV supply chain through 2025. With continued expansion of

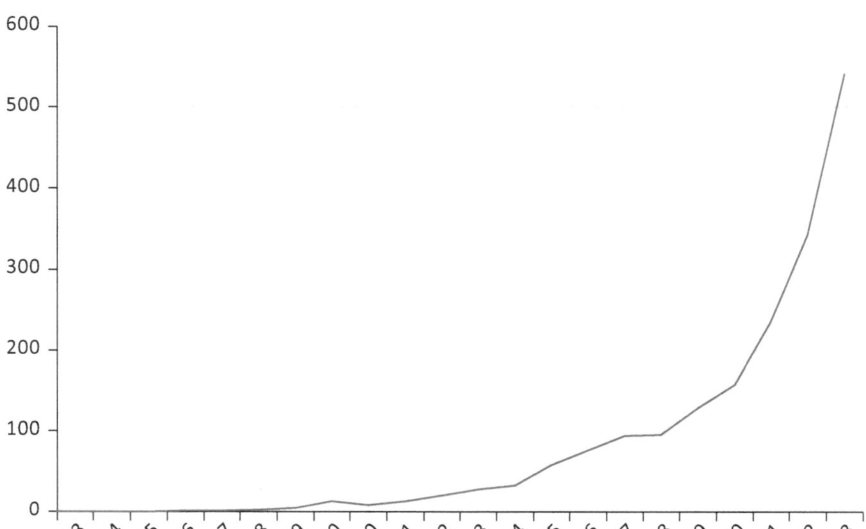

Figure 5.1 Solar Cell Output in China (2003–2023)

(*Note:* The output is measured in gigawatts (GW). *Source:* National Bureau of Statistics of China)

manufacturing capacity, China's share of global polysilicon, ingot, and wafer production is projected to approach 95% (IEA, 2022).

Recent data from China's Customs Authority also highlight the growth of the solar industry, with the total output value surpassing 1.7 trillion *yuan* (about $235 billion) in 2023. Polysilicon production increased to 1.43 million tons, a 67% rise, while silicon wafer production reached 622 gigawatts (GW), growing 67.5% year-on-year. Solar cell production hit 545 GW, marking a growth of 64.9%, and PV module production reached 500 GW, growing by 69.3% [2]

On the export front, Chinese PV products saw significant growth in 2023 despite a decline in prices. Exports of wafers, solar cells, and PV modules reached 70.3 GW, 39.3 GW, and 211.7 GW, respectively, with year-on-year growth rates of 93.6%, 65.5%, and 37.9%. However, the total export value declined to $47.59 billion in 2023, reflecting a 4.9% decrease compared to the previous year. This decline is attributed to the overall drop in PV product prices. Since the second half of 2023, the prices of PV cells and modules have steadily decreased, with cells falling by approximately 51.8% and modules by about 45.6%.[3]

Competitive Advantages of the Chinese Solar Photovoltaic Industry

China boasts abundant solar energy resources, making it an ideal location for PV power generation. Research in solar PV cells began in the early 1960s, but the development of China's solar PV industry remained slow until the 1990s. The high cost of solar cells restricted their use to satellites, communication systems, and off-grid power supplies in remote areas (Zhang & White, 2014). However, over the past two decades, China has emerged as a global leader in the solar industry, gaining a significant competitive advantage by producing high-quality solar products at competitive prices. The price of solar panels in China now ranges from $0.07 to $0.14/W, while the average cost per watt for solar installations in the US is approximately $2.75/W before incentives.[4] Between 2003 and 2023, China saw a remarkable surge in solar PV patent applications, with an average annual growth

2 Data quoted from: China Chamber of Commerce for Import and Export of Machinery and Electric Products(CCCME) 2024. "Analysis and Suggestions for International Trade of China's Photovoltaic Products of 2023" [2023年我国光伏产业对外贸易形势分析及对策建议]. Available at: <https://cccme.org.cn/model5-1/news/details.aspx?id=F505990E0457F444CD4EC929843D18A1&classid=3AFFFDC5D50285DC&xgid=F868932F64EB7AAF>

3 Data quoted from: China Chamber of Commerce for Import and Export of Machinery and Electric Products(CCCME) 2024. "Analysis and Suggestions for International Trade of China's Photovoltaic Products of 2023" [2023年我国光伏产业对外贸易形势分析及对策建议] . Available at: <https://cccme.org.cn/model5-1/news/details.aspx?id=F505990E0457F444CD4EC929843D18A1&classid=3AFFFDC5D50285DC&xgid=F868932F64EB7AAF>

4 Data quoted from: Nieka Ranises, "Solar Panel Price in China 06 October 2024." Available at: <https://jbms360.com/solar-panel-price-in-china/>; Emily Walker, Vikram Aggarwal, "Solar Panel Cost in 2024: It May Be Lower than You Think." *Energy Sage.* (December 10, 2024)

rate of 22.1%. By the end of 2023, China had filed 166,000 cumulative patent applications, with 73,000 valid patents, both ranking first globally.[5]

These lower prices and vast production capacity highlight China's dominance in the global solar market, making renewable energy more accessible and affordable worldwide. Several factors contribute to this edge, including lower labor costs, reduced energy expenses, affordable land prices, access to low-interest loans, and a range of favorable conditions.[6] According to Nahm, Chinese solar companies have leveraged a fragmented policy framework to develop knowledge-intensive capabilities for mass production (Nahm, 2021). By collaborating with global supply chains, they repurposed manufacturing policies to build new capacities, benefiting from resources for technological learning and attracting foreign high-tech manufacturers. This created an ecosystem conducive to innovative manufacturing. Chinese solar companies grew by focusing on scaling up production and commercialization, attracting global innovators and competing on skills rather than labor costs. The sustainability of China's dominance in innovative manufacturing may depend on applying these scaling and commercialization capabilities to other sectors. Studies on China's electronics, machine tools, and automotive industries show similar upgrading trajectories focused on manufacturing. While Beijing recognizes the importance of manufacturing institutions for economic development and innovation, the ultimate responsibility for identifying new applications for advanced manufacturing skills rests with entrepreneurial companies. These companies must leverage a variety of institutional supports to drive future growth and innovation (Nahm, 2021).

Domestic Policies and Strategic Initiatives

Extensive research has highlighted the factors behind China's rise in the PV industry, attributing it to a combination of supportive policies, technological advancements, strategic market approaches, and a large domestic market (Huang et al., 2016; Zhang et al., 2021).

Pursuing Green Energy Goals

China's transition towards sustainable energy systems is driven by multiple factors, with the need to reduce its reliance on coal and imported fossil fuels being paramount. As the world's largest energy consumer, China faced significant environmental challenges due to its dependence on coal. Coal-fired generation alone

5 Data quoted from: "The 2024 Annual Report on the Development of Photovoltaic Industry Patents Released: Intellectual Property Ecosystem Construction Steadily Advancing" [光伏产业专利发展年度报告（2024）》发布　知识产权生态建设稳步向前]. Available at: <http://ipr.mofcom.gov.cn/article/sjzl/gn/202406/1986517.html>>

6 Bradsher, K., "How China Came to Dominate the World in Solar Energy." *The New York Times*. (March 8, 2024); Robinson, Q., "The True Cost of Chinese Solar Panels," *Time Magazine*. (January 18, 2024)

accounted for 75% of its electricity production in 1996.[7] This coal-dominated energy structure not only contributed to severe air pollution but also posed long-term constraints on energy security. The environmental consequences of this energy model – particularly high levels of carbon emissions – made climate change a central issue in both domestic and global policy discussions. As the leading emitter of greenhouse gases and an emerging global power, China views climate change as a strategic priority. Balancing domestic energy needs with international climate goals has allowed China to leverage its position to influence the development of global rules and institutions (He, 2010).

To drive the development of renewable energy, China has implemented a comprehensive legal and policy framework aimed at accelerating the use of renewable sources. This framework has been pivotal in advancing the solar PV industry. From 1994 to 2019, China introduced 253 national-level policies designed to support renewable energy development (Song & Xiao, 2022). These policies have evolved over time, initially focusing on supply-side measures and gradually shifting towards a more balanced approach that includes both supply-side support and environmental policies. Concurrently, demand-side policies have gained increasing momentum, reflecting a more holistic approach to energy policy (Song & Xiao, 2022).

Since the 1990s, the Chinese government has actively supported the growth of renewable energy. The "Ninth Five-Year Plan (1996–2000)" set ambitious targets for "new and renewable energy," marking the start of a sustained governmental push toward cleaner energy sources. In 2001, the "Tenth Five-Year Plan (2001-2005)" emphasized the need to diversify China's energy portfolio by developing new energy sources. In 2005, the enactment of the *Renewable Energy Law* further solidified China's commitment to renewable energy, establishing a comprehensive legal framework to promote the development and use of these resources.

China's renewable energy policies have been built around three core principles. First, the government focused on creating a strong national base of producers and consumers to stimulate both demand and supply for renewable energy. Second, it implemented measures to safeguard emerging green technology markets during their early stages of development, allowing them to grow and mature without being overshadowed by competition from well-established fossil fuel industries. Third, China set ambitious yet achievable renewable energy targets, providing clear direction and motivation for the industry. These principles, coupled with the supportive legal framework established by the Renewable Energy Law, have been instrumental in fostering the success and growth of China's renewable energy sector.[8]

Due to a favorable environment for renewable energy, China has rapidly expanded its capacity in wind, solar, and other clean energy sources. As shown in

7 Data quoted from: "IEA Energy Statistics and Balances of non-OECD countries, 1995–1996." OECD 1998.

8 UNESCAP. Low Carbon Green Growth Roadmap for Asia and the Pacific: Case Study – China's renewable energy policies.

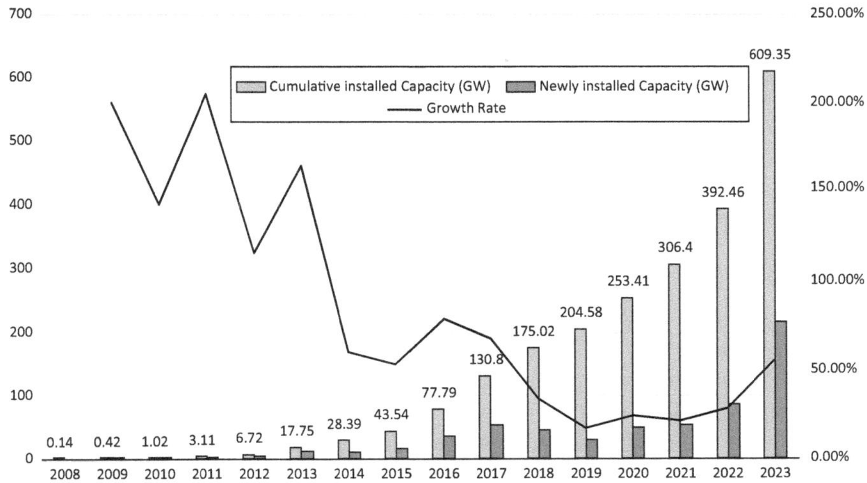

Figure 5.2 Installed Photovoltaic Power Generation Capacity in China (2008–2023)

Source: China Photovoltaic Industry Association

Figure 5.2, the cumulative installed capacity of PV power generation in China has steadily increased from 0.14 GW in 2008 to 609.35 GW in 2023. Notably, in 2023 alone, China added 216.89 GW of solar capacity, representing nearly half of the total new PV installations globally.[9]

Although coal still accounted for nearly 60% of China's electricity supply in 2023, China's newly installed capacity surpassed the cumulative installed capacity of other major economies. For example, according to S&P Global Commodity Insights data, the US had added a total of 157 GW, India 81 GW, Germany 75 GW, and the UK 15 GW by 2023. This remarkable growth highlights the growing potential for power generation from renewable sources. China has also solidified its position as a global leader in the clean energy market.[10] Moreover, green energy has become a significant driver of China's economy. In 2023, the clean energy sector, including the value of goods and services, contributed an estimated 11.4 trillion *yuan* (about $1.6 trillion) to China's economy, marking a 30% increase from the previous year. This means that clean energy now accounts for about 9.0% of China's GDP.[11]

9 According to the International Energy Agency (IEA), between 407.3 GW and 446 GW of PV systems were newly installed worldwide in 2023. See IEA, Snapshot of Global PV Markets 2024 (Report IEA-PVPS P1-42:2024).

10 Ivy Yin, "Coal Still Accounted for Nearly 60% of China's Electricity Supply in 2023: CEC," *S&P Global*, 2024.

11 Data quoted from: Lauri Myllyvirta, "Analysis: Clean Energy was the Top Driver of China's Economic Growth in 2023," Carbon Brief.

Leveraging International Technology Transfer

In the PV industry, Chinese enterprises have adopted a distinctive strategy focused on the commercialization and scale-up of technologies, a model known as *innovative manufacturing*. This approach contrasts with the strategies of US enterprises, which tend to focus on start-ups, and German enterprises, which emphasize supply chain management (Nahm, 2021).

The Transfer of Photovoltaic Production Technology to China

In the early stage of development, China's PV industry faced what was termed "three dependencies abroad" – relying heavily on foreign countries for raw materials, markets, and core technologies. One of the most significant challenges was the production of polysilicon, a high-purity form of silicon crucial to the PV industry. Initially, polysilicon was sourced from the microelectronics sector, but it was produced in limited quantities, with global production ranging from only 30,000 to 40,000 tons between 2001 and 2005. This scarcity severely constrained China's ability to scale its PV industry. As a result, Chinese manufacturers were primarily active in the downstream segments of the PV production chain, such as cell production and module assembly, where the barriers to entry were lower. Meanwhile, Western enterprises dominated the upstream markets, where advanced technological expertise was essential (De La Tour et al., 2011).

When Chinese PV enterprises started up, they largely depended on imported equipment and technology. They acquired the capabilities to produce cells and modules primarily through two main avenues: purchasing manufacturing equipment and the return of high-tech talents from abroad. Other forms of international technology transfer, such as foreign direct investment and intellectual property trade, had a comparatively minor impact. Foreign direct investment in China's PV sector remained limited, hovering around 10%, while major domestic players were predominantly private enterprises (De La Tour et al., 2011; Luo & Yu, 2012).

The purchase of foreign manufacturing equipment was a crucial step in technology acquisition. Through this, Chinese enterprises learned key production techniques and trained a skilled workforce, laying the groundwork for the rapid expansion of their production capacity. In 2000, German suppliers began providing cell and module production lines to China's solar enterprises, and other foreign equipment providers quickly followed suit, establishing sales networks in China (Nahm, 2021). A landmark event occurred in 2006 when the Chinese company Daqiao Group entered into an exclusive technology transfer agreement with a European company to break the Western monopoly on polysilicon production. This collaboration not only alleviated the critical bottleneck in polysilicon production but also positioned China at the forefront of the global PV industry.[12]

12 Emily Feng, "How Did China Become the World's Dominant Polysilicon Producer?," NPR, July 6, 2021.

In addition to technology transfer through equipment purchases, returnee talents played a crucial role in the industry's growth. Many of China's leading PV enterprises were founded by scientists who had studied abroad. Notable figures such as Yang Huaijin, Shi Zhengrong, and Zhao Jianhua – often referred to as the "Three Great Returnees" in the PV industry – studied in Australia during the 1980s and 1990s. Upon returning to China, they established pioneering PV businesses, bringing advanced technology and new business models to the country (Luo & Yu, 2012). These returnees have been instrumental in identifying opportunities in the PV sector, introducing advanced technologies, and accelerating the industrialization of China's solar energy industry.

Fostering Indigenous Innovation and Refinement

Based on international technology transfer and the contributions of returnees, Chinese PV enterprises have made remarkable advancements in indigenous technological innovation within the PV production industry. A prime example of this progress is JinkoSolar, one of China's leading PV enterprises, which boasts an impressive portfolio of over 3,500 patent applications and more than 2,000 granted patents. The company holds one of the industry's largest and most valuable collections of recognized TOPCon (Tunnel Oxide Passivated Contact) patents, a cutting-edge technology in solar cell efficiency. In February 2024, JinkoSolar made headlines when one of its affiliated companies granted rights to certain N-type TOPCon-related patents to another of the world's top ten module manufacturers. This move underscores JinkoSolar's leading role in advancing solar technology and highlights China's growing dominance in the global PV industry.[13]

In the field of polysilicon production, China has also made significant advances. The traditional Siemens Process, developed by German companies Siemens and Wacker in the 1950s, was initially used to produce hyper-pure polysilicon for the semiconductor industry. However, to scale up polysilicon production, China National Chemical Corporation (ChemChina) has refined and optimized this process since 2006. In collaboration with Yongxiang Co. Ltd., a subsidiary of Tongwei Group, China National Chemical developed the Yongxiang Method, a breakthrough innovation that has enabled large-scale polysilicon production. A key feature of this method is the use of a high-efficiency cold hydrogenation fluidized bed reactor, which significantly improves the chemical reaction conversion rates. The Yongxiang Method boasts a single-pass conversion rate of up to 28%, surpassing foreign technologies by more than 20%. This innovation has lowered the cost of polysilicon production and positioned Tongwei as the world's largest polysilicon producer, with a global market share of over 28% in 2022. As a result,

13 Data quoted from: Jinko Solar, "JinkoSolar Promotes Technology Innovation with TOPCon Patent License Transaction."

Tongwei became the first company in the PV industry to enter the Fortune Global 500.[14]

These achievements reflect China's growing capacity for internal innovation, particularly in terms of utility model patents and process innovation patents. While breakthrough innovations are relatively rare, incremental improvements to existing technologies and production processes – such as the Yongxiang Method – have led to substantial advancements in product quality and cost reductions. Indigenous innovation in China's PV manufacturing sector is primarily driven by the need to reduce costs, increase efficiency, and enhance market competitiveness. These "small innovations" may not be groundbreaking, but often result in significant technological and economic benefits, as seen with the impact of the Yongxiang Method on polysilicon production and the broader adoption of solar energy worldwide(Luo & Yu, 2012).

The Evolution of Industrial Policies in China's Photovoltaic Sector

In its early stages, China's solar PV industry was heavily supported by extensive subsidies, which played a key role in its rise as the world's leading manufacturer and market for PV products. These subsidies, combined with strategic industrial policies, were instrumental in fostering the growth of the solar industry and driving technological advancements (Chen & Wang, 2022).

Implementation of the Feed-in Tariff (FiT) Policy

A significant turning point in China's PV policy came after observing the success of Germany's approach to renewable energy. In 2004, Germany made crucial amendments to its *Renewable Energy Sources Act or EEG* (German: Erneuerbare-Energien-Gesetz*)*, which had originally been originally enacted in 2000. These amendments reinforced the feed-in tariff (FiT) system, which guarantees fixed payments to renewable energy producers for the electricity they supply to the grid. The FiT model has proven to be an effective tool for accelerating the installation of renewable energy technologies. Numerous studies have shown that FiT policies can significantly drive growth in renewable energy capacity. For example, research by Leepa and Unfried (2013) found that each increase of 0.1 euros per kWh in Germany's FiT led to a rise of 84,100 kW in total installed PV capacity. In California, it was estimated that increasing rebates by about $470 would boost installations by 10%, with the overall rate of installations being 53% higher due to these subsidies (Hughes & Podolefsky, 2015).

Germany's experience with the FiT policy set a global precedent for the promotion of renewable energy technologies, and this model was adopted by China

14 Data quoted from: "The Innovation in Polysilicon Technology by China National Chemical Corporation Supports the Achievement of the 'Dual Carbon' Goals". [中国化学多晶硅技术创新赋能"双碳"目标]. Available at https://finance.sina.cn/2024-02-07/detail-inaheith1332118.d.html

in its efforts to build a strong PV industry. A key element of China's approach is its *Renewable Energy Law,* which includes an important provision – the "protective full-amount acquisition system clause." This clause mandates that power grid enterprises purchase all electricity generated by renewable energy projects within their grid-connected areas and provide the necessary grid connection services for renewable energy generation (Article 14). This provision serves as the legal foundation for China's FiT policy, ensuring that renewable energy producers receive guaranteed prices for their electricity and have assured access to the power grid. It has been a critical driver of growth in the solar energy sector and supporting China's emergence as a global leader in renewable energy.[15]

To implement the FiT policy, the National Development and Reform Commission (NDRC) issued a trial measure on renewable energy prices and cost-sharing in January 2006, marking the formal establishment of China's renewable energy tariff subsidy policy framework.[16] Article 9 of this measure specifies that the grid-connected electricity prices for solar, ocean, and geothermal power generation projects are set by the government. The price standards are determined by the State Council's price authorities based on principles of reasonable cost and profit. Since the introduction of this measure, China has been subsidizing renewable energy power generation through fixed tariffs. Grid enterprises must compensate renewable energy generation enterprises for economic losses if they fail to fulfill the required purchase of renewable energy electricity. In 2011, China began implementing a nationwide unified FiT policy for the PV industry, establishing a long-term stable selling price for PV power plants to the grid. At the end of 2011, the National Renewable Energy Development Fund was established to support the research and development of renewable energy. If grid connection costs and other related expenses cannot be recovered through electricity sales tariffs, grid enterprises can apply for subsidies from this Fund. The Fund is financed through the national fiscal public budget and the renewable energy tariff surcharge revenue collected from electricity users.

15 In 2009, the Renewable Energy Law was amended, including a revision of the "protective full-amount acquisition system clause." According to the amendment, the State Council Energy Administration, Power Regulatory Authority, and Finance Administrative Department shall determine the proportion of renewable energy power generation relative to the overall generating capacity within a specified timeframe. These departments are tasked with devising the implementing measures for electricity grid enterprises to procure the entire amount of electricity generated from renewable energies. Grid enterprises are obligated to enter agreements with renewable energy power generation enterprises to acquire all eligible renewable energy power complying with grid synchronization standards (Article 14).

16 The Notice of the National Development and Reform Commission (NDRC) on Issuing the "Interim Measures for the Management of Renewable Energy Power Generation Prices and Cost Sharing." (Fagai Price [2006] No. 7)

Transitioning from FiT to Grid Parity

The National Development and Reform Commission (NDRC) released the "13th Five-Year Plan for Solar Energy" in 2016, setting the goal of transitioning to market-driven development without reliance on state subsidies – a policy often referred to as "grid parity." Achieving grid parity means that the cost of producing electricity from renewable sources, such as solar and wind, becomes equal to or lower than the cost of purchasing electricity from the traditional power grid. At this point, renewable energy can compete directly with conventional energy sources like coal, natural gas, and nuclear power, without the need for subsidies or financial incentives. Reaching grid parity is seen as a significant milestone in the global adoption of renewable energy technologies. The Plan aimed to reduce the cost of PV power generation by over 50% by 2020 compared to 2015 levels, ultimately achieving grid parity for consumers.

To support this transition, China introduced a series of policies. On May 31, 2018, the NDRC, the Ministry of Finance, and the National Energy Administration jointly released a new policy cutting subsidies, known as the "531 Policy." This policy focuses on three key areas: (1) controlling the pace of PV industry development, (2) accelerating the reduction of subsidies for PV power generation, and (3) encouraging market-driven development within the solar industry. The "531 Policy" aims to move companies away from government support and towards market-based mechanisms.[17] In January 2019, the NDRC and the National Energy Administration issued a policy aimed at achieving grid parity for both wind and PV power generation, with a focus on pilot projects and low-cost grid connections.[18] By June 2021, the NDRC issued another notice signaling the official termination of subsidies for new centralized PV stations, distributed PV projects, and onshore wind power projects from the central government budget. This marked a key step in the implementation of China's grid parity policy.[19]

Effects of the Reduction of Subsidies

Subsidies, the FiT policy, and local incentive programs have stimulated the rapid development of the PV industry in China. Among these, the FiT policy has been particularly crucial in driving the expansion of PV power capacities. By guaranteeing fixed prices for renewable energy producers, the policy has spurred a significant increase in China's production capacity. For example, an increase of 0.1 yuan/kWh in the PV subsidy has been estimated to result in an additional 5.4-6.6 GW/year of installed capacity in China's PV market. Without the implementation

17 Notice Matters Relevant to PV Power Generation in 2018 (NDPC Energy [2018] No. 823).

18 Notice from the National Development and Reform Commission and the National Energy Administration on Actively Promoting the Subsidy-Free Grid Parity for Wind and Photovoltaic Power Generation (NDPC Energy [2019] No. 19).

19 Notice on the 2021 New Energy Feed-in Tariff Policy (NDRC Price [2021] No. 83).

of any subsidies, the PV market size would have likely shrunk by as much as 85% compared to the actual outcome (Dong et al., 2021).

However, large-scale subsidies have also placed considerable financial pressure on the government and led to issues of unfair competition. Industrial policies, in general, are costly, and not all regions can afford to implement them effectively. Before 2015, subsidies from the National Renewable Energy Development Fund were allocated in an orderly manner. But as the rapid growth in installed capacity exceeded expectations, the available funds became insufficient to meet the actual subsidy needs, resulting in a growing gap in renewable energy subsidies. According to the Wind Energy Special Committee, by the end of 2021, cumulative arrears in renewable energy generation subsidies had reached approximately 400 billion yuan (around $60 billion).[20] This financial strain has prompted a reduction in subsidies and a shift toward grid parity for new projects, meaning they now receive the same base tariff as coal-fired power.

The withdrawal of subsidies has had a profound impact on China's solar industry, particularly affecting the scale of PV installations and pushing the industry into a new adjustment cycle (Yao & Cai, 2019). In the short term, the "531 Policy" created a temporary "freezing point" in the industry, leading to a sharp decline in the market value of PV enterprises. By October 12, 2018, the cumulative market value of 64 listed PV enterprises had dropped by at least 242.3 billion yuan. Among these, 46 enterprises experienced a market value decrease of over 1 billion *yuan*, accounting for 71.88% of the total, while 15 companies saw their market value decline by more than 5 billion yuan. One major company, LONGi Green Energy, saw its market value decrease by 30 billion yuan, nearly halving from its previous high of 53.1 billion yuan. As a result, newly installed PV capacity also dropped significantly. In 2018, China's newly installed PV capacity was 44.22 GW, marking an 18% year-on-year decrease. In 2019, this figure further declined to 29.56 GW, a 33.15% decrease.[21] However, the 531 Policy had a minimal impact on China's PV production capacity and exports. In 2019, Chinese solar cells entered markets in 150 countries and regions, with an annual export value of approximately $1.47 billion, representing an 83.8% increase from the previous year (IEA, 2020).

In the long run, the reduction of subsidies has enhanced the economic competitiveness of China's PV industry, making PV power projects more viable compared to traditional energy sources. The cost of PV power generation in most regions of China dropped to less than 0.2 yuan/kWh in 2023, marking a substantial decline from 2.75 yuan/kWh in 2011 and achieving a total reduction of over 90%. In contrast, the average costs for coal-generated power have increased from 0.33 yuan/

20 <Data quoted from: "How to Fill the 400 Billion Yuan Gap? Renewable Energy Generation Subsidy Review in Progress" (in Chinese), [4000亿缺口如何填补？可再生能源发电补贴核查进行时！]. Available at: <https://www.in-en.com/article/html/energy-2320441.shtml>

21 Data quoted from: "Since the implementation of the "531 Policy," the market value of photovoltaic (PV) companies has evaporated by 242.3 billion yuan, with nearly 60 billion yuan lost just last week." [531至今光伏公司市值蒸发2423亿，上周蒸发近600], Available at: https://www.jiemian.com/article/2537247.html

kWh to 0.55 yuan/kWh during this period. Currently, the cost of PV power generation is lower than that of coal-fired power. By 2050, solar energy is projected to account for 38% of all electricity produced in China.[22]

The Role of Local Governments

Since the reform and opening-up policy, Chinese local governments have played a crucial role in regional economic growth by actively seeking investment and promoting local economic development. Within the Chinese institutional framework, each level of government operates in a competitive growth environment, where the career advancement of officials is closely tied to local economic performance. This intense competition among local governments has driven economic rivalry between regions, fundamentally changing the approach of government departments toward key production factors such as capital. As a result, the monopoly rents of government departments have been significantly reduced (Zhou, 2007).

Chinese local government policies related to the PV industry have primarily focused on the supply side, directly influencing GDP, tax revenue, and employment. Although some regions like Jiangsu Province implemented demand-side policies before 2008, these measures had limited impact. These supply-side policies have been crucial in the development of enterprises in the PV industry (Zhang & White, 2014). Local governments have played a significant role in the development of enterprises in the PV industry. Nearly all Chinese PV enterprises are young companies established after 1997, belonging to the private sector rather than being state-owned. Although these enterprises are not significantly influenced directly by the government, the social capital relationship between PV companies and local governments has been crucial during both the critical startup phase and challenging periods of setbacks (Zhang & White, 2014).

The support provided by the Wuxi municipal government for Suntech has been widely cited as a prime example in the industry. In 2000, Shi Zhengrong, a scientist in PV engineering, returned to China from Australia to start his business. The Wuxi municipal government facilitated Shi's establishment of Suntech by attracting a 6-million-yuan ($0.92 million) investment from eight local state-owned enterprises, collectively holding 75% of Suntech's total equity. With this support, Suntech completed the construction of the first 10-megawatt solar cell production line in Wuxi in September 2002, with a capacity equivalent to China's total solar cell production output in the preceding four years. In addition to attracting investment, the government also facilitated Suntech's access to research funding. Between 2003 and 2004, Suntech received funding exceeding 30 million *yuan* ($4.7 million) from national, provincial, and municipal levels through nine projects. To prepare for

22 Data quoted from: Zhou You. Module Prices have Rebounded, with March Production Schedules Showing a Significant Recovery. The PV Industry is Stabilizing and Steadily Progressing [组件价格回暖3月排产反弹显著 光伏行业企稳回升有序发展]. Available at: <https://finance.eastmoney.com/a/202403123009162840.html>

Suntech's overseas listing, the Wuxi municipal government instructed the local SOEs to divest their investment from Suntech, transforming it into a purely private enterprise. Suntech achieved a historic milestone in December 2005 by becoming the first privately-owned Chinese company to be listed on the New York Stock Exchange. The withdrawal of investment by local SOEs was hailed as a notable example of local government support for private enterprises. Despite Suntech's fall in 2013, some local governments have emulated the Wuxi approach in helping young startups, and Wuxi remains a hub for solar PV manufacturing due to the complete industry chain established by Suntech.[23]

Foreign Responses and Impacts

China has dominated the supply chain of PV products since 2007 due to a combination of effective industrial policies and the competitive advantage of its PV enterprises despite some fluctuations. This rise in the industry has caused losses and bitterness for traditional market players, leading to a series of trade restrictions imposed by foreign governments. As reported by the IEA, restrictions on Chinese solar panels have been steadily rising. Since 2011, there has been a notable surge in the number of antidumping, countervailing, and import duties imposed across different segments of the solar PV supply chain (IEA, 2022). Trade tensions over solar panels between China and other developed economies have persisted since 2011. Recently, the EU, the US, and India have initiated new investigations and imposed trade restrictions on Chinese solar PV products.

Measures in the US

Anti-Dumping and Countervailing Duty Measures

In October 2011, SolarWorld, a German company and, at the time, the largest solar manufacturer in the US, filed an anti-dumping petition against Chinese solar panel manufacturers. In response, the US Department of Commerce (DOC) initiated an investigation and, in its preliminary findings, determined that imports of solar cells from China were subject to anti-dumping ("AD") duties ranging from 31.14% to 249.96%. Additionally, the DOC proposed countervailing duties ("CVD") ranging from 2.9% to 4.73% on all imports of Chinese solar cells. Following further investigations, the DOC issued its final AD and CVD Orders in December 2012. The AD Order imposed weighted-average dumping margins primarily ranging from

23 Wuxi Suntech filed for bankruptcy in 2013 after missing a $541 million payment to bondholders. According to filings, Chinese banks were owed around $2.3 billion by the mainland entity as of the end of 2011. For more details, see Charlie Zhu and Bill Powell, "Special Report: The Rise and Fall of China's Sun King," Reuters, May 20, 2013.

18.32% to 24.48% on Chinese solar cells. The CVD Order established a subsidy rate ranging from 14.78% to 15.97%.[24]

On December 31, 2013, SolarWorld submitted a second petition, urging the DOC to initiate investigations against solar cell manufacturers from Mainland China and Taiwan. The petition argued that the 2012 Orders only applied to modules that contained Chinese solar cells and not to modules assembled in other regions, such as Taiwan, with Chinese-made components. The goal was to expand these measures to cover modules made from specific Chinese-made components that were assembled in other countries. In response to this petition, the DOC issued its affirmative final determination in December 2014, imposing AD duties ranging from 26.71% to 78.42% and CVD ranging from 27.64% to 49.79% on solar products imported from China.[25]

On April 24, 2024, the American Alliance for Solar Manufacturing Trade Committee filed new AD and CVD petitions targeting solar imports from Southeast Asian countries, including Cambodia, Malaysia, Thailand, and Vietnam. The petitioners contend that these countries, under the influence of Chinese industrial policies, are engaging in practices that harm US manufacturers by flooding the market with low-cost solar modules. In response, on May 15, 2024, the DOC announced the initiation of AD and CVD investigations into crystalline PV cells – whether or not assembled into modules – imported from these Southeast Asian nations. The DOC issued preliminary affirmative determinations in the CVD investigations.[26]

Anti-circumvention and Safeguard Measures

The trade diversion phenomenon in the solar industry has prompted the implementation of safeguard measures. On February 8, 2022, Auxin, a US-based solar panel manufacturer, submitted a request for a circumvention inquiry. The inquiry alleged that solar cells and modules assembled in Cambodia, Malaysia, Thailand, or Vietnam using components manufactured in China were circumventing the 2012 AD Order and CVD Order.[27] According to a report by the US Department of Energy, two-thirds of imports of solar modules in 2020 and 2021 to the US were

24 Federal Register, "Crystalline Silicon Photovoltaic Cells, Whether or Not Assembled Into Modules, From the People's Republic of China: Amended Final Determination of Sales at Less Than Fair Value, and Antidumping Duty Order" (77 FR 73018); Federal Register, "Crystalline Silicon Photovoltaic Cells, Whether or Not Assembled Into Modules, From the People's Republic of China: Countervailing Duty Order" (77 FR 73017).

25 International Trade Administration, 2014. Factsheet: Commerce Finds Dumping of Imports of Certain Crystalline Silicon Photovoltaic Products from China and Taiwan and Countervailable Subsidization of Imports of Certain Crystalline Silicon Photovoltaic Products from China.

26 International Trade Administration. *Preliminary Affirmative Determinations in the Countervailing Duty Investigations of Crystalline Photovoltaic Cells, Whether or Not Assembled into Modules, from Cambodia, Malaysia, Thailand, and Vietnam.*

27 Federal Register, "Crystalline Silicon Photovoltaic Cells, Whether or Not Assembled Into Modules, From the People's Republic of China: Initiation of Circumvention Inquiry on the Antidumping Duty and Countervailing Duty Orders" (87 FR 19071).

exported from Cambodia, Malaysia, Thailand, and Vietnam.[28] In response to the request, the DOC initiated the country-wide circumvention inquiry and determined that five companies were attempting to avoid the payment of US duties by completing minor processing in third countries and that three companies were not circumventing. Nonetheless, according to a Presidential Proclamation, tariffs would not be imposed on solar module and cell imports from these four countries until June 2024, provided that the imports are utilized in the US market within six months of the termination of the President's Proclamation.[29] Despite efforts by US lawmakers to revoke the Presidential Proclamation, they have not succeeded.[30]

Moreover, the Trump administration initiated a 30% safeguard tariff on imported solar cells and modules on January 23, 2018, under Section 201 of the Trade Act of 1974. The tariffs decreased by 5% annually over four years, ending at 15% by 2022. President Biden announced an extension and modification of the existing safeguard tariffs for an additional four years on February 4, 2022.[31] In April 2022, the Indian government also implemented a 40% basic customs duty on imported solar modules and a 25% duty on imported solar cells.

China has challenged the US safeguard measure on PV products at the WTO (DS562). The Panel ruled in favor of the US. The panel report circulated on September 2, 2021, concluded that the US had established a causal relationship between increased imports and serious harm to the domestic industry. Moreover, the report acknowledged that the US had appropriately taken into account other factors contributing to the injury of the domestic industry aside from increased imports. The ruling by the Panel marks the US's first successful defense of a general safeguard action before a WTO dispute panel. On September 16, 2021, China informed the Dispute Settlement Body of its decision to appeal certain legal issues and interpretations in the panel report to the Appellate Body.[32]

Restrictions on Xinjiang-Sourced Polysilicon

Since 2021, solar panels made with polysilicon from China have effectively been banned from entering the US due to policies aimed at preventing the importation of goods from Xinjiang. The 2021 *Hoshine Withhold Release Order* (WRO) and the 2022 *Uyghur Forced Labor Prevention Act* (UFLPA) have significantly restricted

28 US Dept. of Energy, *Acute Shortage of Solar Equipment Poses Risks to the Power Sector* (June 2022).

29 Procedures Covering Suspension of Liquidation, Duties, and Estimated Duties in Accord with Presidential Proclamation 10414

30 The US Congress passed a joint resolution disapproving Proclamation 10414 in April 2023, voting 221–202, but Biden vetoed the legislation. Congress failed to garner enough support to override President Joe Biden's veto.

31 Office of the United States Trade Representative, "Section 201-Imposed Solar Cells and Modules," (February 4, 2022)

32 United States - Safeguard Measure on Imports of Crystalline Silicon Photovoltaic Products, WT/DS562/R.

the entry of solar modules and cells into the US, as the vast majority of these components use polysilicon sourced from Xinjiang. The WRO specifically targets the withholding of goods from companies linked to Xinjiang. It doesn't apply to all silica-based products but those specifically connected to such companies. The UFLPA expands on the WRO, presuming that goods from Xinjiang are linked to forced labor unless companies can provide clear evidence that their products are not.

As a result, the US ban on Chinese polysilicon produced in Xinjiang has created a separate, higher-priced market for non-Chinese polysilicon manufacturers. One of the key factors driving higher solar module prices in the US is the limited availability of modules made with non-Chinese polysilicon. Non-Chinese polysilicon is priced approximately three times higher than its Chinese counterpart, with a price difference of $7 to $10 per kilogram. Using Chinese polysilicon would reduce module manufacturing costs by 10-20%.[33]

Investigations in the EU and Other Regions

In the EU, EU Pro Sun, an industry association representing more than 20 European companies manufacturing solar panels and PV components, filed a complaint in July 2012, alleging that solar panels and crucial components imported from China were being sold in the EU market below market value. In response to this complaint, the European Commission initiated two simultaneous investigations: one AD investigation and another for anti-subsidy measures. In June 2013, the Commission imposed provisional measures in the anti-dumping case with an average rate of 47.7%. The Commission accepted a price undertaking proposed by the majority of Chinese solar panel exporters, covering approximately 75% of Chinese solar panel exports to the EU and exempting them from anti-dumping or anti-subsidy duties. In December 2013, the Commission decided to enforce definitive measures on Chinese solar panels not covered by the price undertaking for a two-year period. For cooperating companies, the average duty stood at 47.7%, while non-cooperating companies faced an average duty of 64.9%.[34] These measures were initially imposed for two years but were subsequently extended until they expired in September 2018.

Since the lapse of trade restrictions, the EU has emerged as the largest market for China's solar panels. In 2023, China exported PV products worth $19.24 billion to the EU, accounting for over 40% of China's total exports of PV products for that year.[35] The influx of Chinese solar panel products into the EU market has prompted frustration among European solar manufacturers and policymak-

33 <Sylvia Leyva Martinez & Elissa Pierce, "Turn of the Tide? What the Entry of Chinese Polysilicon to the US Means for the American Solar Supply Chain," Wood Mackenzie, December 18, 2023.>

34 European Commission, "EU Imposes Definitive Measures on Chinese Solar Panels, Confirms Undertaking with Chinese Solar Panels" (December 2, 2013)

35 Supra note 2.

ers. They contended that Chinese manufacturers were benefiting from significant subsidies provided by the government and banks. With the implementation of the *Foreign Subsidy Regulation*, the Commission initiated two in-depth investigations into Chinese solar panel manufacturers in April 2024. As a result of the investigations, the Chinese bidders withdrew from the tenders, citing concerns over potential regulatory scrutiny and the risk of facing anti-subsidy measures (Chapter 3).[36]

Other emerging economies also took measures against PV products from China to protect their domestic industries. India, ranked as the third-largest electricity producer in the world, with an installed capacity of 426.1 GW as of 30 November 2023, has launched a series of AD and CVD investigations against Chinese solar PV products. In 2019, India imposed AD duties on EVA sheets for solar modules imported from China, Malaysia, Saudi Arabia, and Thailand, set to expire in March 2024. However, India decided to extend the AD duties on EVA sheets for solar panels imported from China for an additional five years.[37] In 2022, India imposed AD duties on the import of fluoro back sheets (excluding transparent back sheets) from China. The most recent investigation was launched in February 2024 into imports of solar glass from China and Vietnam, prompted by a complaint from domestic industry stakeholders.[38]

Impacts of Foreign Protectionist Measures

Empirical research has demonstrated that AD/CVD measures directly decrease imports by raising their prices and also have a trade diversion effect, leading to increased imports from other trading partners not targeted by such measures (UNCTAD, 2014). In response to the AD and CVD measures targeting Chinese PV products, certain Chinese manufacturers have opted to outsource their production or establish manufacturing facilities in other countries to mitigate the impact. Over the past decade, Chinese green energy enterprises have consistently expanded into global markets. In 2022, the green energy sector accounted for the majority of China's overseas investments, comprising about 58% of the total. This included eight solar power generation projects, which made up 33% of these ventures, with investments totaling US$1.331 billion.[39]

36 "EC Drops Probe on Romanian Solar Park Tender, After Chinese Companies Withdraw." *Romania Journal*. (May 13, 2024)

37 See Ethylene Vinyl Acetate (EVA) Sheet for Solar Module - Continuation of Anti-Dumping Duty on Imports of "Ethylene Vinyl Acetate (EVA) Sheet for Solar Module" Falling Under Tariff Items 3920 10 11, 3920 10 19, 3920 10 99, 3920 61 90, 3920 62 90, 3920 99 19, 3920 99 39 or 3920 99 99, Originating in or Exported from China PR, Imposed Vide Notification Number 15/2019-Customs (ADD), Dated the 29th March, 2019 [G.S.R. 272(E)].

38 "India Initiates Anti-Dumping Probe into Imports of Solar Glass from China, Vietnam," *The Economic Times*. (February 16, 2024).

39 Data quoted from: "New Energy has Become the Hottest Area for Chinese Power Enterprises to Invest in Abroad," *Concord New* Energy (July 18, 2023).

Foreign protectionist measures have significantly influenced the competitive landscape for Chinese PV companies. The AD and CVD measures imposed by the US and the EU in the early 2010s triggered the first major shakeout in the Chinese PV industry. At the time, many Chinese PV companies were highly dependent on overseas markets. As a result, a large number of small and medium-sized enterprises ceased operations or went bankrupt, while even some major large-scale companies faced financial difficulties. For instance, Suntech's main unit in Wuxi declared bankruptcy in 2013. However, this shakeout also helped identify the top players in the industry. A decade after the initial round of trade remedy measures, some Chinese PV producers not only survived the challenges but have also emerged as dominant global players.

Foreign protectionism has been a driving force behind the development of China's domestic market for PV consumption, laying the foundation for a future where renewable energy dominates the country's electricity supply. The AD and CVD measures have prompted the Chinese government to shift its focus toward cultivating its domestic PV market. As a result, China has become the largest market for PV products. Before the global financial crisis, over 98% of Chinese PV products were exported, but post-crisis, China began prioritizing domestic PV consumption. Over the past 12 years, China's reliance on European and American markets has significantly declined. In 2023, China maintained its position as the global leader in newly installed PV capacity for the 11th consecutive year, adding 216.89 GW – nearly half of the world's total new installations – and utilizing almost half of its production domestically. By comparison, the EU added 56 GW, the US 32 GW, and Japan 6.5 GW in the same period. Notably, China accounted for an impressive 40% of the global cumulative installed PV capacity. By the end of 2023, global cumulative installed PV capacity reached approximately 1.6 TW (estimated between 1,581 GW and 1,624 GW). China's cumulative installed capacity accounted for about 37% of global installations.[40] Despite fierce competition among market players, demand for PV products is expected to continue growing rapidly. Bernreuter, a German research institute specializing in the polysilicon industry, predicts that annual PV installations will increase from 425 GW in 2023 to 1,100 GW by 2027, representing an average annual growth rate of 26.8%.[41] Industry leaders in China share a similar perspective, noting that periodic overcapacity in the PV industry is a normal aspect of market dynamics. The global pursuit of carbon neutrality underpins the potential growth of renewable energy industries, and the significant reduction in PV costs achieved by Chinese enterprises further enhances the prospects of electricity systems dominated by renewables.[42]

40 Data quoted from: IEA. "Snapshot of Global PV Markets 2024". (Report IEA-PVPS T1-42: 2024)

41 Johannes Bernreuter. "The Polysilicon Market Outlook 2027". Available at: <https://www.bernreuter.com/files/data/polysilicon/industry-reports/polysilicon-market-outlook-2027-info.pdf>

42 Wang Fang, "Battle Under the Sun: The Photovoltaic Journey of a 70s-Born Chinese Entrepreneur "[阳光下的较量：一位70后中国人的光伏风云]. Fortune China. <https://www.fortunechina.com/shangye/c/2024-10/14/content_458836.htm>

Conclusion

The rise of China's PV industry illustrates the development trajectory of the country's emerging strategic sectors. The success of the PV industry can be attributed to three key factors: technological advancements, targeted industrial policies, and the resilience of Chinese entrepreneurs. Early on, the return of overseas Chinese talent and the acquisition of advanced production equipment were crucial in facilitating the transfer of PV technology to China. Government support, including the FiT policy, further accelerated sector growth, while local governments provided essential investment incentives and resources, fostering both new and established companies. These policies played a vital role in expanding China's PV industry. As a result, Chinese entrepreneurs have excelled at assimilating foreign technology and driving domestic innovation, with a strong focus on commercialization and large-scale production. The combination of low production costs and high-quality products has afforded China a competitive edge in the global PV market. However, China's rise has provoked resentment among foreign competitors, leading to trade restrictions in several countries. Despite challenges such as trade barriers, subsidy cuts, and market fluctuations, Chinese PV companies have demonstrated resilience and global competitiveness. China's dominance in the PV manufacturing sector has also raised concerns about industrial security in other economies, indicating the intensifying competition within the strategic industries in the global trade and geopolitical landscape.

References

Chen, Z., & Wang, T. (2022). Photovoltaic subsidy withdrawal: An evolutionary game analysis of the impact on Chinese stakeholders' strategic choices. *Solar Energy, 241*, 302–314.

De la Tour, A., Glachant, M., & Ménière, Y. (2011). Innovation and international technology transfer: The case of the Chinese photovoltaic industry. *Energy Policy, 39*(2), 761–770.

Dong, C., Zhou, R., & Li, J. (2021). The effect of feed-in tariff on China's photovoltaic capacity development: An empirical analysis based on panel data regression. *Resources Science, 43*(6), 1065–1076.

He, L. (2010). China's climate-change policy from Kyoto to Copenhagen: Domestic needs and international aspirations. *Asian Perspective, 34*(3), 5–33.

Huang, P., Negro, S. O., Hekkert, M. P., & Bi, K. (2016). How China became a leader in solar PV: An innovation system analysis. *Renewable and Sustainable Energy Reviews, 64*, 777–789.

Hughes, J. E., & Podolefsky, M. (2015). Getting Green with solar subsidies: Evidence from the California Solar Initiative. *Journal of the Association of Environmental and Resource Economists, 2*, 235–275.

International Energy Agency (IEA). (2022). *Solar PV Global Supply Chains*. https://www.iea.org/reports/solar-pv-global-supply-chains.

International Energy Agency (IEA). (2020). National survey report of PV power applications in China 2019. https://www.iea.org/reports/national-survey-report-of-pv-power-applications-in-china-2019.

Leepa, C., & Unfried, M. (2013). Effects of a cut-off in feed-in tariffs on photovoltaic capacity: Evidence from Germany. *Energy Policy, 53*, 536–542.

Luo, S., & Yu, Y. (2012). Returnees' and enterprise technological innovation: An empirical study based on China's photovoltaic industry. *Management World, 11*, 124–132.

Nahm, J. (2021). *Collaborative Advantage: Forging Green Industries in the New Global Economy*. Oxford Academic.

Sen, S., & Ganguly, S. (2017). Opportunities, barriers, and issues with renewable energy development – A discussion. *Renewable and Sustainable Energy Reviews, 69*(May), 1170–1181.

Song, W., & Xiao, R. (2022). Research on the policy instruments' evolution path of China's photovoltaic industry and its enlightenment. *Journal of Intelligence, 1*, 177–184.

UNCTAD. (2014). *Trade Remedies: Targeting the Renewable Energy Sector* (UNCTAD/DITC/TED/2014/3). https://unctad.org/en/PublicationsLibrary/ditcted2014d3_en.pdf.

Wen, D., Gao, W., Qian, F., Gu, Q., & Ren, J. (2021). Development of solar photovoltaic industry and market in China, Germany, Japan, and the United States of America using incentive policies. *Energy Exploration & Exploitation, 5*, 1429–1456.

Yao, M., & Cai, X. (2019). An overview of the photovoltaic industry status and perspective in China. *IEEE Access, 7*, 181051–181060. DOI: 10.1109/ACCESS.2019.2959309.

Zhang, W., & White, S. (2014). *Research Report on China's Solar Photovoltaic Industry Policies* [中国太阳能光伏产业政策研究]. https://www.cideg.tsinghua.edu.cn/upload_files/atta/1445409312405_A4.pdf.

Zhang, Y., Xie, P., Huang, Y., Liao, C., & Zhao, D. (2021). Evolution of solar photovoltaic policies and industry in China. *IOP Conference Series: Earth and Environmental Science, 651*(2), 022050.

Zhao, Y., Wang, S., Wang, W., Li, X., Liu, Z., Qiu, D., Song, S., & Ramsay, G. (2008). *Research Report on the Development of China's Photovoltaic Industry (2006-2007)*. China Renewable Energy Development Project Office.

Zhou, L. (2007). Governing China's local officials: An analysis of the promotion tournament model. *Economic Research, 7*, 36–50.

6 China’s Strategies in Global Trade Governance

Towards Achieving a Win-set?

Approaching WTO Reform Negotiations

China has significantly benefited from the international free trade system and has consistently advocated for preserving the WTO's multilateral framework. The Chinese government has repeatedly advocated for maintaining and reforming the multilateral free trade system, particularly through the WTO. It has submitted two formal documents to the WTO: *China's Position Paper on WTO Reform* (November 2018) and *China's Proposal on WTO Reform* (May 2019), outlining its vision and recommendations for reforming the organization. In these two documents, China has put forward three basic principles for WTO reform: preserving the core values of the multilateral trading system, safeguarding the development interests of developing members, and upholding the practice of consensus decision-making. Regarding specific recommendations, China's proposal outlines several key priorities. It stresses the importance of resolving critical issues that undermine the WTO's functioning, with particular focus on its dispute resolution mechanism. It also advocates for strengthening the WTO's role in global economic governance and enhancing its operational efficiency. Furthermore, the proposal highlights the need to promote greater inclusiveness within the multilateral trading system.

The Prospect of Reforming WTO Consensus Decision-making

From an interdependence perspective, preserving the WTO's free trade system is essential for enhancing economic linkages among countries and fostering a stable and cooperative global trade environment. At the WTO Ministerial Conference in June 2022, ministers committed to conducting a comprehensive review of the WTO's functions. They also agreed to address issues related to the dispute settlement system, aiming to establish a fully operational mechanism accessible to all members by 2024. However, due to the US's ongoing blockade of Appellate Body appointments, the Appellate Body is still not functioning. Neorealist scholars once predicted that international organizations relying on consensus-based decision-making could face collapse (Steinberg, 2003). This concern has materialized in the ongoing deadlock of the WTO Appellate Body, which the US has effectively obstructed by leveraging the consensus rule. These challenges raise questions

DOI: 10.4324/9781003637110-7

about the potential for either relaxing the consensus approach or even replacing it with a voting system.

Moving to a voting system could address some of the inefficiencies caused by the consensus requirement; however, major powers have shown a preference for consensus in instances involving binding commitments. Empirical research indicates that powerful nations generally favor voting systems only for creating non-binding "soft" rules, thus avoiding unfavorable legislative outcomes (Steinberg, 2003). A weighted voting system, better reflecting actual power distributions among member states, could provide a more balanced approach, aligning with the interests of major powers and perhaps gaining acceptance among Western trading powers. However, such a system might allow the US, Japan, and the EU to form a dominant coalition, enabling them to control the WTO's agenda and voting outcomes. China, therefore, is unlikely to support a shift to weighted voting in the WTO. As a result, despite its procedural inefficiencies and potential for misuse, consensus-based decision-making – with its guarantee of veto power for all members – remains the approach most likely to secure acceptance among major powers in today's complex international landscape.

In effect, despite its inefficiencies, consensus-based decision-making embodies the ideal of international sovereign equality by granting each member veto power. In international organizations, veto power gives principals the right to block proposals by agents that may be unfavorable, thereby preserving the status quo. This mechanism allows principals to counter collective decisions with individual preferences, safeguarding their autonomy from being overridden by the group's will. Simultaneously, veto power enables principals to leverage it as a bargaining tool to negotiate and secure additional benefits. Nearly all decisions were made by consensus between 1959 and 1994, except for cases where voting allowed new members to join, approved free trade areas, or convened special meetings (Footer, 1996–1997). In this framework, members of varying economic strengths achieve formal equality, representing the ideal of sovereign equality in international law. The US initially advocated for consensus in GATT to demonstrate goodwill toward smaller economies while retaining veto power to prevent developing countries from using their numbers to push unfavorable decisions. By the late 1950s, developing countries had become a majority within GATT. If these nations formed a bloc, they could easily achieve a simple majority in GATT's administrative and judicial functions, potentially gaining legislative power through judicially created legal obligations, even if all developed countries opposed it. However, an influx of developing nations in GATT aligned with US strategic interests in containing the Soviet Union. Thus, the US proactively supported the adoption of consensus-based decision-making in GATT (Steinberg, 2003). The WTO's foundational document, the Marrakesh Agreement Establishing the World Trade Organization, formalized this approach, following GATT's precedent of a consensus-based system (art. 9.1).

The WTO multilateral system has been going into a collective action dilemma. Amid shifting political and economic power dynamics – particularly with China's emergence as a major trade power – emerging and developed economies often push competing agendas, making collective action and effective governance increasingly difficult to achieve.

China's Proposal for WTO Reform: An Improvement

Many analysts have characterized China's approach to WTO reform as seeking incremental improvements, "a WTO improvement," not "a WTO revolution."[1] In the two documents, China has emphasized resolving the crisis of the Appellate Body as a top priority to maintain an effective dispute resolution system. China's proposal does not directly address critical issues such as industrial subsidies, SOEs, and intellectual property rights, top concerns for Western economies on WTO reform.

At its core, preserving the existing multilateral free trade system aligns with China's development interests. Integration into the global economy, particularly after joining the WTO in 2001, has significantly boosted its trade volume and economic influence. This integration has provided Chinese enterprises with access to advanced technologies through imports, foreign direct investment, talent mobility, and joint ventures, which have in turn stimulated domestic innovation and industrial upgrading. Over the past two decades, the structure of China's exports has transformed significantly. By 2023, China's total trade volume reached $6.3 trillion, with exports amounting to $3.3 trillion. Notably, 90% of these exports comprised mechanical and electronic products, representing nearly $3 trillion in high-tech, high-value-added goods, while labor-intensive products dropped to only 10%[2].

As a result, the Chinese government has been a strong supporter of the WTO framework and an advocate for globalization. In the context of geopolitical competition, the CPC has pursued a "one-sided" market opening strategy, offering access without demanding reciprocity, to foster free trade channels and deepen economic ties.[3]

Engaging with the Multi-Party Interim Appeal Arbitration Arrangement (MPIA)

China and other WTO members have been exploring alternative dispute resolution mechanisms within the existing multilateral framework, notably the MPIA.

1 Lu Xiankun, "China's Perspectives on WTO Reform." (November 16, 2019), available at: <https://iit.adelaide.edu.au/news/list/2019/11/26/chinas-perspectives-on-wto-reform>; Alicia Garcia Herrero, "China and WTO Reform: What to Expect?." (February 24, 2024), available at: <https://www.realinstitutoelcano.org/en/analyses/china-and-wto-reform-what-to-expect/>

2 Data quoted from: Huang Qifan, "New Characteristics and Tasks of China's Opening-Up in the New Era and New Landscape" [新时代、新格局下，中国开放的新特征、新任务]. *China* Daily (December 27, 2023）.

3 The *Decision on Further Deepening Reform and Advancing Chinese Modernization*, adopted at the Third Plenary Session of the 20th Central Committee of the Communist Party of China, emphasizes "expanding independent opening-up" and "strengthening unilateral market access for the least developed countries."

Building on an EU-led initiative, a coalition of 47 WTO members officially notified the WTO of the establishment of the MPIA on April 30, 2020.[4] The US has opposed the creation of a dedicated WTO secretariat division to support the MPIA and the allocation of related expenses from the WTO's regular budget. In a letter to then-Director-General Roberto Azevêdo, the US argued that Article 25 of the *Dispute Settlement Understanding* (DSU) does not authorize the WTO Secretariat to provide exclusive support to arbitrations under the MPIA.[5] For the US, the creation of the MPIA circumvents the ongoing efforts to reform the WTO and address systemic issues with the Appellate Body.

The MPIA is based on Article 25 of the DSU, which provides a framework for arbitration as an alternative "appeal" mechanism.[6] Before the impasse of the Appellate Body, some experts suggested leveraging the existing but underutilized Article 25 as a mechanism to deal with a small number of politically sensitive cases where compliance with a DSB ruling might be uncertain (Jacyk, 2008). Since the onset of the Appellate Body crisis, a group of WTO lawyers proposed arbitration under Article 25 as a potential solution to address the deadlock and ensure the continuation of dispute resolution within the WTO framework (Andersen et al., 2017). In July 2019, the EU finalized a bilateral arbitration agreement with Canada under Article 25 of the WTO DSU, which was later joined by Norway. The MPIA builds on the experiences of such agreements, reaffirming a commitment to the WTO's two-tiered dispute settlement system and the broader rules-based international trading framework.

Under the MPIA provisions, Participating Members are obligated to utilize the MPIA procedure for appeals, rather than relying on Articles 16.4 and 17 of the DSU. If no party appeals a panel report via the MPIA arbitration mechanism, Participating Members expect the panel report to be formally adopted by the DSB through the negative consensus rule, as outlined in Articles 2 and 8 of the MPIA. This framework makes the MPIA not merely an "alternative" to the Appellate Body but a "replacement" – a temporary substitute for appellate review. It directly addresses the "appeal into the void" issue, wherein parties could block the resolution of disputes by appealing panel rulings to the currently non-functioning Appellate Body. The MPIA is expected to serve as a testing ground to explore and trial new methods for making the dispute settlement process more efficient and better aligned with the goals and interests of WTO members (Pauwelyn, 2023).

4 The founding Participating Members of the MPIA include the following countries and regions: Australia; Brazil; Canada; China; Chile; Colombia; Costa Rica; the European Union; Guatemala; Hong Kong (China); Iceland; Mexico; New Zealand; Norway; Pakistan; Singapore; Switzerland; Ukraine; and Uruguay.

5 Quoted from: Caroline Glöckle, *Bridging the Gap: the MPIA as a Valuable Short-term Solution to the Impasse of the WTO's Appellate Body?*, *Völkerrechtsblog* (October 12, 2020) doi: 10.17176/20210107-184051-0.

6 WTO Analytical Index, DSU – Article 25 (DS reports).

The Rising Significance of the MPIA in Global Trade Governance

Colombia's appeal in the dispute "*Colombia – Anti-Dumping Duties on Frozen Fries from Belgium, Germany, and the Netherlands*" *(DS591)* was the first case resolved under the MPIA framework. The arbitrators' award, published on December 21, 2022, on the WTO website, officially concluded the appeal process. Another arbitration case (DS583), involving the EU and Turkey, was resolved under Article 25, even though Turkey is not a member of the MPIA. This highlights Article 25's flexibility as a mechanism for resolving trade disputes, even beyond the formal MPIA membership framework. Additionally, several disputes between members have been concluded without resorting to MPIA appeals, often through withdrawal, expiration, or settlement. Currently, three disputes remain active, two of which involve China. Of the 13 disputes brought under the MPIA framework, China is the respondent in six cases (See Table 6.1).

The EU has been actively working to shape global governance and strengthen its strategic autonomy by exporting its norms through a range of mechanisms. The concept of "Normative Power Europe" put forward by Ian Manners positions the EU as a global actor defined by its commitment to norms and values (Manners, 2002). In response to the WTO Appellate Body crisis, the EU took proactive steps to maintain a functioning dispute resolution mechanism. To further support and promote the MPIA, the EU has made adjustments to its domestic regulations. In 2021, the EU amended its *2014 Trade Enforcement Regulation (Regulation (EU) 2021/167)*, introducing provisions to address the challenges posed by the paralysis of the WTO Appellate Body. According to the revised regulation, if a WTO member refuses to participate in an arrangement like the MPIA and proceeds to file an appeal to the non-functioning WTO Appellate Body, the EU can swiftly suspend concessions or other obligations under international trade agreements,

Table 6.1 MPIA Cases

Case No.	*Complaint*	*Respondent*	*Status*
DS 591	EU	Colombia	Award
DS 583	EU	Turkey	Award
DS522	Brazil	Canada	Withdrawn by complainant
DS524	Mexico	Costa Rica	Panel report adopted
DS537	Australia	Canada	Mutually agreed solution
DS589	Canada	China	Authority for panel lapsed
DS 598	Australia	China	Mutually agreed solution
DS 601	Japan	China	Panel report adopted
DS 602	Australia	China	Mutually agreed solution
DS 603	China	Australia	Panel report adopted
DS 607	Brazil	EU	Ongoing
DS 610	EU	China	Ongoing
DS 611	EU	China	Ongoing

Source: WTO Plurilateral < https://wtoplurilaterals.info/>

including regional or bilateral agreements.[7] In practical terms, this means the EU has granted itself the ability to impose unilateral retaliatory tariffs on WTO members that refuse to join the MPIA but appeal to the Appellate Body to contest a panel report favorable to the EU. This measure indicates the EU's commitment to ensuring enforceability within the rules-based trading system.

Japan decided not to participate in the MPIA in June 2020. This position remained unchanged until March 10, 2023, when the Japanese Cabinet approved the country's accession to the MPIA. On the same day, Japan formally informed the WTO DSB of its decision to join. According to Japan's official statement, this move was motivated by three key considerations: strengthening cooperation with like-minded WTO members such as the EU and Canada, supporting the rules-based multilateral trading system, and taking a leadership role in WTO reform efforts alongside other member nations.[8] Japanese professor Arato Kuno observes that Japan has traditionally refrained from adopting WTO-inconsistent unilateral measures in response to other members' unlawful trade practices.[9] When the Appellate Body is unable to hear appeals of panel reports, Japan faces limited options if other parties "appeal into the void." This situation effectively stalls the resolution of disputes. In two cases where panels ruled in Japan's favor against India and South Korea, both countries, as non-MPIA members, appealed into the void, leaving the disputes unresolved.[10] The DS601 case, involving Japan's challenge to China's anti-dumping measures on stainless steel, was a key factor in Japan's decision to join the MPIA. Japan's steel industry associations strongly urged the government to participate, viewing the MPIA as an essential mechanism to address trade challenges and ensure access to a functional appellate process (Kawase, 2023). Notably, after Japan's accession, China chose not to appeal the panel report, which ruled in Japan's favor.

As of November 2024, the MPIA comprises 54 of the 164 WTO members, among them three of the world's four largest economies: the EU, China, and Japan. The participation of these major trading powers plays a crucial role in resolving trade disputes, adding significant economic weight to the MPIA. Their involvement enhances its credibility and effectiveness as a temporary solution to the ongoing WTO Appellate Body impasse.

7 Regulation (EU) 2021/167 of the European Parliament and of the Council of 10 February 2021 amending Regulation (EU) No 654/2014 concerning the exercise of the Union's rights for the application and enforcement of international trade rules.

8 Ministry of Economy, Trade and Industry, Cabinet Approval on the Participation in the MPIA (Multi-Party Interim Appeal Arbitration Arrangement) [March 10, 2023]. Available at <https://www.meti.go.jp/english/press/2023/0310_001.html>

9 Arata Kuno, "Japan's joining MPIA an outside chance to boost momentum for WTO reform." East Asia Forum. [14 May 2023]

10 *Ibid.*

Strengthening Economic Cooperation through Regional and Bilateral Partnerships

The *World Trade Report 2011* has identified the continuing growth and increasing prominence of preferential free trade agreements (PTAs) as a key trend in recent international trade relations. However, PTAs and the WTO do not operate entirely independently, creating numerous opportunities for inconsistencies and conflicts to arise (WTO, 2011). If PTAs are driven by the goal of deeper integration rather than market segmentation, the WTO could play a role in fostering coherence among them. However, with the intensification of geopolitical competition and the ongoing crisis within the WTO, PTAs have increasingly taken on "exclusive" characteristics, transforming into tools for applying "pressure" on competitors or pursuing other strategic objectives. For instance, the Indo-Pacific Economic Framework for Prosperity (IPEF), introduced by the Biden administration, is widely viewed as a political initiative aimed at excluding China. It seeks to establish a network of "trusted partners" in Asia to decrease economic reliance on China (Dahlman & Lovely, 2023).

China is often seen as a latecomer in signing PTAs, as it was reluctant to pursue such agreements until its WTO accession terms were finalized. However, since then, it has become one of the most active players in negotiating both bilateral and regional PTAs (Ravenhill & Jiang, 2009). As of August 2024, China had signed 22 PTAs involving 29 countries and regions, accounting for a third of its foreign trade. China aims to expand its high-standard PTA network to foster opening up and deeper reforms, targeting approximately 40% of its total foreign trade by 2030.[11] Its PTA strategy aligns with its interests, including gaining market access, promoting domestic opening and reform, and enhancing trade relations with its partners. Among the PTAs, the *Regional Comprehensive Economic Partnership* (RCEP) and Comprehensive and *Progressive Agreement for Trans-Pacific Partnership* (CPTPP) have garnered the most attention, the two so-called "mega-regional" trade agreements in East Asia.

Advancing the Regional Comprehensive Economic Partnership (RCEP)

In November 2020, China, Japan, South Korea, Australia, New Zealand, and ASEAN signed the RCEP, creating one of the largest free trade agreements globally. Encompassing approximately 30% of the world's GDP, RCEP stands as the largest PTA by economic measure. While the agreement was signed in 2020, it officially came into effect on January 1, 2022. As of June 2023, RCEP has been fully implemented across all 15 member countries.[12]

11 Data quoted from: Xinhua, "China Aims for FTAs to Contribute 40 pct of Foreign Trade by 2030." *The State Council of the PRC.* (August 2, 2024)

12 Since January 1, 2022, RCEP has been gradually implemented across seven ASEAN member states, along with the other five countries. On May 1, 2022, it took effect between China and Myanmar.

A defining feature of RCEP is its emphasis on ASEAN centrality. The initiative was first introduced during the 19th ASEAN Summit in 2011, where the ASEAN Framework for RCEP was adopted. This framework emphasizes an "ASEAN-led" process, highlighting ASEAN's central role in shaping the agreement. The focus on ASEAN centrality is rooted in its strategic "balance of influence" approach. As a coalition of smaller nations, ASEAN strategically manages the dynamic interplay of competition and cooperation between the two regional powerhouses, China and Japan (Ciorciari, 2009). By leveraging this strategy, ASEAN has been able to establish itself as a focal point in cooperative initiatives such as the ASEAN Regional Forum, a critical element in its post-Cold War diplomatic strategy (Emmers, 2001). In the aftermath of the 1997 Asian financial crisis, ASEAN ramped up efforts to strengthen regional market integration. The signing of RCEP marks ASEAN's role as a central actor in regional economic and political frameworks. Before RCEP, ASEAN's ten member states had already formed "10+1" free trade agreements with the other five participating nations. However, RCEP marked a significant milestone as it facilitated the first direct free trade agreement between China, Japan, and South Korea. India, the world's fifth-largest economy, also participated in the negotiations but withdrew from the negotiations in November 2019, citing concerns that the agreement did not align with its national interests. Despite India's withdrawal decision, the remaining member states have maintained an open stance and have expressed support for India's potential return to RCEP.[13]

The 20 chapters of RCEP cover a broad spectrum of trade-related areas, including trade in goods, trade in services, investment, economic and technical cooperation, intellectual property, e-commerce, competition, dispute resolution, among others. RCEP places a strong emphasis on regional trade liberalization, focusing on the elimination of tariff and non-tariff barriers. One of the key goals is the gradual elimination of tariffs on over 90% of traded products within about 10 years, which will enhance the flow of goods and services across the region, fostering deeper regional integration. Given the significant economic diversity among its members, the rules of RCEP are less ambitious than those of the TPP or other high-standard agreements. RCEP does not include provisions related to state-owned enterprises (SOEs), labor standards, environmental protection, or government subsidies. As a result, RCEP is not considered a high-standard trade agreement (Francois & Elsig, 2021).

Despite its perceived lack of ambition, joining RCEP holds substantial strategic value for China. First, RCEP strengthens ASEAN-China trade relations. ASEAN has been China's largest trading partner since 2020, and by 2023, bilateral trade between China and ASEAN reached a record high of USD 702 billion, solidifying China's position as ASEAN's largest trading partner for the 15th consecutive

The agreement officially came into force in Indonesia on January 2, 2023, and in the Philippines on June 2, 2023.

13 Daisuke Akimoto, "The RCEP Conundrum: Japan Awaits India's Return." *The Diplomat*. August 27, 2021.

year.[14] Second, RCEP marks a significant milestone as the first PTA between China and Japan, as well as between Japan and South Korea. Under the agreement, 86% of Japan's exports to China will benefit from zero tariffs, while 88% of China's exports to Japan will also enjoy zero tariff treatment. This unprecedented level of tariff reduction not only strengthens bilateral trade relations but also enhances market access for both nations. Moreover, the successful conclusion of the RCEP agreement has renewed optimism for a potential trilateral free trade deal between China, Japan, and South Korea – a negotiation that has been ongoing for as long as the RCEP itself. Such an agreement could pave the way for deeper economic integration within the region.[15]

China's Bid for CPTTP Accession

In March 2018, 11 countries, including Australia, Brunei, Canada, Chile, Japan, Malaysia, Mexico, New Zealand, Peru, Singapore, and Vietnam, signed the CPTPP. The CPTPP emerged from the original TPP after the Trump administration withdrew in 2017. The Obama administration viewed the TPP not just as a trade agreement but as a geopolitical tool to strengthen US influence in the Asia-Pacific region. President Obama emphasized this strategic intent, stating, "China wants to write the rules for the world's fastest-growing region. If we don't write the rules, China will write the rules out in that region. We will be shut out." By establishing the TPP, the administration sought to create "rules of the road" that would shape the regional order and potentially pressure China to adhere to these standards in the future (Ye, 2015).

Approximately 95% of the original TPP text was retained in the CPTPP. The CPTTP entered into force on December 30, 2018, for six original signatories, and has been implemented by all members since July 12, 2023.[16] Notably, seven of the RCEP members are also original signatories of the CPTPP. From an economic perspective, while RCEP covers a significantly larger population – roughly four times that of CPTPP – its per capita GDP is lower (see Table 6.2). This suggests that, despite their smaller population, CPTPP countries are generally wealthier, with

14 Data quoted from: "Overview of ASEAN-China Comprehensive Strategic Partnership," ASEAN Secretariat Information Paper (As of June 2024).

15 The proposal to establish a China-Japan-South Korea PTA was first made in 2002. After a decade of deliberations, the trade ministers of the three nations officially launched negotiations in 2012, with the first round of talks taking place in Seoul in 2013. By 2019, 16 rounds of negotiations had been conducted, addressing key issues such as market access, e-commerce, and intellectual property. However, the negotiations were suspended due to the impact of the COVID-19 pandemic and evolving domestic and international circumstances. It has been reported that the trilateral negotiations were resumed in June 2024. See Yeo Han-koo, "Economic Cooperation by Korean-Japan-China Trilateral Could Ease Tensions," *PIIE Report* (June 13, 2024).

16 For details of the implementation of the CPTTP, see Australian Government, Department of Foreign Affairs and Trade, "Comprehensive and Progressive Agreement for Trans-Pacific Partnership (CPTPP)." Available at: <https://www.dfat.gov.au/trade/agreements/in-force/cptpp/comprehensive-and-progressive-agreement-for-trans-pacific-partnership>

Table 6.2 Comparison of RCEP and CPTTP Economies

Category	*RCEP*	*CPTTP*
Members	15 countries:10 ASEAN states + China, Japan, South Korea, Australia, New Zealand	12 countries (Australia, Brunei Darussalam, Canada, Chile, Japan, Malaysia, Mexico, New Zealand, Peru, Singapore, Vietnam, and UK)
Population	Approx. 2.3 billion people (about 30% of the global population)	Approx. 578 million people (about 7.5% of the global population)
GDP (2023)	$65,079.3 billion (31.6% of the global GDP)	$20,503.8 billion (11.5% of the global GDP)
Per Capital GDP (2023)	$28,300.6	$35,471.3

Source: World Economics

higher per capita income levels than the more populous RCEP bloc. In February 2021, the United Kingdom applied to join the CPTPP and was accepted in July 2023, becoming its 12th member and the first successful accession. In September 2021, China officially applied for membership in the CPTPP; however, China's application was not approved by the CPTPP members until November 2024.

China's motivation for seeking membership in both the CPTPP and RCEP is primarily driven by its desire to promote trade liberalization and participate in the negotiations of mega-regional PTAs. These agreements are viewed as crucial pathways for China's institutional opening up and its active participation in global trade governance.

Hurdles to China's CPTTP Accession

The CPTTP requires members to adopt the negative-list approach for services and investment. From a technical perspective, it is not challenging for China to adopt a negative-list approach after a decade of domestic trials and gradual refinement. The real challenge lies in the opening up of "sensitive sectors," which often involve industries of strategic importance, national security concerns, or strong domestic interests. These sectors may include areas such as finance, telecommunications, energy, and cultural industries, where regulatory frameworks and market dynamics are more complex (Yu & Jiang, 2021).

Candidates for the CPTPP must satisfy the "Auckland Principles," which include a readiness to meet the Agreement's high standards, a proven track record of complying with trade commitments, and an understanding that accession decisions require the consensus of all CPTPP members. China has encountered challenges in meeting these high standards, particularly in areas such as SOEs, intellectual property protection, labor standards, flow of digital data, and environmental regulations (Yu & Jiang, 2021; Fang, 2024). Despite these challenges, the Chinese government has reiterated its readiness and capability to meet the CPTPP's stringent requirements.[17] In 2023, the State Council issued two guidelines aimed at aligning China's Pilot Free Trade Zones (PFTZs) with international high-standard economic and trade rules. One of the guidelines, specifically for the Shanghai PFTZ, focuses on eight key areas: opening up trade in services, liberalizing and facilitating goods trade, establishing rules for digital trade, strengthening intellectual property protection, reforming public procurement practices, advancing "post-border" management reforms, and enhancing risk management. The measures for "post-border" management reforms are tailored to meet CPTPP non-trade concerns, addressing key issues such as SOE reform, labor rights protection, and environmental protection. These guidelines highlight China's readiness to align its economic policies with the high standards set by the CPTPP.

Furthermore, China's accession to the CPTPP requires the unanimous consensus of all members. However, China is widely regarded as a competitor rather than a collaborator in the global trade arena, and its accession would undoubtedly shift the balance of power within the Agreement. This prospect raises concerns among major powers such as the United States and Japan (Fang, 2024). Notably, Canada and Mexico, both members of the US-Mexico-Canada Agreement (USMCA), face an added constraint. The USMCA includes a "poison pill" clause that requires any of the three members to notify the others if it intends to enter trade negotiations with a non-market economy. This clause was explicitly designed to discourage Canada and Mexico from pursuing a PTA with China. Given these hurdles, some believe that China's CPTPP application "will be pending for a long time coming – and possibly forever."[18]

Expanding China's Bilateral PTA Network

Among the 22 PTAs that China has entered into, 20 are bilateral agreements, while two involve multiple parties: RCEP and the *ASEAN-China Free Trade Area* (ACFTA), established in 2002. The bilateral PTAs include agreements with Serbia (2023), Ecuador (2023), Nicaragua (2023), Cambodia (2022), Mauritius (2019), Maldives (2017), Georgia (2015), Australia (2015), South Korea (2015), Switzerland (2013), Iceland (2013), Costa Rica (2010), Taiwan (2010), Peru (2009), Singapore (2008), New Zealand (2008), Chile (2005), Pakistan (2006), Hong Kong SAR (2003), and Macau SAR (2003). A further 10 PTAs are currently under negotiation. Among the PTAs, three are with separate customs territories: Hong Kong, Macau, and Taiwan. The agreements with Hong Kong and Macau, known as the *Closer Economic Partnership Arrangements* (CEPA), were signed in 2003 and remain active, but the one with Taiwan has been largely suspended.[19]

17 See "China to Speed up Accession to CPTTP." *China Daily*. (March 22, 2024).

18 Shannon Tiezzi, "Will China Actually Join the CPTTP?" *The Diplomat* (September 17, 2021).

19 The *Economic Cooperation Framework Agreement* (ECFA) with Taiwan has faced significant suspension. In December 2023, Mainland China revoked tariff concessions on certain Taiwanese products under the ECFA, citing discriminatory trade practices by Taiwan. This suspension was further extended in May 2024, encompassing an additional 134 items, effectively disrupting substantial

China's network of PTAs often overlaps due to the coexistence of bilateral and regional agreements. These overlaps result in multiple agreements governing trade relations with the same countries, a phenomenon commonly referred to as the "spaghetti bowl effect." For example, China and ASEAN signed the ACFTA in 2002 and later entered into bilateral free trade agreements with Singapore and Cambodia, both of which are ASEAN members. Additionally, since all these countries are also participants in RCEP, trade between China and nations such as Singapore or Cambodia is governed not only by the ACFTA and their respective bilateral FTAs, but also by the broader RCEP framework. Similarly, trade relations between China and South Korea are regulated by two agreements: the bilateral China-South Korea Free Trade Agreement and RCEP.

Initially, China's bilateral PTA strategy focused on a localized and small-scale approach, prioritizing easier negotiations and leveraging the opportunity to gain experience through sequential agreements. The first PTAs were signed with Hong Kong and Macao in 2003, while the first PTA with a developed country was concluded with New Zealand in 2008 (Whally & Li, 2014).[20] Aside from the ACFTA and RCEP, the China-South Korea Free Trade Agreement stands out as the largest bilateral trade deal signed by China. It was finalized in June 2015 and took effect on December 20, 2015. Compared to previous PTAs, this agreement features four key advancements: an expanded scope of coverage, a stronger emphasis on trade in services and investment, the inclusion of provisions addressing competition and environmental issues, and a focus on good governance and regulatory standards. Under its terms, 92% of South Korea's export items and 93% of China's export items will enjoy zero tariffs in bilateral trade within 20 years.[21]

Compared to other high-standard trade agreements, China's PTAs are often regarded as having relatively low levels of openness and limited scope, posing challenges to achieving high-level institutional openness (Miao & Feng, 2024). As Ravenhill and Jiang (2009) observe, pragmatism has been a defining feature of China's economic diplomacy. China has leveraged PTAs to advance a wide range of foreign policy objectives. However, its PTAs lack a standardized template and instead vary significantly in structure and scope, reflecting the diverse diplomatic and economic goals China seeks to achieve through its various partnerships (Ravenhill & Jiang 2009). Recent empirical studies indicate that China's PTA policy decisions are largely driven by political considerations, as reflected in aligned voting patterns in the UN General Assembly. These studies also reveal

parts of the agreement. See Xinhua, "Chinese Mainland to Halt Tariff Cuts on Taiwan." *The State Council Information Office of the PRC.* (May 31, 2024)

20 The Mainland and Hong Kong Closer Economic Partnership Arrangement (CEPA) and the Mainland and Macao Closer Economic Partnership Arrangement (CEPA) were signed on June 29, 2023, and October 17, 2023, respectively. The New Zealand-China Free Trade Agreement was signed on April 7, 2008.

21 South Korea and China maintain a robust trade relationship, with bilateral trade volumes exceeding $300 billion annually in recent years. This significant economic interdependence positions China as South Korea's largest trading partner and South Korea among China's top trading partners.

that stronger diplomatic partnerships substantially increase the likelihood of China signing an FTA with a partner country, while fostering deeper and more comprehensive commitments within the agreement's provisions (Zeng, 2016; Miao & Feng, 2024).

Amid the ongoing WTO crisis, China has increasingly focused on expanding and strengthening its regional and bilateral trade network.[22] China has already undertaken efforts to upgrade PTAs with its trade partners, including ASEAN, South Korea, Australia, New Zealand, and Peru.[23] These upgrades aim to modernize the existing PTAs to address emerging challenges and enhance trade ties. Expanding and upgrading PTAs has become a crucial strategy for China to maintain its trade relationships and integrate more effectively into the global division of labor, particularly against the backdrop of shifting geopolitical dynamics. Furthermore, China views these agreements as a platform to engage more actively in global governance, as upgrading PTAs often requires addressing new issues and harmonizing domestic practices with international standards. By pursuing these upgrades, especially with advanced economies such as South Korea and Switzerland, China seeks to play a more influential role in shaping the future of global economic and trade governance.[24]

Prospects for a Win-set

Before joining the WTO, China had already established itself as an active participant in the global division of labor, a process that began with the reform and opening-up policy in the late 1970s. This integration into the global economy spurred rapid economic growth, driven by significant cost advantages such as low labor and land costs, as well as targeted industrial policies aimed at attracting foreign investment and fostering export-led growth. China's accession to the WTO further accelerated this trajectory by granting it access to advanced technologies, global expertise, and deeper integration into international markets. This allowed China to effectively leverage its vast domestic market and skilled labor force, transitioning over time from low-cost, labor-intensive manufacturing to higher-value sectors.

However, China's rapid economic rise has not been without controversy. Its distinctive economic model, characterized by the dominant role of SOEs, government-led industrial strategies, and subsidies, has been widely criticized by its Western trade partners as "unfair." These practices, perceived as distorting global trade, have become a major source of tension in China's trade relations with the West and

22 China is currently negotiating PTAs with the Gulf Cooperation Council (GCC) member states, Israel, Japan, and South Korea (as a trilateral agreement), South Korea (second-phase negotiations), Moldova, Panama, Palestine, Peru (for an upgrade of the existing agreement), and Sri Lanka.

23 See Ministry of Commerce of the PRC, "China FTA Network," available at: <http://fta.mofcom.gov.cn/english/index.shtml>

24 "China's acceleration in upgrading and expanding free trade agreements requires institutional designs that are well-considered and forward-looking" [我国自贸协定升级扩围加速制度设计需多方考虑并具前瞻性]. *21st Century Business Herald.* (December 2, 2024)

a fundamental driver of the WTO crisis. At the same time, similar industrial policies and subsidies are increasingly being adopted by other major economies, driven by intensifying competition in the global economic arena. The rise of high-standard PTAs has further complicated the global trade landscape. WTO rules are now often seen as the baseline for trade regulations, while economic models are evolving into critical tools for governing market access. While WTO rules do not require China to adopt a Western-style economic model, it raises the question: "Does China need to adapt its economic model to achieve full integration into the global trade system?" This highlights a broader challenge: reconciling diverse economic systems within an increasingly complex and competitive global trade environment. As economic models increasingly become prerequisites or tools for regulating market access, China's reliance on foreign markets for exports means that pressures to align its economic practices with international expectations persist.

Aligning with High-Standard Rules

The *Resolution of the Central Committee of the Communist Party of China on Further Deepening Reform Comprehensively to Advance Chinese Modernization*, adopted on July 18, 2024, stresses China's commitment to "steadily expanding institutional opening-up." This concept, first introduced at the 2018 Central Economic Work Conference, represents a higher level of openness. It focuses on aligning domestic institutional frameworks with international trade and economic rules while removing systemic and regulatory barriers, facilitating the free flow and efficient allocation of resources between domestic and international markets.[25] The 2024 Resolution emphasizes China's intention to align with high-standard international economic and trade rules, creating a transparent, stable, and predictable institutional environment. To achieve this, it outlines its efforts to harmonize rules, regulations, management, and standards across key areas, including property rights protection, industrial subsidies, environmental standards, labor protection, government procurement, e-commerce, and the financial sector. Moreover, the 2024 Resolution highlights plans to open China's markets for commodities, services, capital, and labor more broadly to the global economy in an orderly manner, while unilaterally extending wider market access to the world's least-developed countries.

From Small-scale Pressure Tests to Institutional Opening-up

In 2013, the Shanghai PFTZ was launched in response to the pressure of TPP, aiming to test high-standard international rules through institutional innovation, and to align China's economic practices with global standards.[26] This experimental model

25 Cai Rong. "Institutional Opening-up for Global Integration." *China Daily.* (August 9, 2024)
26 Xinhua, "Pilot Free Trade Zones, China's Vanguard of Reform." *The State Council of the PRC.* (July 11, 2021)

has progressively expanded to other regions. Following seven rounds of expansion, China now has 22 PFTZs, establishing them as vital engines for China's reform and opening-up initiatives. After a decade of exploration, the PFTZs have developed a range of institutional innovations. Nationally, 349 of these innovations have been replicated and promoted, while more than 3,200 have been independently implemented at the local level.[27] These measures are primarily aimed at trade liberalization and facilitation, with a focus on enhancing market access for foreign goods and services and simplifying foreign trade and investment procedures. Among these, the "negative list" approach to managing foreign investment, which was first formally incorporated in the North American Free Trade Agreement (NAFTA) of 1994, stands out as one of the most significant innovations.

Under China's WTO Accession Protocol, China initially adopted a "positive list" approach under the General Agreement on Trade in Services (GATS). This approach specifically enumerates the services sectors open to foreign investors within China's territory, along with any limitations or conditions. However, a significant shift occurred in 2013 when the Shanghai PFTZ pioneered the introduction of a "negative list" approach. This approach specifies only the sectors restricted or prohibited for foreign investment, with all other sectors deemed open. The success of the negative list model in the Shanghai PFTZ led to its replication across other PFTZs and its eventual nationwide adoption. China has adopted three national negative lists: the *Negative List for Foreign Investment Access*, the *Negative List for Market Access*, which applies to all market participants, and the *Negative List for Cross-border Trade in Service.* China has constantly shortened its negative list to expand market access. China's Special Administrative Measures for Foreign Investment Access (Negative List) was first introduced in 2018 and has undergone four revisions – in 2019, 2020, 2021, and most recently in 2024. These updates have progressively reduced the number of restricted sectors for foreign investment from 48 to 29. Notably, the 2024 version, effective November 1, 2024, has eliminated all access restrictions in the manufacturing sector, marking a significant step in China's efforts to open its economy to foreign investors.[28]

Under the RCEP, members are permitted to adopt either a positive-list approach or a negative-list approach. However, all countries have committed to transitioning to a negative-list approach for trade in services and investment within six years of the agreement's entry into force. China has opted for a positive-list approach for trade in services. For investment, however, China has implemented a negative-list approach that covers both services and non-services sectors, including manufacturing, agriculture, forestry, fishing, and mining. This dual approach reflects China's ongoing efforts to balance market openness with the protection of key sectors (Park et al., 2021; Francois & Elsig, 2021).

27 Data quoted from: Ren Ping, "Thriving Development of Free Trade Zones, Hainan Free Trade Port Mirrors China's High-level Opening Up," *People's Daily Online* (September 26, 2024).

28 Xinhua, "China to Lift Foreign Investment Access Restrictions in Manufacturing Sector." *The State Council of the PRC.* (September 8, 2024)

The negative-list approach was codified in Article 4 of China's *Foreign Investment Law*, enacted in 2019. The law stipulates that China "shall implement the management systems of pre-establishment national treatment and a negative list for foreign investment." Codifying this approach into national law marks a significant step in China's efforts to foster a more open, transparent, and business-friendly environment for foreign investment. From a governance perspective, adopting a negative-list approach reduces government intervention in market activities. In contrast, the positive-list model allows governments to retain significant control over economic activities, granting them broad discretionary power, particularly in sectors where market access rules are unclear or undefined. This discretion often led to rent-seeking behaviors, which diminished the incentives for governments to improve regulatory frameworks. Consequently, areas like market access and management were often left in a state of prolonged ambiguity (Wang, 2014).

Exploring Alternatives to Subsidies

The recent years have seen a wave of industrial policies in developed economies, particularly in the US and EU. According to research by the IMF, over 2,500 industrial policy interventions were recorded globally in 2022. Of these, two-thirds were driven by goals such as climate mitigation, supply chain resilience, and economic security, while the remaining interventions focused on competitiveness (Evenett et al., 2024). One of the most notable examples is the *Inflation Reduction Act* passed by the Biden Administration in 2022. This legislation represents one of the largest investments in the US economy in a generation, providing substantial place-based incentives to stimulate investment and job creation across the US Since President Biden took office, companies have announced more than $115 billion in manufacturing investments to support the clean energy economy through October 2023.[29] These state-led policies have been implemented to bolster domestic industries amidst intensifying competition in strategic sectors.

Hefei, the capital of Anhui province – once a relatively lesser-known region in China – has rapidly evolved into a major economic and innovation hub. Beginning with the home appliance industry in the late 1970s, Hefei has successfully developed strengths in cutting-edge industries such as semiconductors, display panels, new energy vehicles, intelligent connected vehicles, smart manufacturing, and artificial intelligence. [30]

The remarkable transformation has propelled Hefei as a rising city for technological development in China. The so-called Hefei model essentially represents a government-led investment approach, earning the Hefei municipal government

29 Data quoted from: US Department of the Treasury, Fact Sheet: How the Inflation Reduction Act's Tax Incentives Are Ensuring All Americans Benefit from the Growth of the Clean Energy Economy, October 20, 2023.

30 Jacob Dreyer, "China's Regional Cities are Now Major Players in World Science." *Nature Index 2024 Science Cities* (20 November 2024); Fu Zhaohuan & Hua Ming, "The Miracle of Hefei: From Small to Smart." *China Focus* (6 August 2024);

the reputation of being "the most outstanding investor in China." In 2005, Hefei's government prioritized the development of technology-driven manufacturing, with a landmark investment in the BOE Technology Group in 2008, a financially struggling LCD display manufacturer based in Beijing. The government persuaded BOE to establish a factory in Hefei and allocated one-third of its fiscal revenue to attract the company, enabling the creation of China's first 6th-generation LCD panel production line. This move spurred the establishment of supporting companies specializing in areas such as glass substrates, polarizers, and modules, fostering the growth of a vibrant display industry cluster in the city. Building on the success of investments in BOE and other enterprises, Hefei has undertaken significant restructuring and integration of its state-owned capital operation platforms since 2015. This effort led to the creation of three specialized state-owned investment and financing platforms. A more recent example of Hefei's strategic investment is its backing of NIO, a leading electric vehicle manufacturer. These initiatives reflect Hefei's commitment to leveraging state-led investments to drive industrial development and economic transformation.[31]

The Hefei model emphasizes the leadership role of state-owned capital in driving economic development and innovation. It involves targeted investments in strategic emerging industries, focusing on large-scale, early-stage, and technology-driven projects. The primary objectives are to strengthen, supplement, and extend industrial chains, creating a synergistic effect on local economic growth. A critical factor in the model's success is the alignment of government investment strategies with market logic, ensuring that investments are both effective and sustainable. Once a project reaches maturity and the industry thrives, the "Hefei model" prioritizes a timely exit over retaining majority control, redirecting the funds into new projects.[32]

In China's development narrative, the Hefei model, alongside other development models such as Guangdong, exemplifies the integration of a "facilitating government" and an "efficient market," two of the most critical institutions driving economic development (Acemoglu, 2005; Lin & Wang, 2017; Zhou, 2023). Research on Guangdong highlights China's strong state capacities in areas such as fiscal management, rule of law, and adaptive learning. These capabilities are complemented by effective incubation strategies, including gradual market-oriented reforms, well-ordered and independent opening-up, targeted industry support, and

31 In 2019, NIO was in severe financial distress and sought investment from 18 other cities before ultimately negotiating with Hefei. In April 2020, Hefei invested 7 billion yuan in NIO, which not only helped stabilize NIO but also played a significant role in establishing Hefei as a key hub for electric vehicle manufacturing. See "The 'Hefei Power' in the New Energy Vehicle Industry" [新能源汽车产业的"合肥力量"！] posted by the Hefei People's Government on October 6, 2024.

32 See "Wu Xiaogdong: The Success of the Hefei Model can be attributed to Three Key Factors: a capable government, market logic, and the power of capital"[吴晓东：合肥模式的成功有三点原因，有为的政府+市场的逻辑+资本的力量]. Available at: https://finance.ifeng.com/c/8erGLNAoSwR

prioritizing infrastructure development. Together, these efforts have facilitated the successful cultivation of a resilient market (Guo & Wang, 2019).

Negotiating Rules for Development Models in Global Trade System

This success reinforces its steadfast defense of the free trade system and globalization. Leveraging its large-scale production capacity, cost advantages, and advancements in high-tech industries, China has inevitably faced protectionist measures and strategic containment policies. However, challenges such as a shortage of original technology, inefficient domestic market demand, and increasingly stringent foreign market access requirements loom on the horizon. In response to rising protectionism and technology restrictions, China is resolutely pushing for original innovation and actively working to expand its domestic market to sustain its growth and resilience.

In the context of China-US relations, the escalating economic rivalry between the two powers poses a significant threat to the continuation and progress of globalization, with the potential to slow its momentum or even reverse its trajectory. This shift could fundamentally reshape the international economic landscape in unpredictable ways (Foot & King, 2019). In response, the Chinese government is likely to double down on a state-dominated economic model, resisting deeper integration with the global economy, particularly in key business sectors. To protect its industrial foundation, China is expected to maintain the dominant role of state-owned enterprises (SOEs) in strategic industries (Bekkevold, 2020).

The Dual Circulations Strategy

From 1960 to 2023, China's average exports of goods and services accounted for 14.79% of its GDP. The lowest recorded value was 2.46% in 1970, while the highest was 36.04% in 2006. Meanwhile, the global average during the same period, based on data from 138 countries, was 45.76%.[33] China's exports-to-GDP ratio has been steadily declining since 2006, with it being around 20% in recent years. In its international trade structure, the total value of service trade imports and exports accounts for less than one-fifth of the total trade volume, with service trade imports outweighing exports (Table 6.3). China's exports of goods saw a dramatic decline in 2023, reflecting a 4.6% decrease compared to 2022, marking a decline not seen since 2016.

The reduction in China's trade dependence over the past two decades is largely attributed to irreversible factors, particularly the growth of internal manufacturing and the saturation of market shares for "Made in China" goods (Miura, 2022). Following the global financial crisis, China shifted its focus toward stimulating domestic consumption to create a more balanced growth model. The decline in

33 Data quoted from: "China: Exports, Percent of GDP." Available at: <https://www.theglobaleconomy.com/China/exports/?utm_source=chatgpt.com>

Table 6.3 China's Foreign Trade Structure from 2019 to 2023

Foreign Trade Indicators	*2019*	*2020*	*2021*	*2022*	*2023*
Exports of Goods (million USD)	2,499,457	2,589,952	3,316,022	3,544,434	3,380,024
Exports of Services (million USD)	283,192	280,629	394,273	424,056	381,121
Imports of Goods (million USD)	2,078,386	2,065,962	2,679,412	2,706,507	2,556,802
Imports of Services (million USD)	500,680	381,088	426,998	465,053	551,995
Export of Goods and Services (in % of GDP)	18.41	18.59	19.94	20.7	19.74

Source: Santander/Trade Markets: Chinese Foreign Trade in Figures

exports of goods drives Chinese policymakers to shift focus more on the domestic market in response to evolving international dynamics and is a critical step toward transforming China's economic growth model. China has embraced the "dual circulation" development strategy. On May 14, 2020, the Standing Committee of the Political Bureau of the CPC Central Committee initially proposed to "deepen supply-side structural reform, fully leverage the advantages of China's super-sized market and domestic demand potential, and establish a new development paradigm in which domestic and international circulations mutually reinforce one another." President Xi Jinping described the dual circulation paradigm as "a strategic decision made in view of the changes in China's development stage, environment, and conditions" and "a strategic decision designed to ensure China's economy can move with the times and gain new competitive edges in global economic cooperation and competition."[34]

The Way Forward: Ongoing Competition in Strategic Industries

The resurgence of industrial policy reflects the intensifying competition in advanced industries. As Schumpeter's economic theory suggests, there is a strong link between technological innovation, a nation's scientific and technical capabilities, and its economic strength. A country's ability to compete globally thus largely depends on its innovation capacity (1911, 1942). Until around 2014, China was often viewed as a country lacking in innovation, unable to compete globally with developed nations that had long established their economies on innovation (Abrami et al., 2014). However, this perception has changed significantly in recent years.

34 See Kevin Yao, "Explainer: What We Know about China's 'Dual Circulation' Economic Strategy." *World Economic Forum* (September 14, 2020); Hung Tran, "Dual Circulation in China: A Progress Report." *Atlantic Council* (October 24, 2022).

For instance, WIPO's 2022 Global Innovation Index ranks China as the 11th most innovative country globally, noting that "China stands out for producing innovations comparable to those of high-income countries"(Atkinson, 2024). Unlike the West's focus on original innovation from "zero to one," Chinese entrepreneurs excel at scaling innovations, driving progress from "one to one hundred."

A prime example is the competition within the automotive industry among major economies, a critical sector characterized by its high value-added activities, intensely competitive market dynamics, increasing technological demands, and significant employment opportunities (Judit & Zsófia, 2018). By the 1960s, car manufacturing was largely concentrated in Western Europe and the US, with these markets remaining mostly insulated from foreign competition. At that time, Japan had not yet produced vehicles capable of competing on the international stage. However, starting in the 1970s, Japan demonstrated how high productivity and superior quality could be achieved, reshaping the global automotive industry (Judit & Zsófia, 2018). Japanese expertise in producing fuel-efficient small cars gave them a significant advantage as gasoline prices soared during the mid-1970s oil crisis (Smith, 1987). By 1976, Japanese car sales in the US had risen to 8% of the market, and by 1979, this figure had surged dramatically to around 16% (Berry et al., 1999). In contrast, the market share of American automakers declined from 86% in 1971 to approximately 80% in 1979. Rising labor costs in the US further exacerbated the competitive gap. By 1979, Japanese manufacturers held a $2,000 cost advantage over their American counterparts for each car produced (Smith, 1987).

In 1981, Japanese automakers' market share in the US exceeded 21%, leading the Reagan administration to negotiate a *Voluntary Export Restraint* (VER) agreement with Japan. Under the agreement, Japan voluntarily limited its auto exports to the US to 1.68 million units per year for an initial period of three years. The VER was extended several times and was ultimately lifted in 1992, following shifts in trade dynamics and the establishment of domestic manufacturing plants by many Japanese automakers in the US Studies have shown that the VER significantly influenced market conditions (Berry et al., 1999). It led to higher prices for Japanese vehicles, which indirectly boosted the sales and profits of US domestic automakers. While domestic firms experienced substantial gains in profitability, Japanese firms were less affected, as they adapted by producing higher-margin vehicles and increasing their US-based production (Berry et al., 1999). The 1990s witnessed an unprecedented wave of mergers and acquisitions in the automotive industry, driven by overcapacity and increasing globalization. During this period, the Big Three automakers – General Motors, Ford, and Chrysler – experienced a continuous decline in US market share. Notably, all new assembly capacity added to the US market came exclusively from Japanese, Korean, and European automakers establishing manufacturing plants, further intensifying competition (Holweg, 2008).

The competitive landscape has shifted significantly with the emergence of electric vehicles, driven in large part by China's rapid ascent in the new energy vehicle (NEV) sector – a development often described as a "leapfrog" advancement in

Table 6.4 Annual Production and Export of EVs in China (2020–2023)

Year	*Production (Number of Units)*	*Export (Number of Units)*	*Export-to-Production Ratio*
2023	9.587 million	1.203 million	12.5%
2022	7.058 million	0.679 million	9.62%
2021	3.545 million	0.31 million	8.74%
2020	1.296 million	0.07 million	5.4%

Source: China Association of Automobile Manufacturers

the automotive industry. In 2023, China's automotive industry achieved a historic milestone, with both production and sales exceeding 30 million units – an 11.6% rise in production and a 12% increase in sales from the previous year.[35] A substantial portion of this growth was driven by electric vehicles (EVs), including battery electric, plug-in hybrid, and fuel cell vehicles, which accounted for nearly one-third of China's automotive production. Over just four years, China's EV production surged from 1.296 million units in 2021 to 9.587 million units in 2023, marking a staggering growth rate of approximately 639.74% (Table 6.4). As the world's largest EV market, China captured 59% of global EV sales and accounted for 65% of worldwide EV production in 2023.[36] China's rapid ascendancy in EV production has raised alarms among traditional automakers worldwide. Following the Trump administration's tariffs in 2018–2019, Chinese carmakers largely withdrew from the US market. Currently, only 2% of all imported EVs in the US, valued at around $400 million, are Chinese. This trend was further solidified in May 2024, when the Biden administration implemented a 100% tariff on Chinese EVs, effectively closing the US market to Chinese manufacturers.[37]

The relentless pursuit of economic and leadership advantages has long been a defining feature of market competition throughout history. From the early days of the automotive industry to the present, achieving economies of scale has been essential for minimizing production costs. Many economies, including Japan, South Korea, and China, have historically relied on tariff and quota policies to protect their domestic industries during their development phases (Nagy & Jámbor, 2018). Market competition has been constantly evolving. Ford initially dominated the market through its pioneering leadership in mass production. Japanese automakers later gained prominence with their manufacturing efficiency, while BMW distinguished itself with a focus on the driving experience, and Audi earned recognition for its innovative "quattro" all-wheel-drive technology (Holweg, 2008). Today, the

35 Data quoted from: Xinhua News Agency. "China's Automotive Production and Sales Surpass 30 Million Units for the First Time in 2023" [in Chinese]. Available at: <https://www.gov.cn/yaowen/liebiao/202401/content_6925448.htm>>

36 Data quoted from: Roland Irle, "Global EV Sales for 2023." *EV Volumes.* Available at: <https://ev-volumes.com/news/ev/global-ev-sales-for-2023/>

37 Data quoted from: Mehreen Khan, "Biden's Tariffs against China are about more than Economies." *The Times* (May 20, 2024)

US retains its technological edge, as demonstrated by Tesla's leadership in innovation, while China has secured a dominant position in the global EV supply chain.

Research suggests that globalization has eroded the comparative advantages once held by leading automobile manufacturing nations such as Germany, Japan, and the US (Spatz & Nunnenkamp, 2002). The current competition stands apart from earlier periods due to an intensified strategic rivalry among major global powers, driven by geopolitical tensions, rapid technological advancements, and the race to dominate emerging sectors. This rivalry has profoundly reshaped the global economic landscape, shifting the focus from efficiency-driven supply chains to networks designed to prioritize security and political stability. As supply chain security becomes a national priority, heavily influenced by national security concerns, the likelihood of achieving mutually beneficial, win-win outcomes has significantly diminished.

References

Abrami, R. M., Kirby, W. C., & McFarlan F. W. (2014). Why China can't innovate. *Harvard Business Review*, March. https://hbr.org/2014/03/why-china-cant-innovate.

Acemoglu, D., Johnson, S., & Robinson, J. (2005). Institutions as a fundamental cause of long-run growth. In P. Aghion & S. N. Durlauf (Eds.), *Handbook of Economic Growth* (Vol. 1, Part A, pp. 385–472). Elsevier.

Andersen, S., Friedbacher, T., Lau, C., Lockhart, N., Remy, J. Y., & Sandford, I. (2017). Using arbitration under Article 25 of the DSU to ensure the availability of appeals. CTEI Working Papers, CTEI-2017-17. https://repository.graduateinstitute.ch/record/295745?v=pdf.

Atkinson, R. D. (2024). China is rapidly becoming a leading innovator in advanced industries. Information Technology & Innovation Foundation. https://www2.itif.org/2024-chinese-innovation-full-report.pdf.

Bekkevold, J. I. (2020). The International Politics of Economic Reforms in China, Vietnam, and Laos. In A. Hansen, J. I. Bekkevold & K. Nordhaug (Eds.), *The Socialist Market Economy in Asia* (pp. 27–68). Palgrave Macmillan.

Berry, S., Levinsohn, J., & Pakes, A. (1999). Voluntary export restraints on automobiles: Evaluating a trade policy. *American Economic Review*, 89(3), 400–430.

Ciorciari, J. D. (2009). The balance of great-power influence in contemporary Southeast Asia. *International Relations of the Asia-Pacific*, 9(1), 157–196.

Dahlman, A., & Lovely, M. E. (2023). US-led efforts to diversify Indo-Pacific supply chains away from China runs counter to trends. *PIIE Report*, September 6.

Emmers, R. (2001). The influence of the balance of power factor within the ASEAN regional forum. *Contemporary Southeast Asia*, 23(2), 275–291.

Evenett, S., Jakubik, A., Martín, F., & Ruta, M. The Return of Industrial Policy in Data. IMF Working Papers, 2024(001). https://doi.org/10.5089/9798400260964.001.

Fang, Y. (2024). How would it be possible for china to join the CPTPP: A comprehensive assessment. *Asian Yearbook of International Economic Law*, (forthcoming 2025). Available at SSRN: https://ssrn.com/abstract=4739615.

Foot, R., & King, A. (2019). Assessing the deterioration in China–US relations: US governmental perspectives on the economic-security nexus. *China International Strategy Review*, 1, 39–50.

Footer, M. E. (1996–1997). The role of consensus in GATT/WTO decision-making. *Northwestern Journal of International Law & Business*, 17(1), 653–680.

Francois, J., & Elsig, M. (2021). *Short Overview of the Regional Comprehensive Economic Partnership (RCEP)*. Policy Department for External Relations, EP/EXPO/INTA/FWC/2019-01/LOT5/3/C/06.

Guo, Y., & Wang, J. (2019). 国家能力支撑下的市场孵化——中国道路与广东实践 [Market Incubation Supported by State Capacity: China's Path and Guangdong's Practice]. People's Publishing.

Holweg, M. (2008). The evolution of competition in the automotive industry. In G. Parry & A. Graves (Eds.), *Build to Order* (pp. 13–34). Springer.

Jacyk, D. (2008). The integration of Article 25 arbitration in WTO dispute settlement: The past, present and future. *Australian International Law Journal*, 15, 235–266.

Judit, N., & Jámbor, Z. (2018). Competitiveness in global trade: The case of the automobile industry. *Economic Annals*, 63(218), 61–84.

Kawase, T. (2023). China's ban on imports of Japanese fishery products is an act of economic coercion: Japan should use MPIA and file a WTO complaint. RIETI Report. https://www.rieti.go.jp/en/special/policy-update/112.html.

Lin, J. Y., & Wang, X. (2017). The facilitating state and economic development: The role of the state in new structural economics. *Man and the Economy*, 4(2), 13–14.

Manners, I. (2002). Normative power Europe: A contradiction in terms? *Journal of Common Market Studies*, 40(2), 235–258.

Miao, C., & Feng, Z. (2024). 外交伙伴关系与中国FTA签订 [Diplomatic partnership and the signing of China's FTA]. *International Economic and Trade Research*, 40(7), 37–55.

Miura, Y. (2022). What does China's declining trade dependence mean? Superiority stemming from market size and industrial concentration, and the consequences of this. *Pacific Business and Industries*, XXII(85). https://www.jri.co.jp/en/MediaLibrary/file/english/periodical/rim/2022/85.pdf.

Park, C.-Y., Petri, P. A., & Plummer, M. G. (2021). The economics of conflict and cooperation in the Asia-Pacific: RCEP, CPTPP and the US-China Trade War. *East Asia Economic Review*, 25(3), 233–272.

Pauwelyn, J. (2023). The WTO's multi-party interim appeal arbitration arrangement (MPIA): What's new? *World Trade Review*, 22(5), 693–701.

Ravenhill, J., & Jiang, Y. (2009). China's move to preferential trading: A new direction in China's diplomacy. *Journal of Contemporary China*, 18(58), 27–46.

Schumpeter, J. A. (1911). *The Theory of Economic Development*. Harvard University Press.

Schumpeter, J. A. (1942). *Capitalism, Socialism, and Democracy*. Harper & Brothers.

Smith, P. A. (1987). The US automakers' reaction to the Japanese. *Draftings in Economics: Major Themes*, 2(4). https://scholarworks.uni.edu/draftings/vol2/iss4/3.

Spatz, J., & Nunnenkamp, P. (2002). *Globalization of the automobile industry: Traditional locations under pressure?* Kiel Working Papers, No. 1093. Kiel Institute for the World Economy (IfW Kiel).

Steinberg, R. H. (2003). In the shadow of law or power? Consensus-based bargaining and outcomes in the GATT/WTO. *International Organization*, 2, 339–374.

Wang, L. (2014). The negative list approach and private law autonomy [负面清单模式与私法之治]. *China Legal Science*, 5, 26–60.

Whally, J., & Li, C. (2014). China's regional and bilateral trade agreements. *CERP Report*, March 5.

WTO. (2011). *World Trade Report 2011: The WTO and Preferential Trade Agreements: From Co-existence to Coherence.* WTO World Trade Report. https://www.wto.org/english/res_e/booksp_e/anrep_e/world_trade_report11_e.pdf.

Ye, M. (2015). China and competing cooperation in Asia-Pacific: TPP, RCEP, and the new silk road. *Asia Security*, 11(3), 206–224.

Yu, M., & Jiang, H. (2021). 从RCEP到CPTTP: 差异、挑战及对策 [From RCEP to CPTPP: Differences, challenges and solutions]. *International Economic Review*, 2, 129–144.

Zeng, K. (2016). China's free trade agreement diplomacy. *The Chinese Journal of International Politics*, 9(3), 277–305.

Zhou, H. (2023). State capacity and leadership: Why did China take off? *The Chinese Economy*, 56(1), 50–68.

Index

FSC
www.fsc.org
MIX
Papier | Fördert gute Waldnutzung
FSC® C083411

Kolibri 360 GmbH
Ferdinand-Jühlke-Straße 7
99095 Erfurt, Deutschland
produktsicherheit@kolibri360.de